The Dance

PAVLOWA AND VOLININ IN "AMARILLA"
From a dry-point by Troy Kinney

Frontispiece

THE DANCE

ITS PLACE IN ART AND LIFE

BY

TROY AND MARGARET WEST KINNEY
("THE KINNEYS")

With reproductions of six etchings by Troy Kinney, one hundred and forty-seven line drawings and diagrams by the co-authors and two hundred and seventy-eight illustrations from Photographs

NEW AND REVISED EDITION

NEW YORK
TUDOR PUBLISHING CO.
1935

COPYRIGHT, 1914, 1924, BY
FREDERICK A. STOKES COMPANY

*All rights reserved, including
that of translation into
foreign languages*

New printing, 1935

PRINTED IN THE UNITED STATES OF AMERICA

To
A FELLOW-ENTHUSIAST
J. T. W.
WITH APPRECIATION

PREFACE

The pleasant responsibility of writing about one of our two overwhelming enthusiasms was accepted by us only after consultation with friends in the dancing profession.

"A book of technical instruction is not the idea," we started to explain.

"No," they concurred, "that would not be an undertaking for painters. Only an experienced master of dancing should write such a book, and he would not be likely to, because he would know that execution is taught only by personal criticism of a pupil's work."

We hastened to specify that the proposal involved no more—and no less—than an effort to share our enthusiasm with others. Appreciation of an art requires no faculties not included in the normal human equipment; more than anything else it is a matter of knowing what to look for. When a layman comes to a painter asking what it is that people find so enjoyable in classic mural decoration, the answer is not difficult. A few hours in an art museum, with some direction of his attention to line as a vehicle of beauty, acquaint him with the idea of beauty as a self-sufficient object; and he goes on his way rejoicing in the possession of a lasting process of making happiness for himself.

Great dancing, to us, always had been a gratification of the same senses that are addressed by decoration. The same suggestions, therefore, that convey the power to enjoy classic mural painting, would enable us to communicate our satisfaction in the dance. But the question arose, was our point of view on dancing in accord with its real intent, and that of its performers and composers?

Madame Cavallazi disposed of the doubt at one stroke. "The ballet," she said, "*is* mural decoration."

Sanctioned by such authority, we have followed the lines above indicated, treating the dance from the standpoint of pure optical beauty. Its enjoyment, experience proves, is distinctly sharpened by acquaintance with choreographic technique. One not fairly familiar with the resources of the art, though he be conscious that the dance before his eyes is progressing, like music, in conformity with an artistic argument, is confused by the speed and seeming intricacy of steps. As a result he loses the greater part of the beauty of the succession of pictures unfolded before him. Whereas the ability to grasp the theme of a composition, and then to follow its elaboration through a vocabulary of already familiar steps, is in effect to quicken the vision. Instead of being harassed by a sensation of scrambling to keep up with the argument, the spectator finds himself with abundant time to luxuriate in every movement, every posture. And, like a connoisseur of any other art, he sees a thousand beauties unnoticed by the untrained.

To the end of furnishing the needed acquaintance with the alphabet of the art, the book includes a chapter of explanation of the salient steps of the ballet. These steps, with superficial variations and additions, form the basis also of all natural or "character" dances that can lay claim to any consideration as interpretative art. It is convenient to learn the theories of them as accepted by the great ballet academies, since those institutions alone have defined them clearly, and brought to perfection the ideals for their execution. Incidentally the school of the ballet is made the subject of considerable attention. In the first place, after getting a grasp of its ideals and intent, any one will catch the sentiment of a folk-dance in a moment. Moreover, it is in itself an important institution. During its long history it has undergone several periods of retirement from public attention, the most recent beginning about sixty years ago. From this eclipse it has already returned to the delighted gaze of Europe; as always after its absences, so far evolved beyond the standards within the memory of living men that posterity seems to have been robbed of the chance of discovering anything further. The renaissance is moving westward from St. Petersburg; London is wholly under its influence; America has felt a touch of it.

American love of animated beauty and delight in skill predestine us to be a race of ardent enthusiasts over the dance. Among us, however, there are many who have never accepted it as an art worthy of serious attention. As a gentle answer to that point of view, a historical résumé is included, wherein statesmen, philosophers and monarchs show the high respect in which the art has been held, save in occasional lapses, in all periods of civilised history.

Neither in word nor picture does the book contain any statement not based upon the authors' personal knowledge, or choreographic writings of unquestioned authority, or the word of dancers or ballet-masters of the utmost reliability. To these artists and to certain managers we are greatly indebted. Much of the matter has never before been printed in

English; a considerable portion of it has here its first publication in any language. The illustrations of dances of modern times are made from artists in the very front rank of their respective lines. If the new material so contributed to choreographic literature proves, according to the belief of dancers who have read the manuscript, to be of value to producers, the authors will experience the gratification that comes of having been of service. But their efforts will be more directly repaid if the influence of the book hastens by a day that insistence upon a high choreographic ideal in America, and that unification of dance-lovers which must exist in order that worthy productions may be reasonably insured of recognition in proportion to their quality.

Finally, a word of thanks to those whose aid has made this book possible. Though busy, as successful people always are, they have given time and thought unsparingly to the effort, in co-operation with the authors, to make this a substantial addition to the layman's understanding of the dancing art.

T. K. and M. W. K.

CONTENTS

CHAPTER   PAGE

I. THE DANCING OF ANCIENT EGYPT AND GREECE 3

The dance a primitive emotional expression. Importance in Egyptian religious ritual. Biblical allusions. Its high place in Greek civilisation. Origin attributed to the gods. Employed in observances religious, civic, and private. Practice decreed by Lycurgus for military discipline and cultivation of national stamina. A feature of Plato's "Ideal Republic." Ballet in drama. Interacting influence between dance and sculpture.

II. DANCING IN ROME 22

Simplicity of early Roman taste and manners enforced by poverty. Vulgarity with riches. Degeneration of dancing with other arts, under Empire. Acrobatics, obscenity. Ballet pantomime. Pylades and Bathyllus.

III. THE MIDDLE AGES AND THE RENAISSANCE 29

The Christian Church lifts dance from degradation. Ballet d'action in ritual of worship. A cause of disagreements between ecclesiastical dignitaries. The Seises of Seville Cathedral preservers of dance in religious service. Moralities, etc. Mechanical effects. Ambulatory ballets.

Rebirth of polite society; the masque. Cardinal Riario. Catherine de Medici, direct influence toward modern ballet. Elizabeth of England. Richelieu, composer. Louis XIV, ballet performer, founder of national academy.

Dawn of stars. Sallé. Prévost. Camargo. New standards. Expression. New steps added to those derived from old dances: Gavotte, Minuet, Pavane, Saraband, Tordion, Bourrée, Passecaille, Passepied, Chaconne, Volte, Allemande, Gaillarde, and Courante. Their formality; illustrations.

IV. A GLANCE AT THE BALLET'S TECHNIQUE 59

Visual music: dance steps are notes, an enchainement is a phrase, a dance-composition is a song, the ballet is an orchestra. Ballet dancing, as such, not based on imitation of nature; a convention, analagous to ornamental decoration. Intent: perfect beauty of line and rhythm; abstract qualities exploited. Importance of pantomime unsettled.

CONTENTS

CHAPTER   PAGE

       Ballet dancing can be seen intelligently only by aid of acquaintance with elemental steps. Fundamental positions of feet and hands. Gliding steps: chassé, échappé, coupé, etc. Battements, grand, petit. Changement. Entrechat. Brisé. Balloné. Enchainements. Pas de Bourrée, pas de Basque.

       Turns and pirouettes. Rond de jambe. Fouetté. Sur le cou-de-pied; en l'air. Renversé. En arabesque, etc. Optical illusions. Phrasing. Theme. Motive.

       Standards of form. Exactness. Beneficial relaxation of formality; results of unguided emancipation.

V. THE GOLDEN AGE OF DANCING 100

Early eighteenth century finds ballet profiting by many favourable influences. Royal patronage. Public enthusiasm and discernment. Great-minded artists in co-operation. Fortunate accidents. The Vestris, father and son. Noverre, "the Shakespeare of the dance." Boucher, designer of stage decoration. Gluck. Costuming.

       Rivalries of Camargo and Sallé; Allard and Guimard. Coterie of great performers. French Revolution.

       Dance resumed with return of peace. An ambassador as impresario. Public controversy and enthusiasm over Taglioni and Ellsler; opposites; none to replace them; singing supersedes dancing in opera.

VI. SPANISH DANCING 121

Gaditanae in Roman literature. Spanish dancing resists Roman corruption, Gothic brutality. Favouring influence of Moors. Attitude of the Church. Public taste and discrimination.

       Two schools, Flamenco (Gipsy origin) and Classic. The Gipsy. La Farruca, el Tango, el Garrotin; distinct character. Costume. Classic: Seguidillas family. Las Sevillanas; general character. The Fandango rarely seen. La Malagueña y el Torero. Las Malagueñas. The Bolero. Castanets. Los Panaderos. The Jota of Aragon, character, costume, etc. Other dances.

VII. ITALIAN DANCES 156

The Forlana of Venice: Harlequin, Columbine, Dr. Pantalone. Pantomime and tableaux. The Tarantella, character, costume. The Ciociara of Romagna. Italian fondness for pantomime. The Saltarello. La Siciliana, la Ruggera, la Trescona, etc.

VIII. EUROPEAN FOLK-DANCING IN GENERAL 164

Folk-dancing an expression of social conditions. Scotch nationalism. The Sword Dance; the Highland Fling; the Scotch Reel. Mo-

CONTENTS

CHAPTER   PAGE

tives, basic steps. Reel of Tulloch. The Shean Treuse. England: Sailor's Hornpipe. Morris Dances. Recent revival of old dances. Ireland: Jig, Reel and Hornpipe. Intent, steps, devices of tempo. Irish festivals; Gaelic League. Sweden: recent revival of old dances. The Skralât; Kadriljs. The Vafva Vadna; the Daldans. Holland: the Mâtelot. France: la Bourrée, la Farandole. Specimen freak dances: the Perchtentanz, the Bacchu-ber. The Schuhplatteltanz of Bavaria. Balkan region: the Kolo. Degeneration of dancing in Greece. Russia: Cossack Dance, Court Dance. Slavonic character and steps: the Czardás; the Mazurka; the Szoló; the Obertass. Temperament.

IX. ORIENTAL DANCING 196

Symbolism, decoration, pantomime, story in the dance. Sensational mismanagement in Occidental countries. Mimetic dancing a substitute for newspapers. The Dance of Greeting; welcome, blessings, etc. Structure of Arabic choreography. Handkerchief Dance of Cafés; candour. Flour Dance. Popular narrative dances. Fantasia of Bedoui; religious outbreaks. Dancing for tourists; the Almées. Dance, Awakening of the Soul. Animate sculpture. Oriental technique. Sword Dance of Turkey. Dervishes. Lezginkà of the Caucasus. Ruth St. Denis; Nautch; Spirit of Incense; the Temple; the Five Senses. Antiquity; carvings in India and Java. Hula-Hula of Hawaii. Priestesses trained for religious dancing. Japan: dancing for all occasions. Abstractness of symbols. Dances of war.

X. THE BALLET IN ITS DARK AGE 228

Sterilisation of ballet by struggle for technical virtuosity. Ballet in opera. Vulgarisms and counterfeits: the Can-Can; contortion; high kicking; skirt-dancing; insipid prettiness. A revival of good work; falsifications of it. Loie Fuller, silk scarf, electric lights. Serpentine and Fire dances. Imitators. World's Fair of 1893; stigma on Oriental dancing. One class of managers. Obscure preparation of a new force.

XI. THE ROMANTIC REVOLUTION 241

Isadora Duncan, complete idealist. Her metier. Russia: dissatisfaction with ballet. Duncan in St. Petersburg. Secession from Imperial Academy. The romantic idea; choreography, music, painting united in a radical new school. The Russian ballet. Paris, United States, England. Influence and reception. Management in America.

CONTENTS

CHAPTER   **PAGE**

XII. THE RUSSIAN ACADEMY AND ITS WORKINGS 257
Selection of pupils. Consecration to work. Contract, obligations after graduation. Advantages to the government. General education. Technical training: Italian ballet technique, music, drawing, acting, pantomime, plastic gymnastics, fencing. Care of health. Age of Academy. Russian ballet as distinguished from French-Italian; law-governed freedom. Addition to emotional scope. Recent ballet pantomimes.

XIII. A LAYMAN'S ESTIMATE OF CONDITIONS 269
Re-establishment of great dancing in the United States; will it take and keep a high plane? Loose standards of judgment. Dependence upon commercial management. Managers; their varied influences. Need of endowed ballet and academy. Difficulties of ballet organization in the United States. Insufficient training of American ballet dancers. Ballet in operas; unimportance under old traditions, changing standards. Metropolitan and Russian ballet; ground gained and partly lost. Russians under other auspices. Ballet school; impositions upon it. Need of academy with dancing as primary purpose. General organisation; departures from scheme of Russian Academy.

XIV. TENDENCIES? 288

BIBLIOGRAPHY 361

INDEX 365

ILLUSTRATIONS

PAVLOWA AND VOLININE IN *Amarilla*	*Frontispiece*	
TANAGRA FIGURE	Page	3
GREEK VASE DECORATION	"	3
TANAGRA FIGURE	"	3
TANAGRA FIGURES	*Facing Page*	4
GREEK CERAMICS	" "	5
GREEK VASE DECORATION	Page	8
GREEK COMEDY DANCING	"	9
STATUETTES	"	10
Tanagra (A) — Myrina (B) — Tanagra (C).		
GREEK RELIEF DECORATIONS	*Facing Page*	12
GREEK CERAMIC DECORATIONS	" "	13
STATUETTES	Page	13
Myrina (A) — Tanagra (B) — Myrina (C)		
DANCE OF NYMPHS	"	17
TANAGRA FIGURES	*Facing Page*	20
GREEK COMEDY DANCING	Page	21
DANCE OF PEASANTS	"	36
BALLET OF THE FOUR PARTS OF THE WORLD: *Entrance of the Grand Khan*	"	41
A FOURTEENTH CENTURY BALL	"	46
SEVENTEENTH CENTURY COURT DANCES	*Facing Page*	48
The Tordion (1, 2) — *The Pavane* (3, 4, 5).		
LOUIS XIV AND A COURTIER IN THE BALLET OF NIGHT .	Page	50
SEVENTEENTH CENTURY COURT DANCES	*Facing Page*	54
The Saraband (1) — *The Allemand* (3) — *The Minuet* (2, 4, 5, 6, 7).		
THE GAVOTTE	" "	55
MME. ADELINE GENÉE AND M. ALEXANDER VOLININE . .	" "	64
Ballet Robert le Diable (1) — *Butterfly Dance* (2) — *Pierrot and Columbine* (3).		
MME. GENÉE IN HISTORICAL RE-CREATIONS AND M. VOLININE	" "	65
Sallé (1) — *The Waltz* (2) — *Camargo* (3) — *Guimard* (4).		
FUNDAMENTAL POSITIONS OF THE FEET	Page	66

ILLUSTRATIONS

Positions of the Arms	Page	67
"Glissade"	"	68
"Assemblé"	"	69
"Assemblé" and Changement (*Floor Plan Diagram*) . . .	"	69
"Jeté"	"	70
"Jeté" to the Side	"	71
"Battements"	"	72
Steps of the "Battement" Type	"	74
"Fouetté"	"	75
Start of a "Fouetté Pirouette"	"	76
"Fouetté Pirouette" (*Continued*)	"	77
Optional Finish of a "Fouetté Pirouette"	"	78
The "Pirouette sur le Cou-de-Pied"	"	79
Various "Pirouettes"	"	80
Beginning of the "Renversé"	"	82
The "Renversé" (*Concluded*)	"	83
Two Forms of "Attitude"	"	84
Mechanism of Broad Jump	"	86
Classic Ballet Positions	Facing Page	88
Typical moments in a renversé (*1, 2, 3, 4, 5,*) — Starting a developpé (*6*) — Progress of a rond de jambe (*7, 8, 9*).		
Classic Ballet Positions (*Continued*)	" "	89
Rond de jambe (*10*) — Jeté tour (*11*) — Pas de bourrée (*12*) — Preparation for a pirouette (*13*) — Position sur la pointe (*14*) — A fouetté tour, inward (*14*) — A cabriole à derrière (*16*) — Descent from an entrechat (*17*) — An arabesque (*18*).		
"La Malagueña y el Torero"	" "	122
Typical "Flamenco" Poses	Page	129
"Flamenco" Poses	"	133
"Las Sevillanas"	"	137
"El Bolero"	Facing Page	138
Typical moment in first copla (*1*) — Finish of a phrase (*2*).		
"La Jota Aragonesa"	" "	139
Type of movement (*1*) — Finish of a turn (*2*) — A pirouette (*3*) — Kneeling position (*4*) — Woman's sitting position (*5*).		
Two Groups in "Las Sevillanas"	Page	140
Groups in "La Malagueña y el Torero"	"	145
Miscellaneous Spanish Notes	"	147
Two Groups in "Los Panaderos"	"	149
Part of the "Jota" of Aragon	"	152
"La Tarantella"	Facing Page	156
Opening of the dance (*1*) — A poor collection (*2*) — They gamble for it (la Morra) (*3*) — She wins (*4*) — He wins (*5*).		

ILLUSTRATIONS   xvii

"La Tarantella" . . . . *Facing Page* 157
    An arabesque (1) — Finish of a phrase (2) — Typical moment (3) — Finish of a phrase (4).

"La Tarantella" . . . . " " 158
    Opening of the dance (1) — A turn back-to-back (2) — A pause after rapid foot-work (3) — Characteristic finishes of phrases (4, 5).

"La Forlana" . . . . " " 159
    Doctor Pantalone patronized (1) — Defied (2) — Pleads (3) — Accepts the inevitable (4) — Is ridiculed (5).

"La Ciociara" . . . . " " 160
    Opening promenade (1, 2) — End of promenade (3) — He has "made eyes" at a spectator (4) — Opening of dance (second movement) (5).

"La Ciociara" . . . . " " 161
    Rustic affection (1) — Again caught in perfidy (2) — Tries to make amends (3) — Without success (4) — Removed from temptation (5).

The Scotch Sword Dance . . . . " " 164
    A step over the swords (1, 2) — A jump over the swords (3) — Steps between the swords (4, 5).

The "Scotch Reel" . . . . " " 165
    Use of the Battement (1) — A pirouette (2) — Characteristic style (3, 4) — A turn (5).

The "Shean Treuse" . . . . " " 168
    The promenade (1, 2) — The thematic step (3) — Finish of a phrase (4).

The "Sailor's Hornpipe" . . . . " " 169
    Look-out (1) — Hoisting sail (2) — Hauling in rope (3) — Rowing (4) — Type of step (5) — Type of step (6) — Hoisting sail (7).

Irish Dances . . . . " " 174
    The Jig (1, 3, 4) — The Hornpipe (2, 5) — The Reel (6, 7, 8).

A "Four-Hand Reel" . . . . " " 175
    Preparation for woman's turn under arms (1) — Characteristic style (2) — A turning group figure (3).

The "Irish Jig" and Portrait of Patrick J. Long . . . " " 178
From Various Folk-Dances . . . . *Page* 185
The "Schuhplatteltanz" . . . . *Facing Page* 186
    A swing (1) — A turn (2) — A turn, man passing under woman's arms (3) — A swing, back-to-back (4) — The Mirror (5).

ILLUSTRATIONS

The "Schuhplatteltanz" of Bavaria . . . . Facing Page 187
    Preparing a turn (1) — A lift (2) — Starting woman's series of turns (3) — Start of woman's turns (4) — Man fans her along with hands (5) — Finish of dance (6).
The "Kolo" of Servia . . . . " " 190
    Start of a turn (1) — Progress of a turn (2) — A bridge of arms (3) — An emphasis (4) — A lift (5).
Poses from Slavonic Dances . . . . " " 191
    Coquetry (1) — Petulance (2) — Indifference (3) — Emphasis (4) — Jocular defiance (5).
Poses from Slavonic Dances . . . . " " 192
    Negation (1) — Fear (2) — Supplication (3) — An emphasis (4).
Poses from Slavonic Dances . . . . " " 193
    Characteristic gesture (1) — Characteristic step (2) — Characteristic gesture (3) — Characteristic step (4) — Same, another view (5) — Ecstasy (6) — The claim of beauty (7).
Arabian "Dance of Greeting" . . . . " " 196
    Called upon to dance, she reveals herself (1) — Salutation (2) — Profile view of same (3).
Arabian "Dance of Greeting" (Continued) . . . . " " 197
    "For you I will dance" (4) — "From here you will put away care" (5, 8) — "Here you may sleep" (6) — "Here am I" (7).
Arabian "Dance of Greeting" (Continued) . . . . " " 198
    "And should you go afar" (9) — "May you enjoy Allah's blessing of rain" (10) — "And the earth's fullness" (11).
Arabian "Dance of Greeting" (Continued) . . . . " " 199
    "May winds refresh you" (12) — "Wherever you go" (13) — "Here is your house" (14) — "Here is peace" (15) — "And your slave" (16).
Arabian "Dance of Mourning" . . . . " " 200
    The body approaches (1) — The body passes (2) — "I hold my sorrow to myself" (3).
Arabian "Dance of Mourning" (Continued) . . . . " " 201
    "He has gone out of the house and up to Heaven" (4) — "Farewell" (5).
Arabian "Dance of Mourning" (Continued) . . . . " " 202
    "He slept in my arms" (6) — "The house is empty" (7) — "Woe is in my heart" (8).
Arab Slave Girl's Dance . . . . " " 203
"Handkerchief Dance" of the Cafés . . . . " " 206
    The handkerchiefs symbolizing the lovers are animated with the breath of life, but kept dissociated (1) — Brought into semi-association (2) — Separated and dropped (3).

ILLUSTRATIONS   xix

"Handkerchief Dance" (Continued). . . . . Facing Page 207
    She can dance about, between or away from them, indifferently (4) — Made into panniers, the panniers express her willingness to receive; turned inside out, her willingness to give (5) — One of the two handkerchiefs is thrown to the selected lover (6).

"Dance of the Soul's Journey" . . . . " " 210
    The soulless body (1) — Asks for the light of life (2) — Vision dawns (3) — Inexpert in life, she walks gropingly (4).

"Dance of the Soul's Journey" (Continued) . . . . . . " " 211
    She draws aside the veil of the future (5) — Life is seen full and plenteous (6).

"Dance of the Soul's Journey" (Continued) . . . . . . " " 212
    But old age will come (7) — Grief will visit (8) — She shall walk with her nose close to the camel's foot (9).

"Dance of the Soul's Journey" (Continued) . . . . . . " " 213
    Yet now, from the crown of her head (10) — To the soles of her feet she is perfect (11).

Miscellaneous Oriental Notes . . . . Page 215

"Dance of the Soul's Journey" (Continued) . . . . . . Facing Page 216
    Rejoices in the perfect body (12) — And in all good things (13) — Runs from the scene (14).

Characteristic Pantomime in Dancing of Modern Egypt . . . . " " 217
    Express sorrow (1, 3) — Represents a prayer directed downward and back: i.e., to spirits of evil (2).

"Dance of the Falcon" (Egyptian) . . . . " " 218
    Shock as the bird strikes his quarry (1) — Rejoicing as he overcomes it (2).

Dancing Girls of Algiers . . . . " " 219
Reliefs on Tower of the Temple of Madura (India) . Page 219
Persian Dance. Princess Chirinski-Chichmatoff . . . Facing Page 220
Oriental Poses . . . . " " 221
    Votive offering (3 poses) — Decorative motives (3 poses) — Disclosure of person (1 pose).

Javanese Dancer, Modern . . . . " " 222
Relief Carvings, Temple of Borobodul, Java . . . . . " " 223
    Dance of Greeting (1) — Dance of Worship (2) — An Arrow Dance (3).

"Nautch Dance" . . . . " " 226
Japanese Dance . . . . " " 227
Isadora Duncan . . . . " " 242
Greek Interpretative Dance . . . . " " 243
Impressions of Isadora Duncan . . . . Page 244

ILLUSTRATIONS

MLLE. LOPOUKOWA, MLLE. PAVLOWA, MLLE. NIJINSKA, WITH SR. E. CECCETTI	*Facing Page*	246
MLLE. LYDIA KYASHT AND M. LYTAZKIN	" "	247
"ARABESQUE"	" "	248
"ARROW DANCE"	" "	249
BACCHANAL	" "	252
MLLE. LYDIA LOPOUKOWA	" "	253
MLLE. PAVLOWA IN A BACCHANAL	" "	257
MLLE. LOPOUKOWA IN BOUDOIR	" "	258
LOPOUKOWA AND NIJINSKI IN *les Sylphides*	" "	259
MLLE. LOPOUKOWA IN "LE LAC DES CYGNES"	" "	262
M. ALEXANDER VOLININE	" "	263
REPRESENTATIVE RUSSIAN BALLET POSES AND GROUPS	*Page*	265
REPRESENTATIVE RUSSIAN BALLET POSES AND GROUPS	"	267
"SERENADE." TAKEN FROM *Scéne Dansante*, PERFORMED BY MLLE. BUTSOVA AND M. PIANOWSKI OF THE PAVLOWA COMPANY	*Facing Page*	288
ADELINE GENÉE	" "	304
ADOLF BOLM IN *Prince Igor*	" "	320
ROSHANARA. IN HER *Nautch*, ACCOMPANIED BY RATAN DEVI	" "	352

THE DANCE

The Dance

CHAPTER I

THE DANCING OF ANCIENT EGYPT AND GREECE

BEFORE logic, man knew emotion; before creed, ritual. With leap and mad gesture the savage mimics his triumph, to the accompaniment of crude saltation performed by a hero-worshipping tribe.

Not by argument is the coming storm propitiated, but by a unified expression of tribal humility. To the rhythm of beaten drums, the tribe, as one, performs the genuflexions and prostrations that denote supplication and fear.

So on through the gamut of simple emotions—love and hate, fealty and jealousy, desire and achievement—primitive man expresses his mood in terms of the dance. History shows that dancing persists on a plane with words, paint and music as a means of expression, however far a race may advance along the road of evolution; and that the few exceptions to this rule are to be found among peoples who have allowed a Frankenstein of logic to suppress, for a time, their naturalness of spirit.

Egyptian carvings of six thousand years ago record the use of the dance in religious ritual; and abundant evidence attests the importance in which it was held at all times through the period of Egypt's power. In lines as stately as the columns of a temple, sculptors have traced choreography's majestic poses, its orchestral repetitions and variations. As a dance may be, the religious dances of Egypt were a translation and an equivalent of the spirit of the Pharaohs' monumental architecture; that they were no less imposing than those temples we cannot avoid believing.

Plato, deeply impressed by these hierarchical ballets, finds that their evolutions symbolised the harmonious movements of the stars. Modern deduction carries the astronomical theme still further: the central altar is believed to have represented the sun; the choral movements around it, the movements of the celestial bodies. Apis, the sacred black bull, was honoured in life by dances of adoration, in death by ballets of mourning.

Either dancing was attributed to the divinities (according to a Christian saint of later centuries, it is the practice of angels) or some of the divinities were represented by dancers in the religious ballets. A carving in the Metropolitan Museum of New York shows Anubis and Horus kneeling, their arms completing a pose that is seen to this day in the dances of Spain.

Important as was the dancing of Egypt as the root from which grows the choreography of all the Occident —and of India too, for anything known to the contrary —the carvings reveal little of its philosophy or symbolism. But the history of other peoples at once demon-

ANCIENT EGYPT AND GREECE 5

strates its force as example, at least, if not as teacher of actual technique. (The Hebrews of very early days gave dancing a high place in the ceremony of worship. Moses, after the crossing of the Red Sea, bade the children of Israel dance. David danced before the Ark of the Covenant.)

(Numerous Biblical allusions show that dancing was held in high respect among early leaders of thought. "Praise the Lord . . . praise Him with timbrel and the dance," is commanded.) With dancing the Maccabees celebrated that supremely solemn event, the restoration of the Temple. To honour the slayer of Goliath, the women came out from all the cities of Israel, "singing and dancing . . . with tabrets, with joy and with instruments of musick." Relative to the capture of wives the sons of Benjamin were told: ". . . if the daughters of Shiloh come out to dance in dances, then come ye out of the vineyards, and catch you every man his wife . . . and the children of Benjamin did so, and took them wives, according to their number, of them that danced, whom they caught" (Judges 21:21 and 23). "Thou shalt again be adorned with thy tabrets, and shalt go forth in the dances of them that make merry" (Jeremiah 31:4). "Then shall the virgin rejoice in the dance" (Jeremiah 31:13). "And David danced before the Lord with all his might" (2 Samuel 6:14). In the solemn chapter of Matthew narrating the beheading of John the Baptist we read: "But when Herod's birthday was kept, the daughter of Herodias danced before them, and pleased Herod.) Whereupon he promised with an oath to give her whatever she would ask."

Perhaps with an idea of forestalling discussion of

the art's antiquity, one of the early writers eliminates argument by a simple stroke of the pen. "The stars conform to laws of co-ordinated movement. 'Co-ordinated movement' is the definition of dancing, which therefore is older than humanity." Taking this at its face value, human institutions are thrown together into one period, in which differences of a thousand years are as nothing.

In turning to Greece, years need lend no aid to make the subject attractive. In that little world of thought we find choreography luxuriant, perhaps, as it never has been since; protected by priesthood and state, practised by rich and poor, philosopher and buffoon. Great mimetic ballets memorialised great events; simple rustic dances celebrated the gathering of the crops and the coming of the flowers. Priestesses performed the sacred numbers, the origins of which tradition attributed to Olympian gods; eccentric comedy teams enlivened the streets of Athens; gilded youth held dancing an elegant accomplishment. Philosophers taught it to pupils for its effect on body and mind; it was a means of giving soldiers carriage, agility and health, and cultivating *esprit de corps*. To the development of dancing were turned the Greek ideals of beauty, which in their turn undoubtedly received a mighty and constant uplift from the beauty of harmonised movements of healthy bodies. Technique has evolved new things since the days of classic Greece; scenery, music and costume have created effects undreamed of in the early times. But notwithstanding the lack of incidental factors—and one questions if any such lack were not cancelled by the gain through simplicity—the wide-spread practice of good dancing, the greatness and frequency of munici-

ANCIENT EGYPT AND GREECE 7

pal ballets, the variety of emotional and æsthetic motives that dancing was made to express, all combine to give Greece a rank never surpassed as a dancing nation.

The man-made attributes of man's gods are a synopsis of man's important thoughts. Cybele, mother of the gods and friend of mankind, taught dancing to the corybantes as a fitting gift to be passed along to her mortal foster-children. Apollo, speaking through the mouths of priestesses, dictated further choreographic laws. Orpheus journeyed to Egypt to study its dances, that he might add to the scope of the Hellenic steps and movements. One of the nine muses was devoted to the fostering of this particular art. All of which shows a profound belief in the Greek mind that dancing was worthy of a great deal of divine attention. Certainly no subsequent civilisation has been so well qualified to judge the importance of dancing, for none has experimented so completely in the effect of rhythmic exercise on the body and mind of a nation.

Classic sculpture no more than suggests the importance of dancing in Greek life. An assemblage of a few Greek thinkers' observations on the subject furnishes an idea of the value they gave it as a factor in education. Plato, for instance, specifies it among the necessities for the ideal republic, "for the acquisition of noble, harmonious, and graceful attitudes." Socrates urged it upon his pupils. Physicians of the time of Aristophanes prescribed its rhythmic exercise for many ailments. Lycurgus gave it an important place in the training of youth, military and otherwise. Among the special dances whose teaching he decreed, was one, the *Hormos*, that was traditionally performed without clothing. Plutarch tells of a protest against the nudity of the women. The Law-giver of Athens replied: "I wish them [the women] to perform the same exercises as men, that they may equal men in strength, health, virtue and generosity of soul, and that they may learn to despise the opinion of the vulgar."

Of great men's dancing in public there are instances

FROM A FOURTH CENTURY VASE.
In the Louvre.

in abundance. The very method of choosing the leaders of great civic choreographic spectacles insured the association of people of consequence, for these leaders were always selected from the highest rank of citizens. Epaminondas, Antiochus, and Ptolemæus are variously mentioned for their skill in dancing, as well as their prominence in national affairs. Sophocles danced around the trophies of the battle of Salamis. Æschylus and Aristophanes danced in various performances of their own plays. And Socrates, one of the very fathers of human reasoning, danced among friends after dinner. Aristides danced at a banquet given by Dionysius of Syracuse. Anacreon, in his odes, declares that he is always ready to dance.

Professional dancers enjoyed high prestige. Philip of Macedon had one as a wife; the mother of Nicomedes, king of Bithynia, was a dancer. Aristodemus, a famous

ANCIENT EGYPT AND GREECE

dancer of Athens, at one time was sent to the court of Philip of Macedon as ambassador.

This chapter must not be understood as trying to represent that Athenian civil life was given over to an endless round of choreographic celebration; nor have the later chapters concerning the courts of the Louis any intent to picture a set of beings whose minds were devoted to dancing to the exclusion of all else. What is intended, however, is to call attention to an important omission in the writings of the general historian, who never has given dancing its due proportion of consideration as a force in those and other high civilisations. Literature and the graphic arts followed the coming of civilisation, and are among its results; they have been analysed with all degrees of profundity. The dance is, undoubtedly, among the causes of Greek vigour of mind

GREEK COMEDY DANCING.

and body; but it is of far less concern to the average historical writer than any disputed date. The microscopist charting the pores of the skin knows nothing of the beauty of the figure. And the grammarian's myopic search for eccentricities of verb-forms atrophies his ability to perceive the qualities of literature, until finally he will try to convince his listeners that literary quality is, after all, a subject for the attention of smaller minds.

Greek philosophy, mathematics, political and military

science are part of the structure of Occidental society—a good and useful part. Had the importance of the dance been appreciated—had proper authority recognised its inherent part in the Greek social organism—who can say how much dulness, ugliness and sickliness of body and spirit the world might have escaped?

STATUETTES.
From (A) Tanagra; (B) Myrina—now in the Louvre; (C) Tanagra (disputed).

Folk-dancing has been introduced into the public schools of certain cities; a movement too new to be judged. Let it be neither praised nor censured until results have had time to assert themselves. If at the end of ten years the children who have danced their quota of minutes per day do not excel in freedom from nervous abnormalities, the children who have not danced; if they fail to manifest a better co-ordination of mind and body, and a superior power of receiving and acting upon suggestion—then let public school dancing be abolished as of no value beyond amusement and exercise.

Of recent years a good deal of ingenuity has gone into study of the dances of classic Greece, with view to their re-creation. From paintings on vases, bas-reliefs and the Tanagra statuettes has been gathered a general idea of the character of Greek movement. The results have been pleasing, and in Miss Duncan's case radical, as an influence on contemporary choreographic art. But, beautiful and descriptive as they are, the plastic representations are of scattered poses from dances not as a rule identified. If, therefore, present-day re-creations often fail to show the flights of cumulative interest common in modern ballet, Spanish and Slavonic work, the shortcoming is due at least in part to the lack of explicit records of sequences of step, movement and pantomimic symbol. For it is impossible to believe that the dance composers of the age of Pericles did not equal their successors, even as their contemporaries in the fields of sculpture, architecture and poetry left work never yet excelled.

Of the names and motives of dances the record seems to be pretty complete. Sacred, military and profane are the general categories into which the very numerous Greek dances divide themselves. The sacred group falls into four classes: the *Emmeleia,* the *Hyporchema,* the *Gymnopædia,* and the *Endymatia.* Of these the two latter seem to have been coloured by sentiments more or less apart from the purely religious.

Of the *Emmeleia,* Plato records that some had the character of gentleness, gravity and nobility suitable to the sentiments by which a mortal should be permeated when he invokes the gods. Others were of heroic or tragic aspect, emphasising majesty and strength. A characteristic of this group was its performance without accompaniment of chorus or voice. The origin of the group is attributed to Orpheus, as a fruit of his memories of Colchis and Saïs.

The *Hyporchema,* equally religious, were distinguished by their use of choral accompaniment. In some cases it might be more accurate to say that the dances were an accompaniment to recited poetry; for in very early times the dances seem to have been employed to personify, or materialise, the abstractions of poetic metaphor. Both men and women engaged in dances of this group, and its plane was of lofty dignity. In it were the oldest dances of Greece, besides some composed by the poet Pindar.

The *Gymnopædia* were more or less dedicated to the worship of Apollo, and were especially cultivated in Arcadia. As the name implies, the performers were nude—youths wearing chaplets of palm. A material character seems to have marked this group: Athenæus finds in it points of identity with the *Anapale,* which is known to have been a pantomimic representation of combat.

The *Endymatia* crossed the border-line between the sacred and profane. They were brightly costumed dances, and in demand for general entertainment. In connection with this group we find the first allusion to the highly modern institution of dancers' "private engagements"—professionals aiding in the entertainment of dinner-parties. The Greek and Roman custom of seeing dancers instead of listening to after-dinner speeches is too well known to justify more than a mention.

These four groups are the fundamentals from which numberless other dances were derived, to be variously dedicated to gods, public events, abstract qualities, crops, and fighting. If no particular occasion offered, people would dance for the good reason that they felt like it, as Neapolitans dance the *Tarantella* to-day. To the

Courtesy of The Metropolitan Museum of Art, New York
GREEK RELIEF DECORATIONS

To face page 12

Courtesy of The Metropolitan Museum of Art, New York
GREEK CERAMIC DECORATIONS

ANCIENT EGYPT AND GREECE

glory of Bacchus were the *Dionysia;* the *Iambic* was sacred to Mars, the *Caryatis,* a dance symbolising innocence, and danced nude, to Diana. Hercules, Theseus, the daughters of Jupiter, Castor and Pollux were so honoured—each dance having its special identification of movement, meaning or costume.

Semirelated to the religious group were the dances

STATUETTES.
From (A) Myrina; (B) Tanagra; (C) Myrina.

of mourning. Unlike certain modern dances of the same intent, these are not recorded as having been primarily an individual's pantomimic dance representing qualities of the deceased, or illustrating his relations during life with friends and family; although there was a time in which the *cortège* was headed by an individual dressed in the clothes of the deceased, imitating his virtues and sometimes also his failings. Regularly, however, the dancing was strictly ritualistic, forming a solemn decorative concomitant of the vocal and instrumental music. (At what point in his evolution did the Occidental determine that his ritualistic expressions should be directed almost exclusively to the ear?) A corps of fifteen girls danced before the funeral car, which was surrounded by a band of youths. Naturally the brilliancy of the function was more or less proportionate to the station and estate of the departed.

On dances of war the Greeks relied as an important element in the soldier's training. In their pantomime the veteran lived over the moments of combat, while his children and even his wife caught anew the spirit of Hellenic arms.

Plutarch wrote: "The military dance was an indefinable stimulus which inflamed courage and gave strength to persevere in the paths of honour and valour." It is still known that a body of men moving in step feel fatigue distinctly less than when walking out of step. One of the things learned by the long-distance runner, the wood-cutter, or any other performer of continued work, is the importance of establishing as quickly as possible a regular rhythmic relation between the separate parts of a complete movement, including the intake and expulsion of breath among those parts. Such a rhythm once established, movement succeeds movement with something like momentum; the several steps, or blows of the axe, do not each require a separate effort of the will. Something of this was Plutarch's "indefinable stimulus."

Apart from efficiency of the individual, experience has shown that a command moving "in time" is unified in the fullest sense, with each soldier more or less perfectly proof against any impulse at variance with the *esprit de corps*. To weld a number of men ever more closely into the condition of a military unit is one of the purposes of drill. Drill is in great part a matter of keeping in step. The Greeks carried to a high pitch the unification of a military body in respect to all the movements of attack and defence. History repeatedly

ANCIENT EGYPT AND GREECE

records the demoralisation of the enemy, carried by the assaults of the perfectly organised Greek fighting bodies. But undoubtedly an important value of the study for perfection of corps unity was the disciplinary effect on the Greek soldier himself.

As a means toward such perfection, Greek law prescribed dancing for the soldier. An obvious benefit from his practice of the art was the advantage due to mere muscular exercise; and that in itself is no small thing when the dance is performed in full armour, as the Greek soldier performed it.

Authorities classify the military dances as *Pyrrhic* and *Memphitic;* but the division seems hardly essential, since the meagre technical descriptions draw no distinct line between the two groups. In both, performers carried sword or spear and shield. The movements brought in the manœuvres of individual combat—cutting and thrusting, parrying, dodging and stooping. That they might be carried to a degree of realism is indicated in a description by Xenophon. At the end of a mimic combat between two Thracians, at the conclusion of which the victor sang a song of victory and possessed himself of the vanquished man's weapons, the spectators cried out with emotion, believing that the fallen man was killed.

Of the words "Pyrrhic" and "Memphitic," the latter seems to connote a performance less insistent on the element of combat. To Minerva is credited the origin of the *Memphitic* group, legend having it that the goddess of wisdom composed these dances to celebrate the defeat of the Titans. The usual accompaniment was the flute, according with the idea of comparative tranquillity. Both styles were danced by women; special fame for proficiency was given to the vigorous daughters of Sparta, Argos, and Arcadia, and to the Amazons.

Pantomime was important in most Greek dances. Greek writers interested themselves in an effort to trace pantomime to its origin; but they were not very successful, because they went no further back than the demi-gods. Whereas sign-talk, if inference may be drawn from savages, antedates spoken language—which is beside the point of the present sketch.

Pantomime artists of Greece were of various ranks, according to the plane of thought represented in their work. *Ethologues* represented moralities, or ὑπόθεσες; they "depicted the emotions and the conduct of man so faithfully, that their art served as a rigorous censorship and taught useful lessons," writes De l'Aulnaye, in *De la Saltation Théâtrale*. They were not only artists, but philosophers of a moral standard of the utmost height and purity: the poems of one of them, Sophron of Syracuse, were among the writings kept at hand by Plato during his last hours. Θυμέλικοι were pantomimists of lesser rank, whose work was principally comedy of a farcical nature—though the word seems to have the primitive meaning of "chorister."

Rich in scope was the Greek stage; and, until later days, generally high in plane. For its effects it drew upon poetry, music, dancing, grouping and posing. Little is known of the music; re-creations of it (how authoritative the authors do not know) are simple and melodious, with no attempt at grandeur. But in the other departments, what veritable gods in collaboration! Euripides, Aristophanes, and Æschylus are of those who supplied texts. Sculptors whose works are no less perishable gave their knowledge to grouping and posing.

ANCIENT EGYPT AND GREECE

Of the merit of the performers there is no adequate record, for lack, among other things, of an explicit choreographic terminology. (This deficiency was first made up in the French language, after the organisation of the National Academy of Music and Dancing, in the seventeenth century.) What is known, however, is that dancing was considered a proper medium of expression of great motives, and that great-minded artists chose

DANCE OF NYMPHS.
From an antique frieze in the Louvre.

it as a career; not in spite of a public condescension to it, but with the support of a profound public respect.

Accuracy of rhythm is of an importance obvious to grades of intelligence far below that of the Greeks. They laid stress no less on what may be called rhythmic quality than on mere emphasis of tempo. A time-marker was provided with an assortment of sandals soled with metal or wood of various thicknesses; by means of these he produced sounds consistent with the changing sentiments of the action. (Compare the modes of getting varied sounds from castanets, in chapter on Spanish dancing.) Castanets, too, were used in Greece, essentially the same as those of Spain to-day; also flat sticks in pairs, like clappers, but which unlike clappers were gripped between the thumb and fingers. Little cymbals on the dancers' hands sometimes added their voice, and the tambourine was popular. The variety of these time-marking instruments indicates knowledge of the many effects attainable by tempo alone. Indeed a reading of the poets emphasises this: their selection of words for sound as well as meaning will force even a mediocre reader into an observance of the author's intention of ritard and accelerando, legato and staccato, emphasis and climax. Associated with ballet production, as the ablest poets were, it may be taken as assured that the devices of tempo were made familiar to dancers—unless it was the dance that taught the metre to the poets.

Masks were worn to identify character; but their primary function appears to have been the concealment of a sound-magnifying device to carry the voice through the great spaces of out-door theatres. Women's parts in the ballets were played by men at least frequently; whether the reverse was a conspicuous exception is also uncertain. Both usages were destined to survive in pantomime through centuries. Objection to the mask always was overruled by authority; the Greek play was such an irreproachable organism that deviation from its accepted formulas was deemed an impious and dangerous heresy. In the eighteenth century a premier danseur's absence put a French ballet director temporarily at the mercy of the second dancer, a young radical, who refused to "go on" wearing a mask.* Not until then was the mask tradition disturbed.

Though exact data of the steps of popular dances are lacking, literary allusions record dance names and general character in great number. A complete catalogue

* See also page 101.

ANCIENT EGYPT AND GREECE

of them would offer little inspiration to the lay student or the professional; no more than a hint of their broad scope is necessary. Dances suggesting the life of animals were plentiful. Some were underlaid with a symbolic significance, as that of the crane, the bird's confused wanderings representing the efforts of Theseus to find his way out of the labyrinth, the legend in its turn probably having some relation to life and the tricks it plays on its possessors. The fox was a favourite subject, and the lion was not overlooked. Though the author of *Chanticler* may have been the first to avail himself of the grotesqueries of poultry, the Greeks danced owls and vultures. Similar to the Oriental *Danse du Ventre* was the *Kolia,* probably brought across from Egypt. Another suggestion of North Africa was known in Greek language as the *Dance of Spilled Meal* —what more reasonable than to infer that it was the same in scheme as the *Flour Dance* of present-day Algeria? The flour or meal that identifies this performance is spread on the floor, and a more or less involved design traced in it. What follows is interesting chiefly as a test of a species of virtuosity: the dancer's object is, in her successive turns across and about the design, to plant her feet always within the same spaces, the loose meal exposing any failure. Rapidity of tempo and involution of step may raise the difficulties to a point beyond the reach of any but the most skilful. The children's game of Hop-scotch is a degenerated kinsman of the dance in and over a design.

There were dances of satyrs and goats, nymphs, monkeys, gods and goddesses, flowers, grapes and the winepress. Combat was rendered into poetry in the *Spear Dance,* the *Fight with the Shadow* (σκίαμαχια), the fights with shields, with swords. There were "rounds," performed by an indefinite number of people joining hands in a ring; traces of these are said to survive as peasant dances of the Greece of to-day. There were solos, *pas de deux* and *pas de quatre*. Pythagoras made a period of dancing a part of the daily routine of his pupils, *Hymeneia* were danced to help celebrate a well-conducted wedding. Prayers, sacrifices and funerals, as stated before, were incomplete without their several and special dances.

Movement no less than speech is a vehicle for satire, wit, sensuality and indecency. Theophrastus, with the intent of showing the degree of shamelessness to which erring humanity may fall, tells of a man who performed a dance called the *Cordax* without the excuse of being drunk at the time of the deed. Covering a wide range of light motives was the *Sikinnis,* the word being applied both to a certain dance and to a form of satirical mimodrama. In the latter sense it burlesqued the politics, philosophy and drama of the day. As all peoples divide themselves into masses and classes on lines of taste as well as of money, so also eventually the Athenians. In the hands of the Athens rabble—catered to perhaps by ancestors of certain twentieth-century managers—the *Sikinnis,* as a satire, fell into the slough of vulgarity.

As a dance it may be thought of as a favourite of that Alcibiades type of youth in whom education has not depressed Arcadian frivolity. How such a one vexed the solemnity of a court is the subject of an anecdote compiled by Herodotus. Clisthenes, king of Sicyon, in order to marry his daughter to the greatest advantage, decided to settle the selection of her husband by competition. The invitation met with due interest on the part of the rich and the great. Suitors came from far and near, among them two from Athens. An ominous circumstance, for "Attic salt" was out of the same barrel as the *"sal de Andalucia"* of to-day; both have the record of becoming operative immediately on exposure to any air of oversolemnity.

After days of regal festivity, Clisthenes dedicated a hecatomb to the gods, gave a final banquet, and announced that the suitor-selecting competition would be along the lines of music and poetry. When it came to the turn of Hippoclides, one of the two Athenians, he asked that a table be brought in. On this he mounted, stood on his hands, and traced the figures of a *Sikinnis* in the air with his feet!

Until the king's temper was quite gone, the performance was received in silence. Herodotus supposed that Hippoclides interpreted the silence as encouragement; but Herodotus very clearly did not know that kind of boy. The polished though inverted youth on the table was estimating the horror among his worthy spectators, and luxuriating.

Greece, with her fine simplicity of thought, furnished the pattern on which was cut the civilisation of early Rome; Greek art, the concrete expression of her lofty thought, furnished Rome a model. Which model Rome followed until loot and tribute provided her with means to express the taste that was her own.

GREEK COMEDY DANCING.

CHAPTER II

DANCING IN ROME

AN art that achieves beauty by means of the grace of simple lines, elegance of proportion and other simple resources of composition, is the art of a vigorous nation. Such an art scorns florid treatment, surface realism, triviality; and such an art was that of early Rome. It had that something clumsily called semiasceticism, that attaches to dignity.

A national art quality exists, as is axiomatic, upon a basis and by virtue of a corresponding public state of mind; each influencing the other, but the public state of mind being the force that shapes the art, rather than the reverse. The spirit of simplicity dominated Greece through many centuries of her grandeur. In Rome it endured until Rome grew rich. Its coexistence in the case of the two peoples was no more than a coincidence; they arrived at their common simplicity through wholly different processes.

In Greece, beauty was understood. Action and adornment were restrained because their value was found to be multiplied by sparing use; because, too, any excess of them detracted from the great qualities of line and proportion. In Greece, moreover, beauty dissociated from subject or sentiment could always find an appreciative reception; the Hellenic mind loved beauty for its own sake. And that is the cause of the reserve that governs the best Greek art.

Early Rome, too, instilled into her children the spirit

of simplicity. Not, however, with any understanding of the relation of simplicity to beauty and dignity. War and lust for conquest made the early Roman stern; and simplicity, attached to a very real asceticism, was thrust upon him by the uncompromising hand of poverty. But, after a few centuries of fattening on loot and tribute, what of Rome? Stupidity, degeneracy and vulgarity.

Loot and tribute! In respect to riches both material and mental, other peoples' contributions to Rome's destiny were of a degree of importance sometimes underrated. Her monumental physical structure was built from taxes gathered by the mailed hand. In respect to her thought, expressed in essays, poems, orations, letters, commentaries or whatsoever other form, the extent of other nations' contribution to Rome's apparent originality is, at first glance, less evident. Upon Greek foundations of narrative structure, metre, and form in general, Roman writings are built, Romanised though they be in subject-matter—but Rome's sterility of invention in that field is suited rather to the discussion of literary men than of dance-lovers.

But sculpture is pertinent. The first so-called Roman art was accomplished by carving Roman faces upon thickened figures in Greek poses, executing them in Greek technique of modelling, and naming them Roman gods and senators. Later the Greek simplicity of modelling was discarded; to replace it there was achieved an ostentatious mediocrity. The Pompeian frescoes? The good ones were painted by Greeks, brought across for the purpose. And the vivacious little statues found in Pompeii express the same artistically witty point of view.

In the field of material gain and convenience Rome's contribution to the world is not to be questioned. But water-supply, paving, land laws and fortifications are not related to questions of taste. It is Roman taste of which one tries to form a conception, in order to explain, at least in part, the disappointing history of dancing under the Cæsars. And the mere direction of attention to Rome's relation to the arts anticipates the story of her treatment of the dance, leaving only details to be told.

First in chronology is found the dancing symbolical of war. Then comes a simple religious choreography, under the Salic priests, supplementing the ritual of sacrifice. As time goes on Greek dances are transplanted, with the degree of success to be expected among a race whose minds, though active, are pleased only by material power, gain, and ostentation: by a process of atrophy following non-appreciation, the symbolism disappears from symbolic dances and the ideal of beauty from the purely beautiful dances. They became at best a display of agility to amuse rustics. More generally they fell into the service of sex allurement; not the suggestive merely, nor the provocative, but unbridled depiction of what should not be revealed and of things that should not exist. This condition of affairs is more than hinted in works of some of the much-read Latin writers, stated by archæologists, and confirmed by certain Pompeian statues.

Such offences, despite the resentment they arouse in the feelings of any naturally constituted person, might be partially pardoned by the dance-lover if they contributed anything to the dance. But absolutely they do not. There is latent drama and good drama in sex relationships; but not one accent of its valid expression can be traced to dances of obscenity. The dancer who gives himself over to obscenity loses, every time, the things that made him a dancer: form, truth and beauty of movement and posture. Where the art of dancing is appreciated, artists avoid obscene suggestion. Where it is not, many are forced to it in order to make a living. However, even where the art is appreciated, obscenity furnishes the incompetent a means of pretence of an artist's career; for obscenity is sure of a mixed following of rabblement, some in rags and some in velvet.

Among the Romans themselves, actual participation in the dance was not popular. Propriety forbade so close an association with an art disfigured and dirtied, the Roman reviling as unclean the image soiled by his own hand. From Spain, Greece and Syria people were brought to dance before gourmands and wasters, degraded to the level of their patrons' appreciation, and discarded when they had exhausted the scope of novelties suitable to the demand. Several centuries of Roman employment of dancers contributed not one step, gesture or expression to the art; the plastic and graphic records show only that which is Greek, or, on the other hand inane, vulgar, or degenerate. To the latter levels sank the *Ludiones* and the *Saturnalia;* instituted as religious celebrations, ending as orgies.

It is vaguely asserted that the Roman stage amplified the Greek scope of pantomime. And, notwithstanding the many reasons to distrust such a statement, there were two artists whose work may have been of a class to justify it. They were Pylades and Bathyllus, natives respectively of Silicia and Alexandria. Their names live in the impression they produced. Of the character of their work it is impossible to learn anything explicit; "softly dancing Bathyllus" is as concrete a reference as anything to be found about them in writings of their period. So it is impossible to know whether their great popularity was due to merit, or to ingenious compliance with the taste of their adopted city. Their record, therefore, must stand as the story of a furor, and not necessarily as that of artistic achievement.

"The rivalries of Pylades and Bathyllus occupied the Romans as much as the gravest affairs of state. Every Roman was a Bathyllian or a Pyladian," De l'Aulnaye writes. Vuillier presents a more graphic image of their hold on public attention: "Their theatrical supporters, clad in different liveries, used to fight in the streets, and bloody brawls were frequent throughout the city." For the endless quarrelling and intriguing between the two, Pylades was once taken to task by the emperor. The answer was that of a lofty artist or a publicity-seeking gallery-player, let him decide who can: "Cæsar, it is well for you that the people are occupied with our quarrels; their attention is in that way diverted from your actions."

His arrogance directed itself impartially toward ruler and subject. Representing the madness of Hercules—he combined pantomime with dancing—he shot arrows into the audience. Octavius being present on such an occasion refrained from any expression of disapproval. Was he afraid of offending his people by so much as an implied criticism of their favourite? It is not unlikely. When, unable to control his impatience with Pylades' unsettling influence, the emperor banished him, a revocation of the decree was made imperative by signs of a popular insurrection!

Not the least of the instances of Pyladian insolence was his interruption of the action of a play to scold his audience. During a performance of *Hercules* some one complained loudly that the movement was extravagant. Pylades tore off his mask and shouted back, "I am representing a madman, you fools!"

So much for Pylades and Bathyllus. The jealous, hypertemperamental artist who allows nothing to interfere with the effect of the work to which he is consecrated sometimes falls into eccentricities of conduct. Such eccentricities are copied to admiration by impudent incompetents; and, contrary to P. T. Barnum's aphorism, some of them do "fool all the people all the time"—especially if those people themselves lack the clear vision of simplicity. Impudence to emperors and "shooting up" audiences may mean the utmost of either sincerity or hypocrisy; choice of opinion is free. Certainly the Roman Empire's political intrigues reveal a profound and practical knowledge of the science of publicity; it is an ancient profession.

Artists, advertisers or both, it matters not at all, Pylades and Bathyllus failed to lift dancing from the mire. The self-styled "Eternal City," the Rome of the Cæsars, held it down to her level till her rotted hands could cling no longer, yet treated it from first to last with scorn. Horace, who never allowed his wit to lead him into danger of offending any except those without influence on his patron Mæcenas, repeatedly uses association with dancers as a synonym of disreputability. Cicero takes a fling at the art; Sallust attacks a lady for dancing with a degree of skill unbecoming a virtuous woman. With the logic of a father who locked up his children so that they should not teach bad manners to their parents, successive emperors banished dancers for doing their work according to the taste of their patrons.

Rome's inability to move her imagination on a high plane had decayed her, muscle, brain and bone; wealth slipped away, and all of her that was respected was her remote past. In the meantime she had imposed upon Europe her laws and prejudices. Ears trained to credulous attention were those that heard her complaint of the depravity of dancing—a complaint given colour by the obscenity of the only secular dancing known to Europeans (outside of Spain) in the time of the empire's decadence. With such a combined force of misrepresentation against it, its restoration to a proper position among the great arts was destined to be postponed a thousand years. To this day there persists to its injury an echo of its early defamation.

Yet in the hour of humiliation, the dance gained the respect of the only earthly power that might reasonably hope, in such an extremity, to save it from a miserable end. It was taken under the protection of the Christian Church.

CHAPTER III

THE MIDDLE AGES AND THE RENAISSANCE

CHRISTIANITY, like the religions of the Hebrews of old and the Greeks, employed dancing as an important part of the ritual of worship. During the greater part of a thousand years, the relation was not violently disturbed; the *ballet d'action* served in the mass before the altar, and in the "moralities" that long held favour as an agency of spiritual instruction. A clerical it was who eventually composed and staged the great pantomime which the many authorities place as the first modern ballet.

European society, slowly emerging from the mire of Roman manners, at length found itself hungry for beauty, and capable of intelligent use of pearls. The ballet masque was evolved, and long remained the supremely brilliant feature of noble festivities. Polite society, headed by a king, was the founder of the ballet as it is now known. But this was in modern times. The institution that had conserved choreography through the brutishness of the Dark Ages was the Church.

To one Father Menestrier is owed a compilation of data about dancing, especially in relation to religion. The good father was a Jesuit living in the seventeenth century, his book having been written about 1682. While his own comments are not always contributory to exact knowledge of choreographic detail, the facts he collected from a great variety of sources are important and interesting. In the following passage he definitely attaches dancing to the ritual:

"Divine service was composed of psalms, hymns and canticles, because men sang and danced the praises of God, as they read His oracles in those extracts of the Old and New Testaments which we still know under the name of Lessons. The place in which these acts of worship were offered to God was called the choir, just as those portions of comedies and tragedies in which dancing and singing combined to make up the interludes were called choruses. Prelates were called in the Latin tongue, *Præsules a Præsiliendo,* because in the choir they took that part in the praises of God which he who led the dances, and was called by the Greeks *Choregus,* took in the public games."

The word *"præsul"* was the designation of the chief priest of the Salii, of early Rome.

Quoting from St. Basil's Epistle to St. Gregory, Menestrier writes further: "What could be more blessed than to imitate on earth the rhythm of angels?" (*"Quid itaque beatius esse poterit quam in terra tripudia Angelorum imitari?"*) To this he adds: "Philosophers have also existed who believed that these spirits had no other means of communication among themselves but signs and movements arranged after the manner of dances. After this we need not be surprised that Virgil, in the sixth book of the *Æneid,* makes the spirits dance in the Elysian fields."

The Emperor Julian was reproved by St. Gregory of Nazianzus, not for dancing, but for the kind of dances with which he occupied himself. "If you are fond of dancing," said the saint, "if your inclination leads you to these festivals that you appear to love so passionately, dance as much as you will; I consent. But why revive before our eyes the dissolute dances of the barbarous Herodias and the Pagans? Rather perform the dances of King David before the Ark; dance to the honour of God. Such exercises of peace and piety are worthy of an emperor and a Christian."

No more need be quoted to explain the adoption of dancing by the Church, and the regard in which it was held by the reverend fathers. By some of them, that is. Others held it in different estimation. Odon, Bishop of Paris, proscribed dancing in the twelfth century. Notwithstanding, the fifteenth and sixteenth see in Spain the so-called *Villancicos de Navidad* (a choreographic celebration of the birth of Christ) and the dances of the *Seises,* then as now performed in the Cathedral of Seville. The latter were authorised in 1439 by a Bull of Pope Eugenius IV. Their discontinuance was ordered by Don Jayme de Palafox, Archbishop of Seville. To settle the matter the *Seises* were taken to Rome and their dances shown to the Pope, who as a consequence approved their continuance.

France, too, declined to take the proscription seriously, as almost numberless documents and images attest. In 1584 the Canon of Langres, by name Jehan Tabourot, otherwise Thoinet Arbeau, wrote (in his seventieth year) his work called *Orchesographie.* He refers cheerfully to opposition: "We practice such merrymaking on days of wedding celebrations, and of the solemnities of the feasts of our Church, even though the reformers abhor such things; but in this matter they deserve to be treated like some hind-quarter of goat put into dough without lard." (*"Mais ils mériteroient d'y être traictez de quelque gigot de bouc mis en paste sans lard."*) Not an infelicitous metaphor, after inquiry reveals that dough without lard bakes to the hardness of concrete, so that the aid of a hammer is necessary to crack the shell. What more satisfying disposal of dissenters from one's own opinions?

Proofs of the dance's tenacious inclination to embody itself in the worship of the vital new religion are many. Records of efforts to establish it are mingled with those of counter-efforts to expel it; on the one side a belief that worship is an emotional expression, on the other a leaning toward logic. Whether religious uplift is a matter of emotion or of reason is a question perhaps not wholly settled yet. Certainly the mediæval writers recorded little to reflect a spirit of compromise—no concession that ritual or logic might advantageously be chosen with some reference to the psychology of the individual. At the suggestion of the Council of Toledo, a ritual rich in sacred choreography was composed by Saint Isidore, archbishop of Seville in the seventh century. Another century produced two occurrences of choreographic importance at about the same moment: from Pope Zacharias, a prohibition of dancing; from the Moorish invasion, preservation of the seven churches of Toledo. Of the two influences, the latter was deemed paramount. In the seven churches a mass known as the *Mozarabe* was established, continued in all of them through the generations of Moorish occupancy of the city, and is still celebrated daily in the cathedral. In the other six churches it was discontinued toward the middle of the nineteenth century. With accompaniment of the tambourine, whose resonance Saint Isidore characterised as "the half of melody," the service included solemn dancing of the style of the *Saraband* and the *Pavane*. Whether or not the choreographic features are still retained, the authors are unable to say.

Writing in 1731 a *Discourse on Comedy,* Father Pierre le Brun contributes the information: " . . . that while the preachers were saying their mass, buffoons, histrions, players of instruments and different other *farceurs* were made to come; this disorder is severely forbidden, as well as dances and the presentation of spectacles in the churches and cemeteries. The same prohibition is found in the synodic statutes of the diocese of Soissons, printed in that city in 1561. Dances were sometimes performed before the church, and there was not less objection made against the practice at that time. . . . Meanwhile it is disgracefully tolerated in some of the country parishes."

These "spectacles" were the vehicle that carried the mimetic ballet through the Dark Ages from Rome's licentious theatre and banquet hall to the stately salon of the Medici. Under the name of "moralities" they survive to this day in convents, though clipped as to their choreographic wings. *Everyman,* played a few years ago by Ben Greet and his company, was a re-creation of some of the elements of the early morality, plus speech and minus dancing. Love, aspiration, reverence; envy, fear, remorse and various other elemental abstractions that inhabit the human soul were the source of most of the morality's characters; the dramatic action consisted—usually if not always—in a simple treatment of the influences wrought by the varied forces on the destiny of a man. The man, no more and no less than the abstract qualities, was represented by an actor. Occurrences of man's life, both earthly and subsequent, were equally available as dramatic material. Apostles, angels and even God were of frequent representation.

A start was made in a direction destined to lead to the development of scenery. Whereas the Greek drama established the setting by means of spoken words (and the Roman apparently made no exception to the same practice), the early morality specified the setting by means of words or crude symbols marked on objects, the back wall, and other available surfaces: "forest," "front of house," "Heaven," "street," or whatever was necessary. Elaboration by degrees brought these primitive suggestions up to the point of real scenery, with practical mechanical devices for sensational entrances.

One must infer that the semiconstant opposition of the Church to these representations was necessitated by occasional forgetfulness of their sacred character. The pagan gods persistently lingered among the *dramatis personæ,* undismayed by the fact that they were dead, and unshamed by the treatment their followers had accorded Christianity. Performers no less than authors were sometimes guilty of ribaldry ranging from the frivolous to the impious. "A canon playing entirely nude the rôle of Christ, and a clerk representing Saint Francis in a scene of seduction, undressed in the same manner, were not at all spectacles of which the originators of the *genre* had dreamed."

Yet the good clearly outweighed the bad. And although repeatedly prohibited, no mention is found of dancing being severely penalised. Now at the altar and again at the feast it serves, in whatever capacity is required of it, until at length it comes into prominent connection with the strolling ballet.

For the morality play—or mystery, as it is otherwise

known—becomes an elaborate affair, with casts and mechanical and scenic effects, on such a scale that it must collect more coppers than one town affords, in order to recover the initial expense of the production. On a scale sufficient to make an impression on its times was the spectacle designed to celebrate the canonisation of Carlo Borroméo, at Lisbon in 1610. In the words of Vuillier: "A ship, bearing a statue of St. Carlo, advanced toward Lisbon, as though to take possession of the soil of Portugal, and all the ships in the harbour went out to meet it. St. Anthony of Padua and St. Vincent, patrons of the town, received the newcomer, amid salvoes of artillery from forts and vessels. On his disembarkation, St. Carlo Borroméo was received by the clergy and carried in a procession in which figured four enormous chariots. The first represented Fame, the second the city of Milan, the third Portugal, and the fourth the Church. Each religious body and each brotherhood in the procession carried its patron saint upon a richly decorated litter.

"The statue of St. Carlo Borroméo was enriched with jewels of enormous value, and each saint was decorated with rich ornaments. It is estimated that the value of the jewelry that bedecked these images was not less than four millions of francs (£160,000).

"Between each chariot, bands of dancers enacted various scenes. In Portugal, at that period, processions and religious ceremonies would have been incomplete if they had not been accompanied by dancing in token of joy.

"In order to add brilliancy to these celebrations, tall gilded masts, decorated with crowns and many-coloured banners, were erected at the doors of the churches and along the route of the choreographic procession. These masts also served to show the points at which the procession should halt, for the dancers to perform the principal scenes of their ballet."

A century and a half before this—in 1462—King René of Provence had organised an entertainment, at once religious and social, given on the eve of Corpus Christi. The word *"entremet"* was applied to the alle-

DANCE OF PEASANTS.
After a sixteenth-century engraving.

gorical scenes, denoting "interlude," like the Italian *"intermezzo."* Other components of the representation were combats and dances. The affair as a whole was a mixture of the sacred and profane to which any idea of unity was completely alien: Fame on a winged horse; burlesque representations of the Duke and Duchess of Urbino, riding donkeys (why represented, no one knows—but during three centuries the two were travestied in Corpus Christi processions); Mars and Minerva, Pan and Syrinx, Pluto and Proserpine, fauns, dryads and tritons dancing to drums, fifes and castanets;

MIDDLE AGES AND RENAISSANCE

Jupiter, Juno, Venus and Love following in a chariot. The three Fates, King Herod persecuted by devils, more devils pursuing a soul, it in turn protected by a guardian angel; Jews dancing around a golden calf; the Queen of Sheba and suite; Magi following a star hung at the end of a pole; the Massacre of the Innocents; Christ and the Apostles—all were scattered through and among the groups of legendary beings of Greece. More dancers, a detachment of soldiers, and Death with a scythe following after all others, approximately completed the fantastic catalogue.

The entertainment as a whole was called by the king the *Lou Gué*. A number of the French popular dance airs that lasted for centuries are said to date back to it. Tradition credits the king with the composition of the work in all its branches—conception, ballets, music and all.

The childish lack of theme, or scheme, bars the *Lou Gué* and the entertainments that followed from any comparison with a ballet spectacle of later times, or of antiquity. But it bridged a gap to better things, kept the ballet in existence, and had the merit of being amusing. In eccentricity it may well be coupled with the celebration of the wedding of Charles the Bold and Margaret of England; "fabulous spectacles imprinted with a savage gallantry," as M. Brussel puts it. The procession of the latter affair included a leopard riding a unicorn, a dwarf on a gigantic lion, and a dromedary bearing panniers of birds, "strangely painted as though they came from India," that were released among the company.

The fête organised by Bergonzio de Botta in 1489, showed a step in the direction of the ballet's destined progress. The occasion was the marriage of Galeazzo, Duke of Milan, with Isabel of Aragon. This fête employed the dance, music, poetry and pantomime in the adornment of a banquet; and the whole entertainment was unified with ingenious consistency. The description of it given by Castil-Blaze cannot be improved upon:

"The Amphitryon chose for his theatre a magnificent hall surrounded by a gallery, in which several bands of music had been stationed; an empty table occupied the middle. At the moment when the Duke and Duchess appeared, Jason and the Argonauts advanced proudly to the sound of martial music. They bore the Golden Fleece; this was the tablecloth, with which they covered the table, after having executed a stately dance, expressive of their admiration of so beautiful a princess, and of a sovereign so worthy to possess her. Next came Mercury, who related how he had been clever enough to trick Apollo, shepherd of Admetus, and rob him of a fat calf, which he ventured to present to the newly married pair, after having had it nobly trussed and prepared by the best cook on Olympus. While he was placing it upon the table, three quadrilles that followed him danced round the fatted calf, as the Hebrews had formerly capered round that of gold.

"Diana and her nymphs followed Mercury. It is unnecessary to say that a fanfare of hunting-horns heralded the entrance of Diana, and accompanied the dance of the nymphs.

"The music changed its character; lutes and flutes announced the approach of Orpheus. I would recall to the memory of those who might have forgotten it, that at that period they changed their instruments according to the varying expression of the music played. Each singer, each dancer, had his especial orchestra, which was arranged for him according to the sentiments intended to be expressed by his song or his dance. It was an excellent plan, and served to vary the symphonies; it announced the return of a character who had already appeared, and produced a varied succession of trumpets, of violins with their sharp notes, of the arpeggios of lutes, and of the soft melodies of flutes and reed pipes. The orchestrations of Monteverde prove that the composers at that time varied their instrumentation thus, and this particular artifice was not one of the least causes of the prodigious success of opera in the first years of its creation.

"But to return to the singer of Thrace, whom I left standing somewhat too long at the door. He appeared chanting the praises of the Duchess, and accompanying himself on a lyre.

" 'I wept,' he went on, 'long did I weep on the Apennine mount the death of the gentle Eurydice. I have heard of the union of two lovers worthy to live one for the other, and for the first time since my misfortune I have experienced a feeling of pleasure. My songs changed with the feelings of my heart. A crowd of birds fluttered down to listen to me; I seized these imprudent listeners, and I spitted them all to roast them for the most beautiful princess on earth, since Eurydice is no more.'

"A sound of brass instruments interrupted the bird-snaring virtuoso; Atalanta and Theseus, escorted by a brilliant and agile troop, represented a boar hunt by means of lively dances. It ended in the death of the boar of Calydon, which they offered to the young Duke, executing a triumphal ballet. Iris, in a chariot drawn by peacocks, followed by nymphs clad in light transparent gauze, appeared on one side, and laid on the table dishes of her own superb and delicate birds. Hebe, bearing nectar, appeared on the other side, accompanied by shepherds from Arcady, and by Vertumnus and Pomona, who presented iced creams and cheeses, peaches, apples, oranges and grapes. At the same moment the shade of the gastronomer Apicius rose from the earth. The illustrious professor came to inspect this splendid banquet, and to communicate his discoveries to the guests.

"This spectacle disappeared to give place to a great ballet of Tritons and Rivers laden with the most delicious fish. Crowned with parsley and watercress, these aquatic deities despoiled themselves of their headdresses to make a bed for the turbot, the trout, and the perch that they placed upon the table.

"I know not whether the epicures invited by the host were much amused by these ingenious ceremonies, and whether their tantalised stomachs did not cry out against all the pleasures offered to their eyes and ears; history does not enter into these details. Moreover, Bergonzio de Botta understood too well how to organise a feast not to have put some ballast into his guests in the shape of a copious luncheon, which might serve as a preface, or argument, an introduction if you will, to the dinner prepared by the gods, demigods, Nymphs, Tritons, Fauns and Dryads.

"This memorable repast was followed by a singular spectacle. It was inaugurated by Orpheus, who conducted Hymen and Cupids. The Graces presented Conjugal Fidelity, who offered herself to wait upon the princess. Semiramus, Helen, Phædra, Medea and Cleopatra interrupted the solo of Conjugal Fidelity by singing of their own lapses, and the delights of infidelity. Fidelity, indignant at such audacity, ordered these criminal queens to retire. The Cupids attacked them, pursuing them with their torches, and setting fire to the long veils that covered their heads. Something, clearly, was necessary

BALLET OF THE FOUR PARTS OF THE WORLD: ENTRANCE OF THE GRAND KHAN.
After an old drawing, Bibliothèque Nationale, Paris.

to counterbalance this scene. Lucretia, Penelope, Thomyris, Judith, Portia and Sulpicia advanced, and laid at the feet of the duchess the palms of virtue they had won during their lives. As the graceful and modest dance of the matrons might have seemed a somewhat cold termination to so brilliant a fête, the author had recourse to Bacchus, Silenus and to the Satyrs, and their follies animated the end of the ballet."

The entertainment made a sensation. It was at the time of the Renaissance; the Occidental mind was awakening after a thousand years of sleep, and craved employment. Taste was being reborn, along with mentality. The pleasures of contact between minds was being rediscovered; the institution of Polite Society was rapidly finding itself.

To attempt to repeat the Bergonzio de Botta entertainment would have been to invite comparisons; to surpass it in any point but magnitude would have been excessively difficult. Its influence on entertainments that followed directed itself toward the development of the masque, a form of musical pantomime that remained, through centuries, an indispensable adjunct of festal gatherings in the courts of the Continent and England. The characters in the De Botta production, it will be noted, were, with two or three exceptions, from Greek mythology. This was the culmination of a fashion that had been growing, and is fairly representative of the revival of learning then in progress. It was not until a few years ago that familiarity with classic tradition ceased to be considered a part of the education of a lady or gentleman. There is no reason to believe that the lack of such erudition makes one the less a lady or a gentleman; but its discontinuance is unfortunate for the pantomime ballet. In Greek mythology, both natural manifestations and mental attributes were personified. Not with the completeness of a catalogue, but enough to express a great many points by the mere presence of certain characters. Venus, Minerva, Diana; Dionysius, Orpheus, Apollo, Mercury—all were accepted symbols of certain human qualities. In relegating their acquaintance to the depository of cast-off mental furniture, people have failed to create new symbols to take the place of the old. Harlequin and Columbine we have,

MIDDLE AGES AND RENAISSANCE

and a few others. But how many are the figures whose mere entrance, without the interruption of dramatic action, could be depended upon to introduce definite and recognisable ideas? Pantomime has to be explained on the programme nowadays; and as nobody gets to his seat until after the auditorium lights are down, the programme is unread and people complain that the characters lack meaning. Broadly, Modernism has devised for itself an education that teaches it to earn each day the cost of a thousand pleasures, but by which it is robbed of the power to enjoy any one of them.

Scattered through mediæval choreographic history are allusions to an employment of chivalry as subject-matter of pantomime. But the idea never seems to have taken root, as is natural enough, considering the relation between dancing and armour—and armour was worn by the unfortunate dancers chosen to represent knights. The dance of chivalry was not an influence, and is mentioned only as a choreographic curiosity.

Bergonzio de Botta's great entertainment, as has been shown, led squarely up to the masque, one of the ballet's immediate forerunners. Meantime the Church's contribution to the art was no longer a matter of moralities for the edification of mediæval rustics; high dignitaries, proceeding partly under ecclesiastical inspiration and partly under tolerance, were evolving a choro-dramatic form that took no second place to the masque in preparing the way for the art that was to come. Sixteenth-century Rome and Florence saw "sacred representations" in which were utilised the *Saltarello* [see chapter on Italian dances], the *Pavane,* the *Siciliana, la Gigue,* the *Gaillarde* and *la Moresca.* The last was accompanied by heel-tappings, like many of the dances of

Spain to-day. Its music survives in Monteverde's opera *Orfeo,* written at the beginning of the seventeenth century; in other words, music was beginning to be worth while. More important than any other single acquisition, to say the least, was the alliance of some of the monarchs of form and colour to whom half the glory of the Renaissance is due. Of Ariosto's *Suppositi,* presented in the Vatican in 1518, the decorations were by Raphael. Andrea del Sarto, Brunelleschi and Cecca enriched with their sacred figures the mimo-dramas played in Florence. In Milan, Leonardo da Vinci lent to the reality and beauty of the religious ballet the palette from which was painted the "Mona Lisa." Furthermore, it is not to be supposed that these and other masters of line, colour and the drama of light were not called to the aid of ballet grouping and movement. The period leaves no record of a great ballet composer or director. It does leave reason to believe, nevertheless, that in grouping and evolution, as well as decoration, music and accessories, these sacred representations lacked nothing to entitle them to a respectable place in the annals of opera ballet. Steps were still primitive, but sufficient unto their day.

Authorities disagree as to which one of several performances is entitled to the recognition due the first presentation of modern ballet. As a matter of accuracy, any decision should be made only after considering exactly which of several species of modern ballet is meant. For the organisation of the first ballet spectacle conforming to the multiple standards of modern excellence, the honour seems to be deserved by Catherine de Medici. True to her family traditions, she took it as an expression of beauty for its own sake, and developed it in ac-

MIDDLE AGES AND RENAISSANCE 45

cordance with French genius for order and form, as is described in later pages. But the first production of opera ballet, in the sense of a *divertissement* or intermezzo composed to interpret sentiments of dramatic action that it precedes or follows, the consensus of authority attributes to a work of Cardinal Riario, a nephew of Pope Sixtus IV. He composed and staged in Castel San Angelo a number of productions in which the ballet was important, during the latter part of the fifteenth century. Besides Pope Sixtus IV, Alexander VI and Leo X were strongly in sympathy with the movement to exalt choreography to its ancient and proper estate. The educated aristocracy of various Italian cities gave it support and protection. Important among these champions was Lorenzo de Medici, with his rare combination of means and scholarly understanding of the arts. Savonarola acidly charged him with softening the people by means of pagan spectacles, while Lorenzo went on adapting and composing.

The Jewish element of Italian society contributed its part to the new art's development. At Mantua, where the Jews formed a numerous colony, they built a theatre on the models of antiquity. Productions were directed by Bernard Tasso, father of the author of *Jerusalem Delivered*. Torquato himself went in 1573 to produce *La Pastorale,* which was a feature of a celebration given on the Island of the Belvidere, near Ferrara.

The ballet entertainment was fashionable; no great event was complete without it as a supplement. The visit of the Duke of Anjou (the future Henry III) to Cracow was the occasion of a fête whose historic importance was the discovery of a genius in ballet arrangement, Baltarazini, otherwise known as Beaujoyeulx.

Catherine de Medici sent for him to take charge of the choreographic entertainments of the French court, the Marshal de Brissac acting as intermediary. "Baltarazini dit Beaujoyeulx" had his first great opportunity in 1581, on the occasion of the marriage of the Duc de Joyeuse. *Le Ballet Comique de la Reine* was the designation of the offering; it was an addition to the now growing list of tremendous successes. Full details are

A FOURTEENTH-CENTURY BALL.
After detail of an illuminated MS. in the Bibliothèque Nationale.

recorded in the journal of one L'Estoile, and in *L'Art de la Danse* by Jean Etienne Despréaux. To repeat them in full is neither necessary nor possible: the amiable L'Estoile in particular experiences all the delight of a simple soul surrounded by several days' proceedings of which not a single detail is anything less than amazing. The lords and ladies appeared in a fresh costume every day, a new practice of whose extravagance L'Estoile writes with a mixture of awe and disapproval.

The story of *Le Ballet Comique* was the mixture of

MIDDLE AGES AND RENAISSANCE 47

Old Testament story and mythology already familiar. Fountains, artificial fire and aquatic machines lent their several notes of richness and variety. Important from the point of view of the *amateur* of the ballet is a comment on the geometrical precision that governed the ballet's groupings and corps movements: *"d'une rectitude qu' Archimède n'eut pas desavoué."* The true and modern note of form in grouping had been struck, and the standard of exactness set that was to become the backbone of the ballet of later centuries. As the first artistically logical relation of dancing to the sentiment of the whole work had been effected in the "sacred representations" of Italy, so *Le Ballet Comique de la Reine* seems to have been the first work of the kind to be produced under a modern (which is to say ancient Greek) understanding of the laws of harmony of line.

The performance lasted from ten o'clock in the evening until four in the morning. Estimates of its cost range from six hundred thousand to a million dollars (three to five million francs). Of tournaments, presents and numberless other items of the several days' celebration the cost is reckoned apart from that of producing *Le Ballet Comique*. Apart from lavishness, there is interest in the fact that queen and princesses participated. They represented nereids and naiads.

England, meantime, was in nowise ignoring the example of Continental neighbours. Pantomimes she had under the names of "mysteries," "dumb-shows" and "moralities"—religious, and melodramatic, and variously proportioned mixtures of both. They figure in the history of the English drama, as a source of plots for the early playwright. Though the translation of gesture into word filled a want felt by a part of the people, it subtracted nothing from the popularity of the masque. Henry VIII was its patron, and occasionally took part in it. Elizabeth carried it on. Francis Bacon, with whom love of stage representation was a passion, wrote plots —and dialogue where it was needed. Charles I brought it to a climax of taste and opulence. Inigo Jones—of whose high merits as an artist evidences are extant—designed decorations. Ben Jonson was accustomed to write the book for important productions. A notable work of collaboration of the two, with the addition of Lawes, the musical composer, was a masque presented at Whitehall by the Inns of Court in 1633. The cost is stated as £21,000. Although a ballet was perhaps the principal feature of the production, its composer is not named in the records. England's failure to credit the original genius may or may not bear some relation to her sterility as a contributor to the dance. With support, both sentimental and material, she has been lavish —in the wake of other nations' enthusiasms. Of invention she has given nothing of consequence. We therefore turn our attention again to France, where history was busy.

Henry IV was of a happy disposition; the dance in his reign was happy in motive, and healthy in growth. To give time to its practice none was too high in station or serious in mind. Sully, the philosopher, profiting by training given him by the king's sister, played a part in one of the fêtes. The journal of L'Estoile mentions the production of eighty new ballets during the twenty-one years of the reign.

The nature of Louis XIII was taciturn; an influence that caused the ballet to oscillate between the sombre and the trivial. The monarch himself played "The

MIDDLE AGES AND RENAISSANCE

Demon of Fire" in *La Delivrance de Renault,* in 1617. Of *Le Ballet de la Merlaison* that he produced in 1635, he composed the dance music.

A whim of this reign is to the credit of the Duke of Nemours. To contrive a choreographic composition "docile to his rheumatism," he composed in 1630 a Ballet of the Gouty. Meantime the dance was becoming frivolous, if not licentious. To rectify its shortcomings Richelieu applied himself—not to preaching damnations of dancing in general, but to the creation of an allegorical ballet of the sort he thought suitable. *Quatre Monarchies Chrétiennes,* played in 1635, is a result of his efforts; "full of pageantry the most opulent and morality the most orthodox," in the words of Robert Brussel.

The regency of Anne of Austria developed nothing in particular; a delicate character enveloped the dance in conformity to the regent's disposition and taste. But distinct progress was not destined to take place until the reign of Louis XIV, founder of the national ballet academy, perhaps the most helpful patron the dance ever had, and as devoutly enthusiastic an amateur performer as ever lived. He played prominent parts in ballet pantomimes to the number of twenty-six.

The date of the founding of the school, *L'Académie Nationale de Musique et de la Danse,* is 1661. From that time, through several decades, developments follow with extraordinary rapidity, and in so many different directions that it is impossible to follow them consecutively. Great performers begin to appear; artists whose work enraptures the public by grace of beauty alone, signifying that *execution* had been awakened. Mlles. Prévost and Sallé were contemporaries and rivals, each with a great and ardent supporting faction. Of the latter's personality, it is of interest that she was a friend of Locke, author of *Human Understanding*. Her popularity is gauged by her pay for a single performance in London, namely, something over two hundred thousand francs. The amount probably includes the considerable quantity of gold and jewels thrown to the stage

LOUIS XIV (AS "THE SUN") AND A COURTIER (AS "NIGHT") IN THE BALLET OF NIGHT.

during the performance, for enthusiasm appears to have reached the point of mania. This admiration was won without very rapid movement, Sallé believing only in the majestic; or any high or very broad steps, which did not exist in the ballet in her time. To have stirred the public as she did without these resources argues a degree of grace and expressiveness less earthly than heavenly.

Yet her reputation was to be eclipsed by a girl who was studying during the very hours when Sallé was gathering laurels. Camargo was her name. She was born in Brussels, daughter of a dancing master. To natural grace and health she added an inordinate fondness for dancing, and eager facility for learning its technicalities. Parental vacillation and educational theories cripple many an artist's career at its beginning. But Camargo's father being a dancing teacher, there was just one thing for the child to do in the natural course of events, and that was to learn to dance.

At the age of ten, her art attracted the attention of a patroness, and she was sent to Paris to study under Mlle. Prévost. In the *corps de ballet* at the opera she bolted into public notice by joining impulse to accident. One Dumoulin, on a certain occasion, missed his musical cue for entrance to perform a solo. Mlle. Camargo leaped from her place and executed the solo to the delight of the audience. Introduced at court, her triumph so affected Prévost that she discontinued her pupil's instruction. It was no longer needed. Camargo's genius had carried her beyond the reach of jealousy, or even the active intrigue that her ex-teacher directed against her.

Her matrimonial and other social ventures were conducted with such an air of candour, and were of such a diversity that they are, above all, amusing. She was a much-petted personage at court, and an esteemed friend of the king. In general she was known "as a model of charity, modesty and good conduct." She was given a maiden's funeral.

Castil-Blaze writes of her: "She added to distinction and fire of execution a bewitching gaiety that was all her own. Her figure was very favourable to her talent: hands, feet, limbs, stature, all were perfect. But her face, though expressive, was not remarkably beautiful. And, as in the case of the famous harlequin,

Dominique, her gaiety was a gaiety of the stage only. In private life she was sadness itself."

In a technical sense she may be regarded as the first modern. Her work comprised all that constituted the ballet up to her time; to the resources that came to her as an artistic heritage she began a process of addition that was to be carried on by successors. She is credited with the invention of the *entrechat,* for instance; and here many readers will find themselves confronted by the need of some explanation of ballet technique as a means of intelligent discussion of the dancing of modern times. Before that chapter, however, it is not amiss to glance over the old dances from which the ballet, up to the foundation of the Academy in 1661, derived most of its steps.

The *Gavotte,* the *Minuet,* the *Pavane,* the *Saraband,* the *Tordion,* the *Bourrée,* the *Passecaille,* the *Passepied,* the *Chaconne,* the *Volte,* the *Allemande,* the *Gaillarde,* and the *Courante*—these were the dances whose measures were trod by courtiers of the sixteenth and seventeenth centuries. Among those who have been moved to study these old dances during the past few years to the end of reconstructing them, no one is more fortunately equipped for the task than the only resident of America who has applied himself seriously to the subject, Mr. John Murray Anderson. He is at once a dancer, an educated man, and for years a devoted student of the social aspect of western Europe in the sixteenth and seventeenth centuries. A period of months that he recently spent in the choreographic libraries of Europe, and in joint study with others similarly engaged, has resulted in the opportunity to see in America a fine and true representation of the old court steps. With Miss

Margaret Crawford, Mr. Anderson posed for the accompanying photographs of the *Gavotte,* the *Minuet,* the *Bourrée,* and the *Tordion.* The groupings were selected with view to indicating the character of each dance. Collectively they give a good idea of the school of formality in which the French ballet was conceived, and from which it received its determining influences.

From the beginnings of time, people who give entertainments have followed a practice of employing performers of dances characteristic of various peoples. With appropriate costume, the *danses caracteristiques* give a synopsis, or essence, of the picturesque aspect of the people the dancer represents. Sixteenth-century nobility availed itself of the entertainment value of these folk-dances, as Athens did in its golden days and as London and Newport do to-day. In such manner did French society gather its material for many of the dances that eventually became identified with the ballroom.

The *Gavotte* is of such origin. A few generations of languid cultivation refined the life out of it, though it was at first a comparatively active dance. After dropping nearly into disuse it was revived and popularised by Marie Antoinette, for whose rendering of it Gluck composed music. After the Revolution, with its paralysing influence, the *Gavotte* was once again revived—and revised—by Gardel, *premier danseur* of the Opera, in a composition based on music by Grétry. But this composition was not of a kind for the execution of any but trained dancers of the stage, Gardel having made it a *metier* for the exploitation of his own capabilities. Among new elaborations the simple little jumping steps and the easy *arabesque* that distinguished the *Gavotte* of earlier days were lost.

The *Tordion* is another dance of lively origin. Sometimes it was made a vehicle for the grotesque, such as black-face comedy—let no one be surprised that the "coon comedian" of to-day is an ancient institution. It was stepped briskly, even in the stately environment of court. The position of the foot with the heel on the floor and the toe up was not adopted by the ballet, but is found in folk or "character" dances in all parts of Europe.

The *Allemande* also was a dance of movement; so was the *Volte*. In the former the man turns his partner by her raised hand; in the costume of the time, the whirl is very effective. The *Volte* is supposed to be the immediate ancestor of the *Waltz*.

The *Saraband* came into France from Spain, where it was tremendously popular as *la Zarabanda*. It dates from the twelfth century, and was praised by Cervantes. Its character justifies the belief that it comes from Moorish origins. It is a solo dance making noble use of the arms, and is executed with a plastic relaxation of the body. A distinctly Oriental mannerism is its quick shift of the foot, just as it is placed on the floor, from the customary position of toeing out to a position of toeing in. The foot-work, moreover, has little more than slow glides. Its exotic qualities, nevertheless, are subordinate to its Occidental courtliness; like all the other dances of polite society, it conformed to the etiquette of its time and place, notwithstanding improprieties of which it had been guilty in earlier centuries.

Marguerite de Valois was fond of the *Bourrée* because, according to tradition, she had an extraordinary natural endowment in the shape of feet and ankles. And the skipping step (related to the modern polka-step) of the *Bourrée* necessitated the wearing of a shorter skirt than the mode of her day permitted for ordinary use. It never was a rigorously formulated composition, perhaps because it never became very popular at court. It contributed to the ballet the latter's useful *pas de bourrée,* and continues as a diversion of the peasants of Auvergne, where it originated.

The *Passepied* was one of a family known as *les branles,* whose family characteristics are ill defined, despite the frequency with which the term is used by seventeenth-century writers. In England the word became "brawl." It was the *Branle du Haut Barrois* in which gentry costumed themselves as the shepherds and shepherdesses perpetuated by Watteau. Another, the *Branle des Lavandières,* was based on pantomime of the operations of the laundress. In the *Branle des Ermites,* monk's dress was worn. In that of the *Flambeaux,* torches were passed to newly selected partners, as in a present-day cotillion figure; it was a fashionable figure at wedding celebrations.

Tabourot's amiable hints for the elegant execution of *branles* probably are not directed at the court. But they are illuminating. "Talk gracefully, and be clean and well shod; be sure that the hose is straight, and that the slipper is clean . . . do not use your handkerchief more than is necessary, but if you use it, be sure it is very clean." There is more; but, after all, why violate illusions?

The *Chaconne,* like the *Saraband,* came to France from across the Pyrenees. The dance of the *Seises* in the Seville Cathedral is said to be a *Chacona* unchanged from its sixteenth-century form.

The *Gaillarde* is sometimes grouped with the *Tordion,*

from which it differs in the respect that the theme of its steps is little jumps, while the *Tordion* is, for the most part, glided. One form of it, however, *"Si je t'aime ou non,"* contained some energetic kicks. Indeed, it was of a character to exercise heart and muscle; excellence in some of its steps "was looked upon as an accomplishment equal to riding or fencing." To that form of it known as *"Baisons-nous Belle"* was attached interest of another variety, in the shape of kisses exchanged between partners. "A pleasant variation," comments the venerable Thoinet-Arbeau. A variation employed to prevent monotony in some of the other dances as well, among them the early *Gavotte*.

The *Courante* was one of the more formal dances, never having been popular even in its origin. It was the *Courante* that was favoured by Louis XIV, during his many years of study under a dancing master. He is credited, before he was overtaken by the demon of adiposity, with having executed the *Courante* better than any one else of his time. In style it has been compared to the *Seguidillas* (q. v.) of Spain.

Of all, the dances most typical of the formality of the most formal society western civilisation has produced are the *Minuet* and the *Pavane*. Both might be characterised as variations of deep bows and curtsies. In the *Pavane* photographs it will be noted that instead of taking hold of her partner's hand, the lady rests her hand on the back of his.

Hernando Cortez is said to have composed the *Pavane* (Spanish *Pavana*) and introduced it in the court of his land on returning from America. If so, he was a solemn person, as well as dignified; to the imposing grace of majesty the dance joins the aloof grandeur of a ritual.

These qualities gave to it the office of opening great court functions. Brocades and armour and swords promenaded very slowly around the room, each couple making its reverence to the monarchs before proceeding to the steps of the dance. These were few, simple, and slow; there were many curtsies, retreats and advances, during which last the gentleman led the lady by the upraised hand, while following her. Poses and groups were held, statue-like, for a space of time that allowed them to impress themselves on the vision. So fond was Elizabeth of England of the *Pavane* (in writings of her land and period spelled *Pavin* and otherwise) that it was more than whispered that excellence in its performance was more valued than statesmanship as a basis of political favour.

The *Minuet's* formality was graded. *Le Menuet du Dauphin, le Menuet de la Reine, le Menuet d' Exaudet* and *le Menuet de la Cour* were its four species, the stateliness increasing in the sequence mentioned. The accompanying *Minuet* photographs of Mr. Anderson and Miss Crawford are of the form *de la Reine*. The "mirror" figure is perhaps its most salient feature—a pretty bit of expression accompanying an interlacement of arms whose composition comes as a climax to strikingly ingenious and gracious arm movements.

The popularity of the *Minuet,* in its various forms, was practically unlimited; lonely and cheerless indeed must have been the social life of the man who did not dance. After the decline of the *Pavane* it continued as an inseparable adjunct of gatherings of all degrees of conventionality within the scope of a polite mode of living. At court balls, at the romping Christmas parties of English country places; in the remote homes of Virginia planters, at governor-generals' receptions, in the palaces of *intendants* in the far North it saluted, made coquetry with fan and eye, incarnated in gallant figures the brave and reverent spirit of chivalry. Pictures represent its performance in home surroundings during daylight; slight pretext seems to have served as occasion for its performance. In connection with this popularity it must be remembered that, even in its simpler forms, so much as a passable execution of the *Minuet* was far from easy to acquire.

Let it be understood that the *grand ballet* of to-day did not spring full-grown from the dances above enumerated. Some of their forms continued unchanged through years of academic influence. Present-day "elevation," as scope of high and low level is called, the great leaps, great turns, and, in short, most of the dazzling elements of to-day's ballet are the accumulated contribution of individual artists from time to time. Taglioni, of the middle nineteenth century, is the last to add notably to the classic ballet's alphabet of steps. It is not unsafe to say that the next few years will see its range increased: the Russians, avid for new things, have ransacked Egyptian carvings and Greek vases. Trained to perfection in the technique and philosophy of their art, they are incorporating intelligently the newly rediscovered with the long familiar. But a concrete idea of their relation to the art, or of the art itself, cannot be had without some acquaintance with its actual mechanics; it is time to consider the salient steps on which most Occidental dancing is based, and which the ballet has reduced to perfect definition.

CHAPTER IV

A GLANCE AT THE BALLET'S TECHNIQUE

THE name of Camargo, which arose in the first half of the eighteenth century, may be taken as the milestone that marks the progress of dancing into its modern development. Predecessors had brought to it pleasing execution and a good spirit; Camargo appears to have surpassed them in both qualities, and, in addition, to have added immensely to the art's scope both of expression and of technique. Her relation to the dancing of her time has been profoundly studied by Mme. Genée, whose fascinating programme of re-creations is the result. After the work attributed to Sallé and Prévost, that of the re-created Camargo shows a very striking emancipation from former limitations. Sallé and Prévost, charmingly graceful, consummately skilful, performed their Dresden-china steps evenly, coolly, in full conformity to the fastidious etiquette of the aristocracy of their day. Camargo, without bruising a petal of the hot-house flower that was her artistic inheritance, first freed it from a fungus of affectation that others had mistaken for the bloom of daintiness. Then she arranged it to show the play of light and shade, to make it surprising—in short, to make it a vehicle of interpretation.

The material at her disposal, as noted before, was limited. To her advantage in "elevation," she replaced high-heeled shoes with ballet slippers; she was the first, since antiquity, to dance on the toes. Nevertheless her changes of level were not exciting; of big leaps she had none. The day of vivid *pirouettes* was yet to dawn. Her most extended step was a little *balloné*. Her *entrechat* was almost the only step that raised both her feet distinctly off the floor; it, with *petits battements,* gave brilliancy but nothing of grandeur. Hers was a dance of simple and little steps. But they were composed, those steps, with appreciation of the value of contrast. By contrast, movement was made long or short in effect. Movements soft and crisp were juxtaposed. We may believe that Camargo's knowledge of composition compensated for the meagre step-vocabulary of her day; that she commanded cumulative interest, surprise, and climax. In short, that she produced an expression; limited to the lyrical, but none the less real.

That there may be no risk of misunderstanding the present use of the word "expression," let it be agreed that the word here has the same application that it has in relation to instrumental music; also let it be agreed emphatically that it has nothing to do with the imitation of nature. Wagner makes a composition of tones portray the attributes of heroes and gods. Grieg's gnomes are of the same tissue: suggested attributes as distinguished from specified facts of the concrete. Broadly, such suggestion is called music. For present clearness let it be known as *music of the ear*. Because, the very same mental sensations produced by rhythm and sound variously juxtaposed and combined, acting through the medium of *hearing,* are susceptible of stimulation by means of rhythm and line, in suitable juxtapositions and combinations, acting through the medium of *vision*. It follows that dancing, in effect, is *music of the eye*. The

THE BALLET'S TECHNIQUE 61

familiar musical resources serve both choreographer and composer impartially. As will be understood before the reading of this chapter is completed, the equivalent of long and short notes is found in steps of varying length; musical phrases are, to the mind, the same as step-combinations, or *enchainements;* argument toward expression of motive is as possible to the silent music as to music of the ear. Indeed the values of the several orchestral instruments have their parallels in steps; the light staccato of the clarinet is no more playful than are certain delicate steps executed *sur les pointes,* nor is the blare of brass more stirring than the noble *renversé.* The scope of expression, in short, that is attainable by the orchestra is identical with that within range of pure dancing—dancing without pantomime. Add pantomime, and in effect you add to your music the explanatory accompaniment of words. Broadly, music is sentiment, while the words of a song are supplementary description. In the ballet, the dance, as such, is the sentiment (or its representation), the pantomime the accompanying description.

Added expression in this musical sense was among Camargo's contribution to the art, definitely restoring to it a quality it had held in a grasp at best precarious since the passing of the glory of Athens. Belief in pantomime rises and recedes from one decade to another. But purely orchestral or æsthetic expression continues at all times (with interruptions) as the fundamental intent of the classic French and Italian ballets. To demand that the figures in a composition conceived in this idea should act and look like the people of every-day life, owing to the mere coincidence of their being human beings, would be like asking the composer of *Pagliacci* to rewrite his score to include the sound of squeaking wheels, because of the latter's pertinence to the wagon of the strolling players represented in the opera. The function of the composer of the opera is to *suggest* by such tonal symbols as have been found effective, the various *emotions* undergone by his characters. Identically, the function of the ballet-master is to suggest by the countless combinations of line—majestic and playful, severe and gracious—and by the infinite variety of movements and postures, the emotions he would arouse in the spectators of his work. At his disposal he has a number of plastic, sentient and sympathetic figures, trained to movements of grace. They are the instruments of his orchestra, the paint on his palette. That they also are human beings is absolutely a coincidence and beside the point.

Pantomime, to be sure, is carried to a high development in both French and Italian academies; they present mimo-dramas calling for practically unlimited scope of expression. Pantomime they added to the dance without departure from the ballet's basic intent. Both schools well know that the introduction of one pose or gesture *imitating* an act of human life, automatically throws the work into another category; that which was purely interpretative mural decoration verges toward the story-telling picture.

The argument is put rather insistently because of the periodical complaint that the ballet "looks artificial." "In real life," people say, "you never see hands held as they are held in the ballet." Mother of all the muses, why should they be? In real life hands are doctoring fountain pens, hewing wood and drawing water, reaching out for things; in real life hands are concerned with

THE BALLET'S TECHNIQUE 63

their practical occupation, and quite disregardful of their grace or expression while so engaged. Whereas the ballet uses hands as the vehicle for lines of grace, exaltation, vivacity, or whatever emotion you will, expressed in terms of the abstract. It is the same in regard to work on the toe: in real life people have no occasion to walk on the tip ends of their feet, because as a means of locomotion it is inconvenient. The ballet's use of it is not based on a belief in the minds of ballet-masters that it is a fashion either in polite society or among nymphs of the primeval forest. The position "on the point" makes possible an agreeable change in elevation, and can instantaneously eliminate the appearance of avoirdupois. The ballet art is a convention, strictly; the figures in it are changing units of a moving design, and not people. A *ballerina* does not ask, "How do I look in this pose?" She asks, "What kind of a line does this pose make?"

Of late years the classic ballet has suffered from public indifference. Doubtless this has been due in part to an insufficiency of competent performers; a great work requires great execution, and the difficulties created by the ballet's ideals are tremendous. But failure on the part of the public to consider the ballet's intent has certainly contributed to an unsatisfactory state of its affairs.

A general acquaintance with the individual steps adds in various ways to the spectator's enjoyment. Relieved of effort to decipher a dancer's means and methods, he who understands the mechanics of the steps can surrender himself to a luxuriance in their grace of execution, and be the more susceptible to the hypnotic charm of the rhythmic movement playing upon his eye. To him who has taken the trouble to learn some of the elemental theories, that which was once a bewildering maze of movement, which he mentally scrambled to follow, becomes an ordered and deliberate sequence, whose argument he follows with ease; instead of a kaleidoscope, he sees phrasing, repetition, and progress of interest, theme, enrichment and climax. With bits of special virtuosity he is instantly gratified; shortcomings he instantly detects. To communicate his observations he has a vocabulary of specific expression; and there is satisfaction in that, for a ballet performance is just as fruitful a subject of controversy among its connoisseurs as a new novel among its readers. Furthermore, the need of a general power of expression as an essential to the betterment of American choreographic conditions is self-evident.

While the ensuing analysis of ballet steps is far from complete from the point of view of the academy, it should give the reader a comprehension of the steps that make an impression on the layman's eye. The material that follows is selected with that end in view. Some description of simple fundamentals, though not in themselves "showy," is included in order to facilitate analysis of the great steps and turns. Moreover, since character dancing includes nothing of technical note that is not also used in the ballet, it is confidently hoped that the subjoined analysis will serve as a useful lens through which to look at dancing of all kinds.

Those whose interest in the subject leads them to seek a more complete knowledge are referred to Zorn, *Grammar of the Art of Dancing;* by means of his choreographic stenography he goes into sub-variations of ballet steps with the utmost exactness. Naturally a course of instruction under a good ballet teacher is best of all;

THE BALLET'S TECHNIQUE   65

theory is best understood by its application. And execution, it should go without saying, is acquired only by long practice under expert and watchful eyes.

Before considering actual movements, it must be borne in mind that separately they are incomplete. Like tones that unite to form chords of music, each in itself may seem lacking in richness. Interdependence of successive parts is more marked in the classic ballet than in any other great school of choreography. The dance of the Moor is a series of statues, each self-sufficient. Of the ballet movements, almost the reverse is true. Their magic comes of the flow of one unit into another.

As France is the mother and nurse of the ballet, it follows that French is its language. Few of the terms translate successfully. To rename the movements would be superfluous—and in practical use, worse; for a big *corps de ballet* is often a gathering from many nations. Being explicit and sufficient, the French terms are the accepted designation of the steps in all lands where the ballet is danced.

To describe steps with precision, it is necessary to use a system of choro-stenography not easily learned, or to refer to positions of the feet. The latter is the usual method, and long usage proves its adequacy. The cut on the following page shows the fundamental positions of the feet, with the designations that are standard wherever Occidental dancing is taught. These are modified in a great variety of ways. (Two modifications which were diagrammed in the first edition of this work are here omitted on the advice of Mme. Genée, as tending to complication.)

The weight may be upon both feet, or either.

In third, fourth and fifth positions: speaking of either

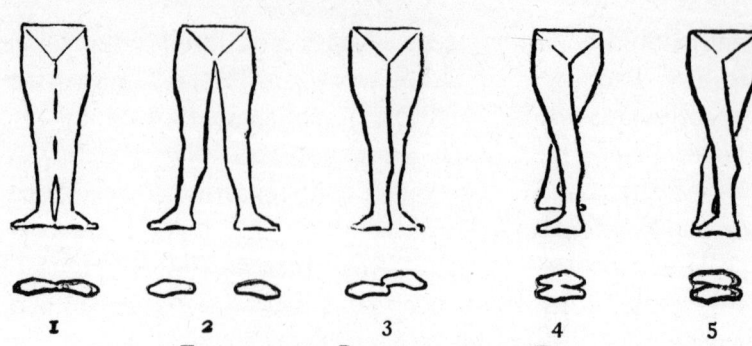

FUNDAMENTAL POSITIONS OF THE FEET.
Fig. 1, first position; 2, second position; 3, third position; 4, fourth position; 5, fifth position.

foot (say the right) it is said to be in anterior or posterior third, fourth or fifth position.

Second and fourth positions are defined as closed or amplified, according as the feet are separated by the length of a foot, or more.

The positions, unless otherwise specified, indicate both feet on the floor. But the second, third and fourth positions sometimes relate to positions in which one foot is raised; for instance, *right foot* in *raised second position*.

The same designations apply whether the feet be flat on the floor, on the ball, on the point, or a composite of these: as for instance, second position, right foot on the point, left foot flat, etc.

Heights are definitely divided; ankle, calf and knee serve as the measures. But as the subjoined explanations are aided by diagrams, the terms to measure heights may be disregarded for the sake of simplicity. Likewise we need not go into the enumeration and names of crossed positions and other complications. The five fundamental positions, however, are important

THE BALLET'S TECHNIQUE 67

and should be memorised. Apart from their importance in any discussion of ballet work, familiarity with them greatly aids the acquisition of ballroom dances. (The latter place the feet at an angle of 45° to the line in which the dancer's body faces, instead of 90°, the form of the French-Italian ballet.)

The school of the ballet also defines the positions of the arms, in the same manner. They need not be memorised as a preliminary to reading this chapter; but they are interesting as a matter of record of the limitations of the classic school, and as a measure of the distance to which the Russians have departed in the direction of freedom of arm movement.

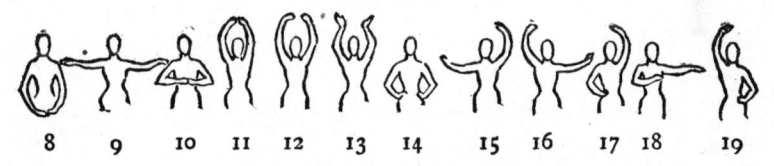

POSITIONS OF THE ARMS.

Figure 8, arms in repose, sustained; 9, extended; 10, rounded in front of the chest; 11, rounded above the head; 12, high and open; 13, *à la lyre;* 14, on the hips; 15, 16, one arm high, one extended; 18, one arm rounded in front of the chest, one open horizontal; 17, 19, one arm high, one on the hip.

Steps, which are now to be considered, fall naturally into the classes of *gliding, beating, turning* and *jumping*. Each class ranges from simplicity to more or less complexity, and certain steps have a composite character, partaking of the nature of more than one of the above general classes.

Dancers distinguish between a step and a *temps*, whose relation to each other is that between a word and a syllable. A *temps* is a single movement. By definition, a step must effect a transfer of weight; subject to that definition, a single movement may be a step.

The simple gliding step is the *pas glissé*. It is executed by gliding the foot along the floor. It may move in any direction. Used as indicated in figures 20, 21 and 22, the step becomes a *glissade*.

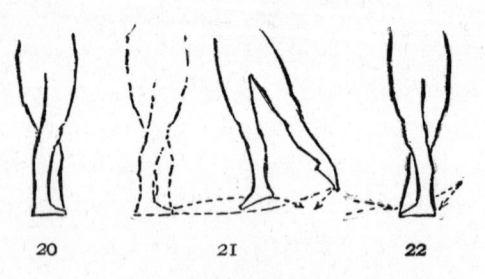

20   21   22

"Glissade."

The essential gliding feature of the step is indicated in the movement of the left foot along the floor, figure 21.

A *chassé,* in effect, "chases" one foot from its place by means of a touch from the other. For instance: the feet are in second position, weight on the right foot; bring the left foot sharply up to this position behind the right foot; at the instant of contact, let the right foot glide sharply out to second position on the right side. The step also may be executed toward the front or toward the rear. It keeps both feet on the floor.

Executing a series of *chassés: simple chassés* commence the step, each repetition, with the same foot. *Alternating chassés* are begun with each foot in turn.

A *coupé* is analogous to a *chassé;* but the foot that is displaced leaves the floor and goes to more or less height in the air. Both *coupé* and *chassé* give an impression of one foot kicking the other out of place.

THE BALLET'S TECHNIQUE 69

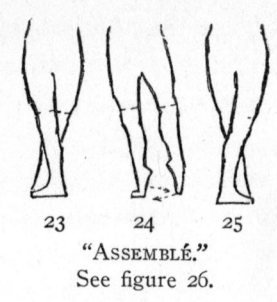

23 24 25
"Assemblé."
See figure 26.

An *assemblé,* starting with the feet in fifth position, effects a reversal of their position. Example (see diagram): the left foot is behind. A little jump upward raises both feet from the floor. Kick out with the left foot to the left, bring it back to fifth position *in front* of the right foot, at the moment of alighting. The right foot, instead of the left, will *dégage,* or "wing out," in the next step, if the step is repeated.

A *changement* is similar to an *assemblé;* its difference is in the fact that it causes both feet to "beat."

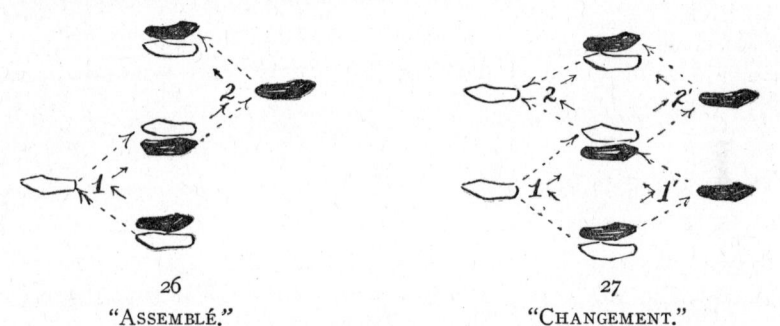

26 27
"Assemblé." "Changement."

Each diagram shows two performances of its step. Both steps take both feet off the floor. In the *assemblé,* one foot remains passive. In the *changement,* both are active.

A *relevé* consists of a simultaneous (a) rise to the ball or point of the supporting foot, while the active foot is raised to the height (usually) of the knee of the supporting leg. The active foot usually is kept close to the supporting leg.

This step furnishes an interesting example of the changes wrought by the Russians. The classic turn-out of the foot confines the movement of the active leg to a plane cutting the performer laterally; i. e., as the classic performer advances *en relevant* toward the spectator, the legs' movements are seen to have their extension out to the sides. Whereas the Russian "toes out" (with exceptions) at a much smaller angle. His knees therefore may rise in front of him; in which case the step, as seen by the spectator, is most effective while the performer crosses the stage from side to side. It is made the thematic step of some of the new Russian dance-poems of Greek nature. It is executed sharply, lightly.

An *échappé* moves the feet from closed to second position by means of moving both feet simultaneously outward.

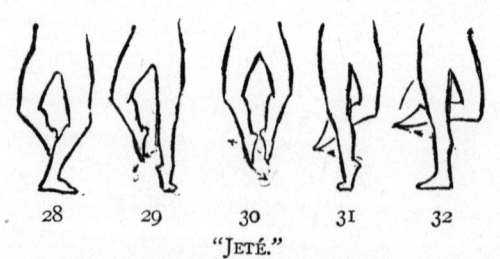

28   29   30   31   32
"Jeté."
Essentials: both feet off the floor simultaneously, and receipt of the descending weight on one foot.

The *jeté* is a step that is simple in principle, at the same time subject to so wide a range of use that it creates the most varied effects. Essentially, it is the step that is used in running.

The *jeté* also may be executed to the side—*à côté*.

THE BALLET'S TECHNIQUE 71

From its use in that manner it is easy to understand its employment as a means of turning in the air: i. e., with both feet off the floor. The *jeté en tournant* is one of the much-used means of producing an effect of big, easy sweep; it lends itself to the embellishment of any one of several *beating* steps—*pas battus;* or others, yet to be described.

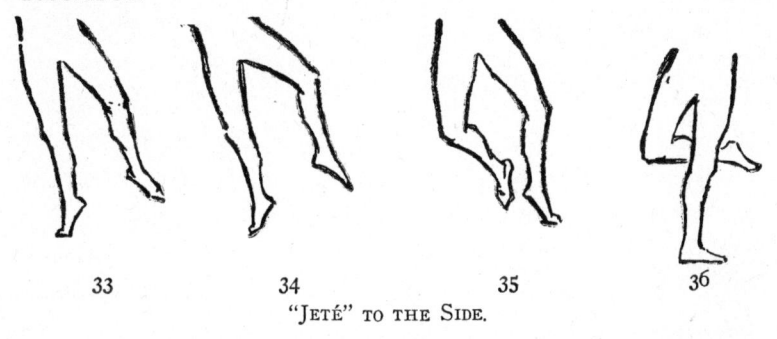

33   34   35   36
"Jeté" to the Side.

Of the "beating" type of step, the fundamental is the *battement:* a beating movement of the free leg, the supporting leg remaining stationary. The accent is not on the up-stroke, as in a kick, but sharply on the down-stroke. The beats may be made from side, front, or (less usually) back. The foot may be raised to the height of the head (though it is not often done), to horizontal, to the height of the knee, or the distance of a foot's length away from the supporting leg. Executed with a straight knee, the movement is a *grand battement*. A *petit battement* is action of the lower leg only, working from the knee as a stationary pivot, while the foot strikes the supporting ankle, calf, or knee. It is a movement designed for brilliancy, and should be executed rapidly. With practice it can be carried to such a degree of speed that the active foot seems to shimmer. It is the basic step of Scotch dances. Modified to allow the sole of the active foot to touch the floor, it provides the shuffle-step of the Irish *Jigs* and *Reels*. *Petits battements,* it should be added, are usually employed in a sequence of several in succession.

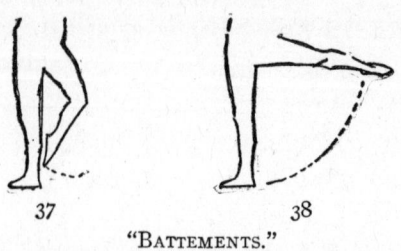

"BATTEMENTS."
Petit battement, 37. *Grand battement,* 38.

Correctly speaking, a *battement* does not constitute a step, but a *temps*.

The *cabriole* is a development of the *battement*. In the latter, only one leg is active; it leaves the supporting leg, and rejoins it. The *cabriole* is executed with both feet in the air; both legs act in the beating movement, rapidly separating and coming together, but not crossing.

A further development of the same theme brings us to the gem which, of the ballet's entire collection, is the most dazzling: the *entrechat*. Instead of merely bringing the legs together, as in the *cabriole,* it uses a jump as the occasion for repeatedly crossing the feet. Cleanly done, it is as the sparkle of a humming-bird.

The word is derived from the Italian *intrecciare,* to weave or braid. The French compound it with numerals, to indicate the number of times the feet cross: as, *entrechat-quatre, entrechat-six, entrechat-huit.* The number includes the movements of each foot; an *entrechat-huit* implies four crossings. Prodigious stories are told about the number of beats that various artists have

THE BALLET'S TECHNIQUE 73

accomplished in their *entrechat*. It forms an attractive centre for choreographic myths. In general, the number of beats said to have been accomplished by a given artist is in direct ratio to the number of years that artist has been dead. In reality there is small object in going beyond an *entrechat-six;* the three crossings (always assuming performance by a master of the technique) are quite sufficient to prove that the law of gravity has ceased to exist. When their staccato twinkle is added as a fin-

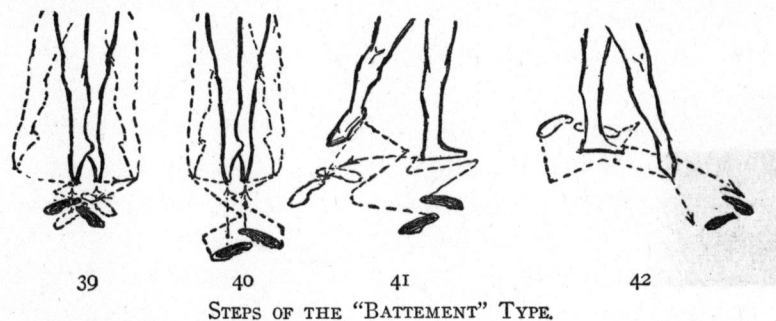

STEPS OF THE "BATTEMENT" TYPE.
Changement, 39; entrechat-quatre, 40; brisé dessus, 41; brisé dessous, 42.
In the *brisé dessus,* the active foot beats in front of the passive foot; in the *brisé dessous,* behind it.

ish to the long pendulum swing of a big *glissade,* or a long *jeté en tournant,* the effect is that of a swift *pizzicato* following a long-sustained note—always surprising, always merry.

The *brisé* is of the category of movements executed while both feet are off the floor. It is so closely related to the *entrechat-quatre* that the layman who can distinguish between the two, during the speed of performance, may conscientiously congratulate himself on having developed a passably quick and sure eye. The difference between the two lies in this: that in the *brisé* only one foot really "beats"; the other makes only a slight complementary or counter-movement. Starting as it does in an open position, it lends itself to the embellishment of broad leaps.

The *balloné* is, in a broad sense, related to the beating steps; its accent, however, is on the up-stroke, which makes it a kick. Start in third position; *pliez* slightly (as preparation); jump, and simultaneously kick forward, bending the knee in raising the leg, straightening it when it has reached the necessary height; usually the *balloné* leads into another step.

(As this description is at variance with that of two eminent choreographic writers, it should be added that it is made from the step as demonstrated and explained by Sr. Luigi Albertieri, ballet-master of the Century Opera Company, an unquestioned authority; his traditions are those of La Scala, and of Sr. E. Cecchetti. Mlle. Louise La Gai, former pupil of Leo Staats, onetime ballet-master of l'Opéra, demonstrates the step in the same manner.)

A phrase of steps (*enchainement*) is rarely made up of big or difficult steps exclusively; the value of the latter would soon be lost in monotony were they not contrasted with work of a simpler nature. The *pas de bourrée* and the *pas de Basque* are among the little steps useful in furnishing such contrasts, in giving the dancer a renewed equilibrium, and in the capacity of connecting links between other steps. They are like prepositions in a sentence—insufficient in themselves, but none the less indispensable.

The *pas de bourrée* (the name is taken from an old French dance) is essentially the familiar polka-step late of the ballroom, with varied applications. Forward, backward or to the side, it "covers stage"—or gives the dancer progress in a given direction. It furnishes a

THE BALLET'S TECHNIQUE 75

means of turning, or preserving the continuity of a dance while the performer keeps his place. Always it is useful as a filler when interest is to be directed away from the foot-work—in such case, for instance, as when the hands have important pantomime.

The *pas de Basque* is of similar value, but commits the dancer to a swinging movement from side to side. Like the *pas de bourrée* it is an alternating step, with one foot on the floor all the time, and executed without much *"elevation"*—i. e., variety of level. It runs through many of the dances of Spain, and presumably is, as its name suggests, a native of the Basque provinces. Probably, too, it is a remote ancestor of the *Waltz*.

"FOUETTÉ."

In contrast to the sharp, dry quality of the beating steps is the fluid, swinging *fouetté*. Its many variations conform to the principles indicated in the diagram figures 43 to 46.

The word *"fouetté"* means literally, whip; the movement, a swing with a snap at the finish, is well named. A relaxed manner of execution gives it a feeling of pliancy, while lightness is preserved by the smart termination.

Start with a *plié* of both knees, for preparation; sharply lift the active leg sidewise to horizontal (i. e., raised second position); *snap* the lower leg back, in a movement curving downward, to the crossed leg position in figure 46. There it is prepared to enter into another step, or to lead to an *arabesque,* or to continue

47   48   49   50

START OF A "FOUETTÉ PIROUETTE."
Figures 47–50 inclusive serve also to describe a *developpé.*

to finish in third or fifth position of the feet. The body has remained facing the spectator.

Now, let it be understood that a *pirouette* is a turn, or spin, on one foot only, or else in the air. One species of *pirouette* is made in conjunction with the *fouetté,* the body being permitted to turn with the impulse of the leg's backward sweep. The making of a *pirouette,* however, requires its own preparations, as shown in the first four figures of the diagram. In figure 47 the legs are *pliés.* Figures 48, 49 and 50 represent a *developpé,* or unfolding—a device of frequent use in the present conditions, namely, the need of bringing the active leg to horizontal in preparation for a step. The exten-

THE BALLET'S TECHNIQUE 77

sion of the arms as indicated enables them to give a vigourous start to the revolving movement; the leg, by a sharp sweep "outward," contributes to the same impulse. The turn started, the *fouetté* is executed as it proceeds. The free foot drops to position behind the supporting leg. But note that as the body continues turning, the foot changes from position behind to position in front; very simple, in performance very effective—and until

51 52 53 54
"FOUETTÉ PIROUETTE," CONTINUED.

Right leg sweeps "out" in horizontal plane (51) continuing as in 52, turning the body with its revolution. As the body completes the turn from 52 to 53, the right foot is brought to crossed position in front of the ankle.

understood, puzzling in its illusion of winding up and unwinding. It is permissible, in the position of figure 52, to drop to the heel of the supporting foot, for a momentary renewal of equilibrium; but there is merit in going through without that aid. The position at finish leaves the dancer prepared to repeat the *tour*, which can be done an indefinite number of times in succession; to continue into an *arabesque* (figures 55, 56); or to enter a different step.

Among the variations of the above typical *fouetté pirouette* is its execution "in" instead of "out": that is, to sweep the active leg across in front of the supporting leg, to start the turn, instead of raising it out to the side. Again using the left foot as support, the turn of the body is now toward the left, instead of toward the right as when the step is executed "out." The active foot arrives at its position of crossing the supporting leg when it has described a half-circle.

Tradition makes the *fouetté pirouette* a step for men, although it is not intrinsically less feminine than any other of the great steps. Nevertheless, tradition is often a thing to respect. So, a *fouetté pirouette* performed by

55 56
OPTIONAL FINISH OF A "FOUETTÉ PIROUETTE."
Continues (55) into *arabesque* (56).

a woman is customarily called a *rond de jambe tour*. Mlle. Zambeli, the *première* of l'Opéra in Paris, has on occasion performed a succession of thirty-two such turns in a steadily accelerating tempo. The result, instead of monotony, is a cumulative excitement little short of overpowering.

The *fouetté pirouette* leads into the subject of *pirouettes* in general. By their common definition, they are turns made on one supporting foot only, or without support (i. e., turns in the air). The definition serves to

THE BALLET'S TECHNIQUE 79

distinguish a true *pirouette* from a turn made by means of alternating steps, such as a *pas bourrée* turn.

The purest example of *pirouette* is that performed "on the crossed ankle"—*sur le cou-de-pied.* (Figures 57 to 61.) This turn is made without the aid of impulse from either leg after the free foot goes into its position, in distinction from the *fouetté pirouette,* for instance, in which the active leg's movement in the air furnishes the motive power by which the body is turned.

The *pirouette sur le cou-de-pied* here diagrammed is

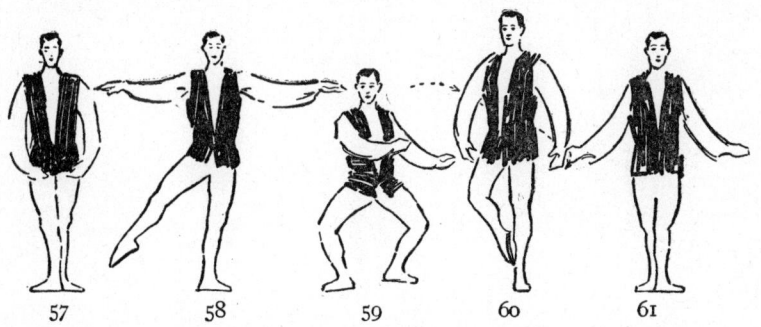

THE "PIROUETTE SUR LE COU-DE-PIED."

Figures 57, 58, 59, preparation; 60 represents the completion of the turn, and the position the feet have occupied during the act of turning; 61, finish.

according to the specifications of Herr Otto Stoige, ballet-master and dancing teacher at the University of Königsberg, as quoted by Zorn. Raise the arms and the active leg (figure 58). Drop the active foot to anterior fourth position (figure 59), *plié,* and at the same time dispose the arms to give the twisting impulse to the body. The same impulse is aided by the sharp straightening of the left leg, coming into position as support. The arms drop (figure 60) as the free foot is placed *sur le cou-de-pied* of the supporting leg. Comparing the finish (figure 61) with figure 57, it is seen that the feet have resumed third position but exchanged places. In making the turn, the face is turned away from the spectator as short a time as possible.

The ability to do a double turn in this form is not rare, and a few men make it triple. The Prussian Stullmueller brought it to seven revolutions. An amusing conventionality of gender in *pirouettes* makes it man's prerogative to do the *pirouette en l'air*—i. e., with both feet off the floor. This too is doubled by some of the men now dancing: Leo Staats, formerly of l'Opéra in Paris, is said to triple it!

VARIOUS "PIROUETTES."
À la seconde, 62; *en attitude,* 63; *en arabesque,* 64;

A *pirouette* of this sort is one of the few *pas* that have a value independent of what precedes and follows; it is a beautiful thing by itself. In combination it gives a feeling of ecstasy; or, in other conditions, of happy eccentricity. A few years ago Angelo Romeo used it as the theme of his solo in a *Ballet of Birds* (under Fred Thompson's management, the New York Hippodrome staged some real ballets). As King of the Birds, Romeo gave his part a gallantry at once amusing and brilliant by the reiteration of double *pirouettes* as a refrain.

Between the two extremes of *fouetté pirouette* and *pirouette sur le cou-de-pied* lie such a variety of manners of turning that experts fail to agree on any definition of the word *"pirouette,"* more explicit than the one already given. A half-turn *sur le cou-de-pied, pas de bourrée,* and complete the turn with a *fouetté:*—there, for instance, is a turn that is a *pirouette* or not, according to arbitrary definition. There are half as many subvarieties of *pirouette* and other turns as there are solo dancers. Turns of mixed type, partaking of the natures of both pure *pirouette* and the *rond de jambe* character of movement, are known collectively as *pirouettes composées.*

A *rond de jambe,* it should be explained parenthetically, is a circle described by the foot. A *grand rond de jambe* is a circle (in any plane) described by the straight leg. A *petit rond de jambe* is made by the lower leg, working from a stationary knee as pivot. Cf. *grands* and *petits battements.*

As the *pirouette sur le cou-de-pied* has its virtue of sparkle, its cousin the *renversé* is endowed with a species of bewildering, bacchanalian ecstasy. Words and diagrams fail to convey an impression of its qualities; but analysis of its mechanics is worth while, in order that it may be recognised when seen, and not allowed to pass without yielding its full and due pleasure to him who sees it.

Preceding the position indicated in figure 65, the dancer, placing his weight on the left foot, has raised the right foot in a *developpé* forward, and around on a horizontal plane "outward." Figure 65 shows the right foot at a point that may be conveniently designated as the quarter-circle. In figure 66 the right foot continues to sweep back, and the body begins to lean forward—or away from the active leg. This lean of the body has become more pronounced in figure 67, in which the active foot has reached the three-quarter circle. Note the sweep of the left hand accelerating the movement of the turn, and its continuance through the remaining figures.

65   66   67

BEGINNING OF THE "RENVERSÉ."
A *developpé* has preceded the position in figure 65, as indicated in vertical dotted line. The body begins to turn as the active foot completes a half-circle (66). In 67, note that the body leans forward.

Up to the position in figure 68 the body has leaned forward—or in other words, has been chest down. In figure 69 it is seen chest up. Figure 68 is the intermediate position. In performance the turn-over takes place so quickly that only a trained eye sees just when it is done.

The right foot touches the floor at the point of completing the half-circle. The body continues leaning back, straightening up in figure 70 after describing a round body-sweep started in figure 69. Figure 70 finds the weight on the right foot; the left is raised on the first *temps* of a *pas de bourrée,* very quick, which brings the

THE BALLET'S TECHNIQUE 83

feet to fifth position as in figure 71. The right-hand-sweep upward, meantime, has been continuous.

Another variation of the *pirouette* is based on the *rond de jambe* described on a previous page. The *rond de jambe pirouette* is executed with the aid and embellishment of a horizontal leg. It usually starts with a *developpé,* like the *fouetté tour.* A *pirouette à la seconde*

68   69   70   71
THE "RENVERSÉ" CONCLUDED.

Figures 68 and 69 trace the over-turning of the body, without interruption to the movement of rotation. A rapid *pas de bourrée* intervenes between 70 and 71.

is so called by reason of the active foot's continuance in raised second position. If the heel is touched at the half-circles for equilibrium, the turns can be continued ad libitum. Still another *tour* is the *pirouette en arabesque,* the pose being entered into (usually) on completion of a half-circle of a *rond de jambe tour,* the revolution being kept continuous while the necessary changes are made in the position of the body. A turn in the air that may be included among *pirouettes* is a *jeté en tournant;* and it may be adorned with an *entrechat,* a *brisé,* or whatever "beats" may suit the artist's taste and abilities.

THE DANCE

The words *"arabesque"* and *"attitude"* do not refer to steps, but to postures. Their composition is as exactly defined as that of any step. Figure 56 shows a typical *arabesque*.

The *developpé* above referred to is a usual means of bringing a leg to horizontal, as a preliminary to fur-

72   73
Two Forms of "Attitude."
Open (*ouverte*) 72; crossed (*croisé*) 73. The position of the supporting leg is the same in both.

ther work. It is the opening step of many a dance-poem, and a pretty accurate index of the class of work to follow. If the leg rises without hurry or faltering, and unfolds with its proper sense of proud elegance; if always the body keeps the serene relaxation that accompanies only the perfection of equilibrium, there is coming a feast for the gods. Far from the least of Genée's manifestations of virtuosity is the legato poise of her entrance *stepping down* from a picture frame: so deliberate

THE BALLET'S TECHNIQUE 85

and even is her *developpé* that the eye at first fails to discern movement, as though it were watching the opening of a morning glory. Never the twitch of a muscle, never an impulse of hurry, never the suspicion of hesitation—through bar after bar of music, the ethereal one makes that first step reverence-compelling in its incredible beauty of movement.

Analogous to the *developpé* in execution is the *pas de cheval,* the latter, however, serving to change the dancer's place on the floor. It is proud, strong, triumphant; used in an advance of a *corps de ballet* toward the spectator, the motive of dominance is strongly felt. Though effective, it is not one of the structural parts, like the steps heretofore described. It is, rather, a decorative unit superadded. The same may be said of the *pas de chat,* which is a jerky, short and very rapid simple alternating step; bending the knees sharply, but not bringing them high; the feet crossing at each step. It is not the physical locomotion of a cat, but it is a good interpretation of the spirit of an especially capricious one. It expresses well the idea of witchcraft or mischievous spirits.

Going to the extreme contrast of this step, a fortissimo effect is attained by the male dancer's form of extended jump. It is necessarily high; but it emphasises especially its effect of length horizontally. (See figures 74 and 75.) Auguste Vestris, the eighteenth-century virtuoso, owed a part of his reputation to his power in this step; "suspended in the air" was the phrase attaching to his performance of it. Its function is, in great part, to astonish. Women accomplish its effect with the aid of a supporting man; the change of level attained by this leap aided by a "lift" is indeed a harmonised explosion, especially if it follows an arrangement of little steps.

Stories of the impression created by Vestris' leap would be quite incredible were their possibility not confirmed in our own time. In *Scheherazade* Volinine jumped a distance that seemed literally more than half the width of a big stage. An illusion, of course. The world's record in the broad jump is less than twenty-five feet, and the broad jumper's covered distance does not look so impressive in actuality as it does on paper, at

74 75

MECHANISM OF BROAD JUMP.
As the body descends, the advanced leg and arm are raised, producing the illusion of sustained horizontal flight.

that. Whereas the dancer's leap seems to be under no particular limit—when adequately performed, which is rare. Being typical of the trickery by which dancing plays with the eye, it may be worth analysing.

The magic is based on two illusions. First, horizontal lines are insisted upon and preserved as continuous; while lines not horizontal are "broken up" into short lengths, to the end that they make comparatively little impression on the eye. The pose itself, then, is horizontal, which practically coincides with the direction of the dancer's flight. Every one has seen the experiment of apparently shortening one of two equal pencil lines by means of cutting short lines across it: the converse of the same principle governs the jump. As the pencil line was shortened by cross lines, the jump is lengthened by long lines parallel to its direction.

As the dancer passes the top of his flight, the second illusion begins to go into effect. Contradicting the eye's observation of the gradual descent of the body, the long lines of the artist's arms and legs are steadily raised to point more and more upward. Be the reason whatever it may, the spectator is much less conscious of the body's descent than of the level—or even rising—direction of those long lines; lines which, by the time the step is half completed, have come to appear a good deal longer than they are. The dancer lowers his foot just in time to alight properly. The eye meantime has been so impressed by the sweep of horizontals that it conveys to the mind an agreeably exaggerated statement of the length of leap they represent. Also it probably has been so puzzled that its owner, unless he knows something of dancing, has failed to catch the value of the step as a thing of beauty.

Reasonable familiarity with the foregoing descriptions of steps will, it is hoped, enable the reader to look at great dancing with the added joy that comes of intelligent sympathy with the ballet's intent as decoration, as well as insight into its technical means. The résumé of steps includes the ballet's fundamentals. Each step has its variations, as has been suggested; some of the variations diverge far enough from the basic step to have earned a special designation. For the sake of simplicity, the special names of subvarieties of steps have been eliminated from this little discussion; but not at the sacrifice of anything that a well-informed connoisseur of the ballet need know.

It is a subject whose study is accompanied by the satisfaction that time spent on it is not being frittered away on an affair of a day. Some of the steps are coeval with the earliest graphic records of social life; Emmanuel (*La Danse Grecque Antique*) has made a fascinating book showing the use of many present-day ballet steps (including "toe-work") by the figures on early Greek ceramics, carvings, etc. Various ages have added to the vocabulary of choreographic material; the national academies of France and Italy have preserved that which is contributory to their ideals of almost architectural style, and rejected that which lacks form, even though expressive. The *tours* and *pas* of which ballet eloquence is composed, therefore, represent a selection based on generations of careful and accurately recorded experiment in the interest of pure beauty. The designation "classic," attached to French and Italian ballets, is in all ways correct and deserved. The watchful care of guardians keeps both schools aloof from passing caprices of the public, and uncorrupted by vulgar fashions. There is a present and growing movement toward naturalistic pantomime—a mode combining with popularity enough intrinsic good to occasion anxiety lest the classic ballet perish under its momentum. In reply to which let it be emphasised at this point that the old schools never have failed to incorporate the good of whatever has offered; whereas that which was not of intrinsic value always has passed away through its own lack of æsthetic soundness. The Russian academy bases its technique on the French-Italian, and insists on it rigourously as a groundwork; Madame Pavlowa's practice is conducted daily under the eye of her Italian maestro, Ceccetti. Lydia Lopoukowa, Alexander Volinine—perfect, both, in academic form; their romantic pantomime is an addition, *not a corruption*. These are among the great artistic intelligences in the new Russian movement. Meantime arises a horde of beings possessed of "soul," "God-given individuality," "natural and unhampered grace," boasting of their self-evident innocence of all instruction. These last constitute the tidal wave that excites alarmists, on behalf of the classic ballet!

No less subject to rule and form than steps and their elements is choreographic composition. Steps are phrased and phrases repeated, exactly as in music. By the same formality of construction, each movement of the composition is dominated by a fixed theme. Suppose an entrance is in the coquettish mood: it is not unlikely that the ballet-master will elect to interpret that mood by whirls—in other words, the horizontal circle. The girl may approach the man in a wide *piqué tour* (a stage-covering circle, the dancer *picking* her steps with emphasised daintiness), elude his grasp by means of a series of rapid *pas de bourrée* turns, and perhaps finally spin into his arms at the finish of a *pirouette*. Everything is kept in turns, and in little vivacious steps; no great elevation, no open or sweeping movements; nothing of the glorious, everything to secure daintiness. Again, the same motive might be rendered in quite another way, namely, by short advances, retreats and steps to the side. The passage might start with a series of *relevés*—quick, sharp rises to the toe, the free foot crossing to pose in front of the ankle of the supporting foot, after describing (each step) a *petit battement en avant;* short, crisp, dainty movements, all. In this group might appropriately be included *pas de bourrée dessus-dessous* (i. e., in front and behind); *glissades; petits battements;* and the devilish-looking little *pas-de-chat*. In the same *enchainement* might easily be grouped the *entrechat*. All these steps may unite in a similarity of action: slight elevation, and a short, saucy movement in which the horizontal direction predominates.

If the mood to be expressed were the triumphant, its interpretation might begin with a series of *pas de cheval*. With this the *balloné* and a *rond de jambe* finishing *en arabesque* would unite coherently, their movements all being based on the general form of an arch.

To multiply instances of arrangement by theme is needless. A ballet-master would admit a greater variety of steps together in sequence than the foregoing paragraphs indicate; whirling dervishes produce an effect by turns alone. The instances are given with view only to emphasising the principle of theme unity. What is not obvious to him who never has seen the horrible example of lack of observance of this principle is, that it is not an arbitrary convention, but a fundamental necessity. It is no uncommon thing to see good execution completely wasted in a helter-skelter throwing together of steps that lead to nothing. Cumulative development—with adornment but not digression—along a certain line, will coax the spectator into a mood of full sympathy with the performance. But a series of unrelated turns, jumps sidewise and up in the air, *entrechats* and kicks, bears about the same relation to choreographic argument as a cat's antics on the keyboard of a piano does to the work of a musician.

It will of course be understood that the ballet-master's problem is complicated by requirements and limi-

THE BALLET'S TECHNIQUE 91

tations not even touched upon in this work. Conformity to his accompanying music, for instance, is alone a matter of careful study. In former generations, before the present relative importance of music, the musical composer followed the scenario of the ballet, which was composed first and independently. Nowadays—owing to causes as to which speculation is free—the procedure is reversed. The ballet-master must not only follow phrasing as it is written; he must move his people about the stage in felicitous group evolutions, basing their steps on a fixed number of musical bars and beats. This requirement disposed of, he should interpret the music's changing moods with appropriate steps. Taking as an example a bit of the Ballet of the Hours in *Gioconda:* the music of the hours before dawn is largo and dreamy, breaking into a sparkling allegro as the light comes, increasing in speed and strength until a forte tells of the full-fledged new day. There are steps and combinations to render these motives with the utmost expressiveness. Failure to employ them does not represent lack of competence on the part of the director, so often as it does inadequacy of the human material at his disposal. In America, at present, the task of producing effects with people whose incapability he must conceal is perhaps the most serious embarrassment the ballet-master has to face.

The dancer's supreme virtue is style. If, beginning as a naturally graceful youngster, he has been diligent for from four to seven years in ballet school, he will have it; some acquire it by study alone. With practice from two to four hours every morning, and half an hour to an hour before each performance, he is likely to keep it. What style is, is not for words to define. To preserve mathematical precision in a series of definitely prescribed movements, while executing those movements with the flowing sweep of perfect relaxation; to move through the air like a breeze-wafted leaf, and alight with a leaf's airiness; to ennoble the violence of a savage with a demi-god's dignity; to combine woman's seductiveness with the illusiveness of a spirit—these things are not style, but the kind of thing that style makes possible, the magic results from the perfect co-ordination of many forces, both æsthetic and mechanical. Some of the latter, as to theory, are readily enough understood.

Of the ballet dancer's ever-surprising defiance of the law of gravity, the more obvious means are the *plié,* to soften a descent, and a manner of picking up the weight so quickly that the body seems buoyant. Of perhaps no less value, though not so obvious, is the straight knee. To the eye it gives a sensation of sure architectural support—doubtless through the suggestion of a column. The mechanical importance of the straight supporting knee is no less than the æsthetic, since a firm foundation is essential to perfect control of body, arms and head. When the knee "slumps," the usual consequence is a softened back and a collapsed chest. The muscles of the body "let down," the fine, hypersensitive control of head and arms is gone. Crisp movement being impossible to them without a sound, springy body as a base to work on, the work becomes monotonous and soggy.

The theory of a straight supporting axis applies also to the foot as soon as it rises *sur la pointe.* The foot of Madame Pavlowa *en arabesque* (see reproduction of her photograph) illustrates the principle. Mechanically, there is definite advantage in an absolutely vertical support; while the spectator's visual impression asserts without hesitation that the figure above the foot is without weight whatever. The superb line of the ankle, continuous in sweep over the instep, is not the least of the wonders of what, if one were writing in Spanish, one could without extravagance refer to as "that little foot of gold."

It should not in the least modify admiration of this superlative bit of technique to dispel the not uncommon belief that rising on the toes is a cause of physical torment, a feat requiring extraordinary strength, or in itself an achievement to insist upon. Quite the contrary. Like every other position in the dance, any half-trained performer or student can get it, all except the quality. As soon as a pupil has acquired the equilibrium that ought to precede toe-work, the necessary muscular development has taken care of itself, as a general rule; and she takes position on the point without special effort. Help is given the foot by the hard-toe slipper, combining as it does the support of a well-fitted shoe with a square, blunt toe. The latter, though of small area, furnishes some base to stand on. Stiffening in the fore-part of the shoe protects the toes against bruising in the descent from leaps.

Position on the point justly claims attention as an acrobatic wonder, when it is taken barefooted. And a dancer who, barefooted, can perform steps on the point, supporting herself easily with one foot off the floor, is simply hyper-normal in strength of ankles, feet, and legs. Miss Bessie Clayton is such a one, and very likely the only one. It is a feat whose absence from formal dancing is not felt, though its use would be effective in some of the re-creations of Greek work. There is evidence that the early Greeks practiced it, as before noted. In our own times, there is only one instance, among the stories ever heard by the authors, of barefoot work on the point being done in public; and that performance, oddly enough, took place in precedent-worshipping Spain. The occasion was one of those competitions that Spaniards love to arrange when two or more good dancers happen to play the same town at the same time. Tremendous affairs; not only does rivalry approach the line of physical hostilities among the spectators, but the competition draws out feats of special virtuosity that the dancers have practiced secretly, in anticipation of such contingencies. La Gitanita (the Little Gipsy), one of the competitors in the event referred to, had, for some years, put in a patient half-hour a day on the ends of her bare toes, without the knowledge of any but the members of her family. When, therefore, at the coming of her turn in the competition, she threw her shoes to the audience, and her stockings behind a wing, and danced a *copla* of *las Sevillanas* on the point, the contest was settled. Most of the spectators never had heard even of the existence of such a thing as toe-work, because it does not exist in Spanish dancing. The experience to them was like witnessing a miracle; so it happens that La Gitanita, many years dead, is still talked of when Spanish conversation turns to incredible feats of dancing.

With such rare exceptions as the above, however, the person who is happy in seeing difficulties overcome is best repaid by watching the manner instead of the matter. There is hardly a step but can be floundered through, if real execution be disregarded. The difficulties that take years to master, that keep the front rank

THE BALLET'S TECHNIQUE 95

thin, are those of nobility, ease and precision of action. Naturally, it is harder to preserve these qualities through a *renversé* than in a *pas de Basque;* but there is no merit in exhibiting a *renversé* badly done. The latter is a pertinent instance of things difficult to do well. A *fouetté tour* "inward" is not safely attempted by any but the most skilful; nor is either a *fouetté* or a *rond de jambe*, finishing in *arabesque*. To keep the movement continuous, imperceptibly slowing it down as the *arabesque* settles into its final pose, requires ability of a rare grade.

As the little alternating steps furnish the means of regaining equilibrium after a big *pas* or *tour*, it follows that their elimination from an *enchainement* represents a tour de force. This is especially true if the big steps be taken at a slow tempo (as an *adagio*, so called); and difficulties are compounded if the artist performs the entire *adagio* on the point. Few there are in any generation who can attempt such a flight.

But there are many qualities justly to be demanded of any artist who steps before an audience. Crisp, straight-line movements should be cleanly differentiated from the soft and flowing. An *entrechat* not as sharp-cut as a diamond represents incompetent or slovenly workmanship. The same applies to other steps of the staccato character—as *battements, brisés, pirouettes sur le cou-de-pied*. Each dancer rightly has his own individuality; and the movements of one will be dominated by a liquid quality, while another's will be brilliant, or "snappy." But a dancer who is truly an artist has, within his scope, a good contrast between the several types of movement. Lack of such contrast may cause a sense of monotony even in very skilful work. Elevation also is important in preserving a sense of variety. Not only *plié* and rise are made to serve; raisings of the arms add immensely to the sense of vertical uplift when height is sought.

A certain conformity to geometrical exactness is necessary to the satisfaction of the spectator's eye, and is observed by all but the incompetent. Not that movement should be rigid—very much to the contrary. "Geometry" is a sinister word; interpreted in a sense in which it is not meant, it would be misleading. An example is sometimes clearer than attempted definitions or descriptions.

If, having given an order for a grandfather's clock, the recipient found on delivery that it did not stand quite straight, he would be annoyed. Suppose then that further observation revealed that the face of the clock was not in the middle, that the centre of the circle described by the hands was not the centre of the face, that the face was no more than an indeterminate approximation of a circle, and that the numerals were placed at random intervals; the eye of the clock's owner would be offended. Various æsthetic and psychological arguments might be applied to the justification of his feeling, but they are not needed. The futility of near-circles, approximate right angles and wobbly lines is felt instinctively. Yet the eye rejoices in the "free-hand" sweep of line correct in placement, though not subjected to the restrictions of straight-edge and compass. Asking for acceptance in such sense of the terms "geometrical" and "precision," we may return to our discussion of the ballet.

The decorative iniquity of the hypothetical clock attaches to all dancing that fails to give to precision the most rigourous consideration. The imaginary circle described in a *pirouette,* for example, is divided into halves

THE BALLET'S TECHNIQUE 97

and quarters. Let us suppose the *pirouette* to end in *arabesque,* stopping on the half-circle, bringing the dancer in profile to the audience: a very few degrees off the half-circle are, from the ballet-master's point of view, about of a kind with a few centimetres separating the misplaced clock hands from their proper situation in the centre of the dial. The *petit rond de jambe* has its imaginary quarter of the great circle in which to play, and which it must fill. In a *fouetté,* the sweep of the foot starts at the quarter-circle (marked by an imaginary lateral plane through the dancer's body), and reaches back just to the half-circle (defined by a similar plane, drawn longitudinally). The lateral elevations of the legs are likewise subject to law, the imaginary vertical circle described by the leg as radius being divided into eighths, to allow the leg to use the angle of forty-five degrees; experience shows that this diagonal, half a right angle, is pleasing to the eye and not disturbing to the senses.

The hands and forearms are turned in such a way as to eliminate elbows, the coincidence of a contour of the arm with an arc of a big (imaginary) circle being always sought.

The convention of "toeing out" has as an object the showing of ankles and legs to the best advantage. On the flat foot the advantage is not so apparent; but experiment shows that pointing out and down greatly helps the appearance of a foot in the air. The supporting foot and leg also show the benefit of the device as soon as the dancer rises to the ball of the foot or the point. Moreover, it is obvious that the pointing of a supporting foot forward would necessitate changes from the classic form of many steps.

Recent years have brought out a volume of protest

to the effect that the classic ballet's **restriction of movement** too severely limits expression. The protest is right or wrong according to point of view, and point of view is a matter of historical period. The French school comes to us from a time when men kissed hands and drew swords in exact accordance with accepted forms, and the favoured house-decoration was a tapestry designed on lines purely architectural. The present is a moment of much concern about freedom of the individual, and its expression. Curiosity is at boiling-point. Narrative is sought. We want something to happen, all the time. And those who fail to see the actual occurrence want the story of it to be graphic. Moving pictures are very satisfying to the majority. Acres of popular pictures are painted in boisterous disregard of order or harmony of line and form. It would be very pleasant for those who enjoy optical beauty, if public taste required beauty as a first requisite for popularity. Nevertheless, popular pictures as they are do no particular harm, probably, either to those who like them or to those who do not.

But, if the world's great and beautiful mural decorations were suddenly painted over with frenzied or sentimental illustrations, to "modernise" them, it would be a different matter. That little public to whom beauty is as a necessary sustenance—by coincidence the same public that includes the leaders of thought in each generation—would have a good deal to say in the line of objection to such desecration. Now, the ballet is essentially a mural decoration, potentially very great in power to exalt. If a large element should have its way, the next few years would see that decoration painted over

THE BALLET'S TECHNIQUE   99

with a huge choreographic story-picture, sentimental or frenzied, realistic; and beauty be hanged.

This anarchistic mania is in no wise a doctrine of the Russians. But their undiscerning admirers, seeing in their work only the lines of departure from old-established formulæ, shout to heaven that any restraint of individual caprice is wrong. Innocent of suspicion that such things as æsthetic principles exist, they force their expression of "individuality" to the limit of their invention. And some of them certainly are inventive.

Fortunately the great dancer is great largely because of his perception of the value of order and form. The best of the Russians are great dancers; great artists in the full sense of the word. They are the ones who will profoundly influence the æsthetic thought of the present generation, and their influence will be sound and good. Opposing it will be many a "hit" by skilful characters, and a dangerous numerical force among the public. It is easily possible that the latter influence may prevail. The grand ballet is still an experiment in the America of this generation. It was here thirty years ago, and fell into the hands of Philistines, who shaped it into the silly thing they thought they wanted, and then were forced to abandon it because it was silly.

Than the present, there never was a more important crisis in the cause of choreographic good taste. The outcome depends upon the manner and degree in which those who stand for good taste assert themselves during the next few years.

CHAPTER V

THE GOLDEN AGE OF DANCING

LOUIS XIV brought public interest in the ballet to a point of eager excitement; indeed, the influence of a monarch's consistent patronage, including the foundation of a national academy, added to the example of his prominent participation in about thirty allegorical dancing spectacles, could not fail to be powerful.

With the growth of public interest and intelligence, the ballet and the technique of dancing developed commensurately. The two enthusiasms of public and artists reacted on each other to the advantage of both; in the uninterrupted enrichment of the ballet the public never failed to find its attention repaid in ever-increasing fascination. Dancers, composers and directors, on their side, abandoned themselves to their work with the zeal that comes of certainty that no good thing will pass unnoticed.

Such conditions bring good results more than can be foreseen even by those actively engaged. As, in fiction, the miner in trying to loosen a nugget usually uncovers a vein, so it may occur in the arts. For instance, Camargo found that her *entrechat* was difficult and ineffectual under the weight and length of the fashionable skirt of the period. She therefore had a skirt made reaching midway from knee to foot. A simple solution? Certainly. But it was thought of only after centuries of submission to clothes that considered fashion and disregarded the problems and possibilities of the dancer's art. And it represented the species of decision that risks acting counter to an accepted, unquestioned institution. It was not an effort to draw attention by means of a spurious originality. Camargo's work explained the change. The public understood and approved. The ballet was directed toward its costume; a long journey lay ahead of it, but it was rightly started.

Liberty of movement so attained at once put a premium on higher and more open steps; technical invention was set to work as never before. The *balloné,* various *pas battus* and *ronds-de-jambe* that followed immeasurably enhanced the scope of the ballet as an instrument of ocular-orchestral expression. New *enchainements,* striking in the contrast of little work with big, soon made the court dances—which for a period had constituted the ballet's working material—look old-fashioned. The stage now required considerable elevation, decided contrasts, increasing scope. And, whatever the cost in skill and energy, there were dancers eager to expend the energy and to give the needed years to acquiring the skill.

Since the days of the Roman Empire, masks had been worn to identify characters. Not a bit of cloth to cover the face, merely; but cumbersome things with plumes, wings, metallic spikes (i. e., the rays of the sun worn by Louis XIV in the Ballet of Night) or what-not, so extended that they restricted the action of the the arms, so heavy as to interfere with steps. It was a clumsy convention, but it was as integrally a part of stage representation as scenery is to-day, and the few who wished its abolition were outvoted by a cautious majority. At last, according to her custom of helping an enterprise that is doing well, Fate took a hand. Auguste Vestris failed to appear for a certain performance; as the time for his entrance drew near, the anxious stage director asked Gardel to "go on" in Vestris' part. Gardel, an until-that-time ineffectual rebel against the mask, consented; but with the condition that the mask be omitted. In default of arrangements more to his satisfaction, the director consented. The public at once saw the advantage of the change, and were pleased with Gardel's appearance. So began the end of the dominion of the mask.

Of the notable personalities that the early rays of the eighteenth century illuminated, the aforementioned Auguste Vestris was the interesting son of a more interesting father. The latter was a genius of the very first water, with a conceit so incredibly exaggerated that it is almost lovable. "This century," he was accustomed to observe, "has produced but three great men—myself, Voltaire, and Frederick the Great." He sometimes signed himself *"le Diou de la Danse"*; himself a Florentine, the relation of French spelling to pronunciation was contrary to his ideas. The phrase as he put it had a special merit, and as *"le Diou de la Danse"* he was known through his long life. A lady, having stepped on his foot, expressed a hope that she had not hurt him. "Le Diou" depreciated the hurt to himself, but informed the lady that she had put Paris into a two-weeks' mourning. Of his son's leaps he said that if Auguste did not remain in the air forever, it was because he did not wish to humiliate his comrades.

The foundation of the Opera was another of the impulses to act favourably, if indirectly, upon the interests of dancing. Its modest beginning had been made a few years after that of the ballet academy. The two arts at once combined to produce a new variety of musical spectacle, namely, opera. Great music came to the fore in response to the added encouragement—but digressions must be repressed.

Contemporary with Camargo and Sallé was a dreamer of dreams too great to be realized in his own time, but whose ideas take place among the lasting good influences in art. Garrick called him "the Shakespeare of the Dance"; his name was Noverre.

To the post of ballet-master at the Opera he brought the experience of years in similar service in Stuttgart, Vienna and St. Petersburg. His work he regarded with the broad vision of cultivated understanding of painting, music, story, acting and dancing, and the functions of each. His genius was, above all else, constructive; his ideal was to bring the arts into a harmonious union, to which each should contribute its utmost, while all should be informed with and dominated by a single æsthetic purpose.

The obstacle always blocking his path was not incompetence of aides and artists, not lack of money, nor any of the *bêtes noires* to which more recent idealists are accustomed. His enemy was the inert, impalpable and almost invincible force of custom, paradoxically persistent despite the public's demand for new things. It was custom that the composer of a ballet should always arrange for the introduction of the specialties of the several principals, irrespective of motives. Custom obliged him to arrange entrances in the inverse order of the artists' relative ranks—he of least rank "going on" first, the star being the last to appear. Noverre broke up this usage, and characters thereafter entered at times consistent with plot-development. Plots had been crippled by accepted beliefs that certain dance sequences were unalterable; a *Gavotte,* for instance, had to be followed by a *Tambourin* and a *Musette;* the sequence had not been questioned. Noverre saw the possibilities of dancing as an instrument of expression; he insisted that steps and *enchainements* should be composed to intensify the motive of the passage. Scenery, he held, should contribute in the same way to the mood of the act it decorates. Pretty it had been, and executed by capable painters; but Noverre found its composition lacking in consideration of proper relationship to the other elements of the production. With himself he associated Boucher and one or two other decorators of lesser name; under his comprehension of the scene's dramatic intent, settings were designed that reasserted in line, form and colour the argument of the scene's plot, music and dance. In this department he was less successful than in others. Boucher made beautiful sketches, some of which are extant. But one has only to consider opera in his own day to realise that any influence Noverre exercised toward the unification of scenery with music and plot, was not strong enough to last. Stories taken from legend, set among surroundings as realistic as skill can paint them; tragic scenes among architecture and foliage coloured in the key of care-free frivolity—to enumerate the familiar discrepancies is unnecessary. Tradition specifies a bright first-act "set" for *Carmen,* and grey for the prison interior in *Faust.* But the profound correlation of colour and line with the explicit mood of the piece has remained for the Russian, Léon Bakst. In the recent volcanic renaissance of dancing effected by his fellow-countrymen, M. Bakst and his ideas have been a force second only to the marvellous work of the dancers themselves. His scenery strikes the note of the drama, attunes the spectator with its mood, at the rise of the curtain. His knowledge of pictorial composition he has extended to the designing of costumes; his broad artist's intelligence he has applied to the composition and direction of ballets! It is his happy rôle to realise Noverre's dream.

In music Noverre worked with Gluck, in certain productions at least; and happily. "Instead of writing the steps on prescribed airs," in a free translation of his own words, "as is done with couplets of familiar tunes, I composed—if I may so express myself—the dialogue of my ballet and had the music made for each phrase and each idea. It was just so that I dictated to Gluck the characteristic air of the ballet of the savages in *Iphigenia in Tauris;* the steps, the gestures, the expressions of the different personages that I designed for him gave to the celebrated composer the character of the composition of that beautiful bit of music."

The abolition of the mask was among Noverre's desires; its fortuitous accomplishment at a later time already has been described. In his ideals for costume reform in general he was only partly successful. What he strove for seems to have been costuming in something of the sense of its present-day interpretation by the Russians; garments wholly in character with the beings represented, in regard to race and period, yet conceding enough in line and colour to enable them to be used as part of the material of abstract interpretation. At the beginning of his administration of the Opera he found each performer dressed, for the most part, according to individual choice: either the drawing-room costume of the period, or the same with shortened skirt, à la Camargo. To this was added the mask, an enormous wig (unrelated to the character) and some such symbol as a leopard skin, a wreath of flowers, or more likely a property such as a bow and quiver of arrows, or a pair of bellows. In the order mentioned, such articles represented a bacchante, Flora, Cupid, and Zephyrus. Excepting the superadded marks of identification, artists provided their own wardrobe. The lack of consistent supervision and its natural consequence is exemplified in an anecdote of a member of the *corps de ballet* in *Le Carnaval et la Folie:* in the performance she exhibited a series of gowns of Adrienne Lecouvreur, which she had thriftily picked up at a sale of the recently deceased tragedienne's effects.

In the ballet of *The Horatii,* of Noverre's own composition, "*Camilla* wore a huge hooped petticoat, her hair piled up three feet high with flowers and ribbons. Her brothers wore long-skirt coats, set out from their hips by padding." And so forth.

It is to be noted that Roman and Greek mythology lived and flourished, but no longer excluded other lore from the composer's use. A list of Noverre's *ballets d'action* includes *The Death of Ajax, The Judgment of Paris, Orpheus' Descent into Hell, Rinaldo and Armida, The Caprices of Galatea, The Toilette of Venus and the Roses of Love, The Jealousies of the Seraglio, The Death of Agamemnon, The Clemency of Titus, Cupid the Pirate* and *The Embarkation for Cythera.* His work of permanent value, still read by composers and ballet-masters, is his book *Letters on the Imitative Arts.* For his light composition, *Les Petits Riens,* the music was by Mozart.

Notwithstanding his failure to accomplish all he hoped

in the several departments of his organisation, and in spite of his rather pessimistic opinions of early eighteenth-century conditions affecting the ballet, the dance was entering its golden age. Pantomime—largely owing to the enrichment he had given it out of the fruits of his study of Garrick's methods—had exponents who could touch the heart. Writings began to show intelligent and explicit criticism, and that of a nature to prove that choreographic execution had reached a high point. The added scope afforded by new acquisitions of material in the steps allowed artists to go far in development of individuality. Camargo charmed by perfection of technique; "she danced to dance, not to stir emotion." Her special steps are enumerated: besides the *entrechat*, she shone in *jetés battus* and a frictionless *entrechat coupé*. About her work there was a healthy public controversy, a vigourous minority protesting against idolisation of one who they asserted had virtuosity only. And the protests show analytical understanding of the dance.

Sallé's more deliberate, probably more feeling work, has been noted in an earlier chapter. Her popularity hardly could have been less, all told, than that of her rival.

Mlles. Allard and Guimard were two stars who followed a little later in the same period. The former combined extraordinary vigour with pathetic pantomime. The work of Guimard was delicate, pretty, light. "She is a shadow, flitting through Elysian groves," one of her contemporaries wrote of her. Certainly she had the art of pleasing, on the stage or off. The list of eminent competitors for her affection is eloquent not in its length, but in the number of occupants of high station

—including three princes of the Church. With a passion for theatrical and political intrigue she combined a spirit of the utmost generosity. To her the painter David owed his professional beginnings; he was an art student without means to study, and engaged in house-painting for a livelihood, when Guimard secured him a pension that afforded him study at Rome. Some of Fragonard's best decorations were made for her establishments.

Her refusal to have any rival about her kept the Opera in an uproar. Perfectly appointed little theatres in both her country and city homes enabled her, with her taste, means, and popularity among the people of the stage, to give performances for which invitations were most highly prized. For these performances she made a practice of setting dates to coincide with court receptions, knowing from experience that the best wit and most of the elegance of Paris would make excuses to the court. From this estate she was reduced, partly by the storm of the Revolution, to a condition of miserable poverty lasting until her death; which was delayed until her seventy-fourth year.

Men did not fall short of women in merit and recognition. Beside the Vestris, father and son, fame touched Javillier, Dauberval, and the comedy dancer Lany. Maximilian Gardel, he who substituted for Auguste Vestris on condition of appearing without the mask (Apollo, in *Castor and Pollux* was the rôle), was a composer of note as well as a dancer. His brother Pierre added to these qualities skill as a violinist.

* * * *

The progress of the ballet was halted by the Revolution. Gardel headed an effort to keep it in motion with

THE GOLDEN AGE

the aid of a spectacle *La Marseillaise* as vehicle; but the people were on the streets, dancing *la Carmagnole*, and nobility were as far from Paris as possible. It is probable that the ballet was set down as an aristocratic institution. Napoleon included a *corps de ballet* in the equipment of the campaign in Egypt; but it signified nothing to the advantage of the art. Immediately after the Terror, eighteen hundred dance-halls were opened in Paris, to furnish, seven nights a week, relief for fever and frenzy. Even England was too preoccupied to offer the ballet a dwelling; its organisation, for the time being, was lost.

But only for the time being. History records a bit of international negotiation indicating Europe's readiness to return to the realities of life and the happiness thereof. In 1821 an ambassador of a great power acted officially as an impresario of dancers.

England, whose best public taste never has been satisfied with the work of her own people, was, within a few years after the peace, again seeking dancers in France. Efforts to get the best were handicapped. The national character of the French Academy makes its pupils and graduates wards of their government, in effect; government permission is and was necessary as a condition to leaving the country. Negotiations therefore were put into the hands of the British ambassador, less formal dealings apparently having failed to produce results. The agreement was incorporated in the form of a treaty, France agreeing to lend England two first and two second dancers, England in return agreeing not to attempt to engage any others without the Academy's consent.

M. Albert and Mlle. Noblet were the first two artists to be taken to London under the new arrangement, at salaries of £1700 and £1500 respectively. During the same period, and for years after, Her Majesty's Theatre had the services of Carlo Blasis, one of the most capable ballet-masters of his time, father of several virtuosi, and the writer of books of lasting value on the subject of his profession. Dancing reached a popularity that would seem the utmost attainable, were it not for disclosures to be made in the years soon to come.

Beauty and its appreciation will carry a public to a condition of ecstasy. If to this be added the incessant discussion attendant on a controversy, with the hot partisanship that accompanies the coexistence of rival stars, the devotional flame is augmented by fuel of high calorific value. Not without cause were the hostilities of Pylades and Bathyllus, of Sallé and Camargo, associated with great public enthusiasm. To artistic appreciation they added the element of sporting interest.

In Marie Taglioni and Fanny Ellsler, Europe had the parties to a years-long competition that was Olympian in quality and incredible in its hold on the sympathies of the public. Both goddesses in art, their personalities and the *genres* of their work were at opposite extremes. In *Pendennis* Thackeray asks, "Will the young folks ever see anything so charming, anything so classic, anything like Taglioni?" Of Ellsler, Flitch quotes words equally enthusiastic—and less coherent—from the pen of Theophile Gautier, who was an incurable maniac and copious writer on the subject of dancing: "Now she darts forward; the castanets commence their sonorous clatter; with her hands she seems to shake down clusters of rhythm. How she twists! how she bends! what fire! what voluptuousness of motion! what eager zest! Her arms seem to swoon, her head droops, her body curves backward until her white shoulders almost graze the ground. What charm of gesture! And with that hand which sweeps over the dazzle of the footlights would not one say that she gathered all the desires and all the enthusiasms of those that watch her?"

This referred to a *Cachucha* that she had brought from Spain; a dance whose steps have been recomposed under other names, its original name forgotten except in association with the name and the art of Ellsler. It was a perfect vehicle for the exploitation of the ardent qualities that the little Austrian was made of, and on her rendering of it was based a great part of her fame.

Taglioni, in contrast, was a being of spirit, innocent of mortal experience, free from ties of the earth. Her training was strictly within the bounds of the classic ballet; during her career she greatly amplified its range, yet she always kept within its premise. Though born in Stockholm, her father was an Italian ballet-master, and two of her aunts were dancers of reputation. Her achievements represented a triumph of choreographic inheritance and training over an ill-formed body; in childhood she is said to have been a hunchback. With training her figure became normal in strength, and attained a quality of form in keeping with her selected rôles. But overstrong features deprived her of the dancer's adventitious aid of facial beauty. Her triumphs were achieved by art alone.

Vienna she conquered at the age of twenty, in 1822, the year of her début. Paris was not so readily moved; but a success in that capital was a practical necessity to a great career, and Taglioni never rested until she secured its approval, expressed in terms that penetrated Europe. Business generalship was not the least of the attributes of the Taglioni, father and daughter; they recognised the propitious hour for an engagement in London. The contract included pensioning a number of their family, and £100 a performance. Results more than justified the terms; ticket sales for Taglioni's nights usually were of the nature of riots. It is as fair to connect with this box-office success, as with any quality of the artist herself, the story of her "holding up" a performance until the management of the theatre should make a substantial payment on an account due. It is unlovable in an artist to keep an audience waiting, and put a manager to the necessity of making explanations. It is unlovable in a coal dealer to discontinue supplies until a debt is settled.

Taglioni paid as heavily for the excellence she put into her work as ever did miner or merchant for the goods he put on his scales. Her training began in early childhood, and covered probably twelve years before her début. Her professional career, with its inevitable anxieties, in no wise reduced the rigour of study, discipline, and precaution. Under her father's eye she practiced hours daily. She went to the length of having installed in her London lodgings a stage built to duplicate the slope of the stage in the theatre.

Apart from the possession of ideals of sheer execution that undoubtedly were higher than any that her predecessors had dreamed of, and whose attainment involved almost superhuman effort and patience, Taglioni was a productive inventor of new steps. Flying *brisés* and other aërial work make their first appearance in her work, according to Mme. Genée's historical programme of ballet evolution. We infer that her effort was directed toward the illusion of flight; a writer of the period refers to an *arabesque* that conveyed that sensation with striking reality. The great addition she made to elevation may naturally be attributed not to any interest in that property for its own sake, but rather to an endless search for lightness. And that, above all others, was the quality she made her own. *La Sylphide* (not the composition recently popularised by the Russians) was the part with which she was most unified in the minds of the public. Her work appears always to have had the creation of fairy fantasy as a definite purpose. In pantomime she was limited. She had none of the stage artist's familiar tricks devised to capture the audience, nor did she avail herself of any vivid contrasts in her costume. She dressed her hair in Madonna fashion, surrounded by a wreath of little roses; further adornment she deliberately avoided.

Ellsler was six years the younger; and, at some sacrifice of time in the acquisition of fame, she reserved Paris as the last of the great cities in which to appear. Taglioni therefore was well established when her destined rival first showed her steps to the Parisians. In fact, she occupied a box at Ellsler's first Paris performance, where it is said she silently wept before the end of the other's first number.

The Swede had succeeded almost in spite of circumstances; Ellsler's natural endowment contained almost everything the gods in a generous mood can give. The perfection of proportion of hands, feet, wrists and ankles were hers, as well as a Greek perfection of figure. Though her legs were of steel, and her strength in general that of an athlete, not a line suffered in sculptural grace nor a movement in freedom. Her face had a beauty that captivated an audience at the moment of her entrance on the stage, and a range of expression covering the moods of the human mind. Her training, like Taglioni's, had begun early. Mozart, for whom Ellsler's father worked as copyist and otherwise, had interested himself in her to the extent at least that her early years were not misspent. With her technical tuition—whatever it may have been—she absorbed stage experience almost from the days of infancy. She danced in a children's ballet in Vienna when she was six years old. Before appearing in Paris she had succeeded in Naples, Berlin and London. The audience of l'Opéra therefore saw her first at the full maturity of her art and equipped with ample knowledge of how to present it to the best advantage.

Her success was not in doubt for a moment. The opening number was a riotous triumph, the morning papers were undivided in praise of the newcomer. Taglioni felt that Ellsler had been brought to Paris expressly to undermine her, and the appearances are that Ellsler lost no time in putting herself on a war footing.

London theatre-goers soon were in a position to question whether, after their elaborate provisions to get good dancers, they had not made a rather embarrassing misplay. Ellsler had danced at Her Majesty's Theatre; the public had enjoyed her work, but, owing either to her lack of a great continental reputation or their own misgivings about the soundness of her work, had refrained from very hearty demonstration. On the first night of the engagement, the manager of l'Opéra—who was in London to form an estimate of the Austrian's work—signed her for the following season.

Contrary to the *metier* of her rival, Ellsler's art consisted of a romantic glorification of life's physique. One gathers that she gave, instead of an ordered and consecutive poem, a thrill of delighted astonishment. She was of a newly forming romantic cult that worshipped the torrid, the savage, the violent. Her most pronounced success was on her rendering of the dances of Spain; she used her hips and her smile, and men—more than women—went into rhapsodies. Gautier, who had seen the best dancers in Spain, wrote that none of them equalled Ellsler. Which is credible, with reservations and conditions. If the sole aim of Spanish dancing is to express fire and temperament, to astonish and inflame, it is more likely to be realised by a clever Northerner than by a Spaniard. The headlong enthusiast is not bothered by delicate considerations of shading, development, and truth of form; seizing the salient and exotic, an exaggeration of these and the elimination of all else is sure to produce a startling result. Execution at an abnormally rapid tempo will conceal inaccuracies from all eyes but those trained to the dance, and backed by a knowledge of its true forms.

All this by no means intends to assert that Ellsler was not a dancer of a high degree of skill, and perhaps of some degree of greatness. It is significant, however, that her encomiums concern themselves only with that which, boiled down, amounts to praise of a beautiful woman, performing evolutions at that time novel and surprising, and frankly—withal in a perfectly clean manner—appealing to sex. The quality that might be called decorative truth does not appear to have been an impressive element of her work. Assuredly that is the foundation of dancing entitled to any consideration in connection with the quality of greatness. Temperament, expressing what it will, of course is as necessary to animate the form as true form is to begin with; but temperamental exuberance cannot take the place of a proper substructure. Granting the inadequacy of data, and speculating on a basis of indications only, one is justified in wondering if Ellsler coming to life to-day could repeat her impression on Paris, with its present knowledge not only of Spanish dancing, but also of feats of supreme virtuosity.

Years only augmented the heat of the feud between the two goddesses. Europe divided itself into acrimonious factions of Taglionites and Ellslerites. The latter were shocked, however, when, to bring to a flat comparison the question of merit, Ellsler announced her intention to play *La Sylphide*. Taglioni had made the part her own; for another to undertake it was at least an act of doubtful delicacy. Nor was the idea better advised on grounds of strategy. *La Sylphide* in its composition was a tissue of the ethereal, even if Taglioni had not made it so by association with herself. Ellsler was insistently concrete. Effects followed causes. Her most ardent partisans could not say after the performance that the attempt spelled anything but failure.

America's first vision of a star dancer was the direct consequence of Ellsler's vexation over the fiasco. Our fathers and grandfathers unharnessed the horses from her carriage, and counted it an honour to get a hand on the rope by which the carriage was drawn; carpeted the streets where the carriage was to pass, strewed flowers where the divinity was to set her foot, and in all ways comported themselves as became the circumstances, during the period of two years that she stayed on this side of the Atlantic.

Ellsler's professional collapse was connected not with art, but politics. After her return from America she danced several seasons in Milan. The ballet academy of la Scala had been founded in 1811, interest in the art ran high, and was fed by the Austrian government as a hoped-for means of distracting the public mind from the revolutionary sentiment of the mid-century. In 1848, on the occasion of a performance especially provided to smooth over a crisis, it was arranged that the people of the ballet should wear a medal recently struck, representing the pope blessing a united Italy. Ellsler conceived a suspicion that the idea represented an intent to insult her as an Austrian; she refused to go on unless the medals be taken off. Meantime the *corps de ballet* had made its entrance, wearing the medals. They were removed at the first opportunity, and promptly missed at the ballet's next entrance. The explanation of the change travelled through the house; the *première*, when she entered, was received with hisses. Tense with political excitement, the audience saw in her only the representative of the power that controlled the Italian sceptre. Her efforts received no answer but furious insults. She fainted.

After three comparatively uneventful years she retired, rich and—in the main—popular. Her contributions to religion and charity had been impressive and so continued until her death in 1884. Her wealth was estimated at one and a quarter million dollars. Taglioni's end was in miserable contrast; during part of her latter years she held a petty position as teacher of deportment in a young ladies' school in England. She died lonely and forgotten, after a most unhappy old age.

Among the many dancers brought out by the period

of enthusiasm were three women of whose work the records have only the highest praise. To Carlotta Grisi, Gautier gave the credit of combining the fiery abandon and the light exquisiteness of the two great luminaries of the day. Fanny Cerito and Lucille Grahn were ranked with her. For Queen Victoria there was arranged a *pas de quatre* by Taglioni, Grisi, Cerito, and Grahn. That performance, in 1845, represents one of the climaxes of ballet history, including as it probably did the greatest sum total of choreographic ability that ever had been brought together.

But it was the milestone at the top of a high mountain, from which the road turned downward. Except in England, Taglioni's prestige was dimmed. Queen Victoria's reign, however uplifting in various important respects, undeniably was depressing in its influence on all the imaginative arts; and it was an influence that reached far. Furthermore, the elements that constituted opera began to assume new relative proportions. The voice of Jenny Lind called attention to the factor of singing. In the present day of subordination of the dancer to the singer, it is almost incredible that opera of seventy years ago assigned to the dancer the relative importance that the singer enjoys now; especially difficult is this conception to any one whose acquaintance with opera is confined to its production in America. General indifference has reduced operatic ballet in this land to a level compared to which its condition in continental Europe is enviable. Though reduced from past importance, in countries that support academies it has at least retained standards of execution.

But the strictly modern interpretation of opera, minimising choreography, has been accepted. New operas are written in conformity with the altered model. It is likely that the present renaissance of dancing, though no less vital than any that have gone before, will effect little change in the art's importance in opera structure, which has become a distinct organism to be heard rather than seen. Aroused interest and intelligence inevitably will force improvement on old organisations, new appreciation will justify it from the box-office point of view. But the American dance-lover's hope lies in the new-old form of ballet pantomime. This is the expression that the great new romantic movement has taken, as though in express recognition of those of us to whom the use of ears has not atrophied eyes.

Against the suddenly discovered passion for singing, the art of Grisi, Cerito, Grahn and their colleagues could not hold public attention. Steadfastly the French and Italian academies held to their creeds of choreographic purity. Upon their fidelity to ideals the latter nineteenth-century reign of artistic terror made no impression; to their preservation of the good is due the ability of the present romantic renaissance to come into its complete expression without the intervention of a century of rebuilding. Russia and Austria too had founded national academies for instruction along the lines made classic by Paris and Milan. Others followed. But it appears that the technical virtuosity of Taglioni had set a pace that was both difficult and misleading. Being a genius, perfection meant to her a means of expression. During a period in which no great genius appeared, efforts to win back the lost kingdom took the form of striving for technique as an object. The public was unjustly damned for failure to respond to marvellously executed students' exercises. With equal lack of justice, it became fashionable to include the whole school of the ballet's art in the accusation of stiffness and artificiality.

The half-century ending about 1908, during which the stage was given over to all the flashy choreographic counterfeits that mediocrity could invent, was saved from complete sterility by the dances that are rooted in the soil. *Jigs* and *Reels, Hornpipes* and *Tarantellas* held their own like hardy wild flowers in a garden of weeds; like golden, opulent lilies, the *Seguidillas* of Spain held their heads above malformation and decadence. This is a fitting point at which to consider the nature of some of these ancient expressions of the heart of men who dwell away from courts.

CHAPTER VI

SPANISH DANCING

SINCE earliest Occidental history, the dances of Spain have been famous. To-day their richness, variety and fundamental nobility give them a position in advance of any other group of national dances of the Occidental type. Whether certain of the Oriental expressions are superior to the Spanish is wholly a matter of point of view on dancing. But dancers and dance-lovers, of all beliefs and prejudices, unite in conceding to Spain the highest development of "characteristic" or national dancing. More even: though the French and Italian ballets in general hold their schools to be the very fountainhead of the choreographic art, not a few disciples of the academies of Milan or Paris concede to Spanish dancing superiority over all, in that aspect of beauty that is concerned with majesty of line and posture.

It is as though Terpsichore herself had chosen the dwellers of Iberia to guard her gifts to mankind. Gadir, the city now called Cadiz, was a little Paris in the day of the Carthaginian, with dancing as its most highly developed art and notable among its diversions. When the Romans took the city they were delighted with the dancers they found there; for centuries after, Spanish dancers remained a fashionable adjunct of great entertainment in the capital, and Cadiz the inexhaustible source of their supply.

When Rome, too infirm to resist, left Spain to be overrun by the Visigoth, she left the arts of the peninsula to the mercy of a destroying barbarian. Architecture and statuary he demolished, books he burned. Dancing eluded his clumsy hand; in places of retirement children were taught the steps and gestures that had crossed the sea from Egypt in the days of the Phœnicians.

In the eighth century came the Moor: slayer, organiser, builder; fanatic, dreamer, poet; lover and creator of beauty in all its manifestations. His verses were epigrams of agreeable and unexpected sounds, formed into phrases of eloquent metaphor. His architecture and its ornament, too, were epigrams; combinations of graceful and simple lines and forms into harmonious symbols more eloquent than description. To him the dance was verse and decoration united, with music added; entertainment and stimulus to contemplation. Under his guardianship and tuition the Spanish dance strengthened its hold on the people, and increased in scope. A certain class of it retains to-day a distinctly Moorish flavour.

The "Century of Gold" that followed the expulsion of the Moors and the discovery of America found the dance surrounded by conditions than which none could have been more favourable. Gold looted from the new continent was lavished on masques and *fiestas* that emulated those of neighbouring monarchies; courtiers were so preoccupied with the diversion that a memoir of the period contains a complaint that "sleep in any part of the palace has become impossible, since persons of all degrees have taken to continuous strumming of the music of the *zarabanda*." The less exalted had in the dance

"La Malagueña y el Torero"
Eduardo and Elisa Cansino

an expression for every emotion, an exercise whose magic ennobled, and a magic whose exercise raised them above the reach of sordid cares. In the Church, while bishops in other parts of Europe were questioning or protesting the dance as an act of worship, their brothers in *"la tierra de Maria Santisima"* were insisting upon it as a most appropriate part of the highest ritual.

Colonies and dependencies fell away; the stream of gold flows in other channels. Uncomplaining the Spaniard retires into the house that once was animated with great companies of guests and hordes of servants. Reduced? Not at all! A few intimates drop in after dinner, bringing friendship and wit. There is always a glass of wine. His daughters will step some of the old dances in the patio; their younger brother has "hands of gold to touch the guitar." An entertainment at once agreeable and becoming—the latter, if for no other reason, because it is Spanish!

To an extent there are grounds for the anxiety, sometimes expressed, that modernism is melting away this tradition-worship. In Madrid there is an English queen; tennis and tea become a cult to be followed with what semblance of gusto one can assume. San Sebastian is the summer resort of royalty, and of pleasure-seekers from all parts of Europe; its modernism is that of Paris or Vienna. Other cities, to the number of perhaps half a dozen, show consciousness of twentieth-century conditions. Among which conditions is, of course, an indiscriminating fondness for novelties for their own sake. And there is always at hand a numerous class of dancers to provide novelties in exchange for a moment's applause.

In another country the national art would deteriorate

under these hostile influences. But in Spain, not readily. Her dances are an organism, rooted in the soil, with forms as definite as the growth of a flower. Mention dancing to an *Aragones,* and it means to him the *jota* of his province. Let other steps be added to it, he will resent them; in his eyes they occupy about the same place as a third arm would on a drawing of the human figure—a monstrosity, and uninteresting. No less than Aragon have other regions their local dances and their choreographic creed, with stupendous pride in both. The steps are handed down like the tunes of old music, with the ideals for their execution. And, high in importance as conservers of their classic national forms, there exists a fine spirit of artistry among a number of the prominent masters. Jose Otero of Seville and Antonio Cansino, a *Sevillano* who for some years has taught in Madrid, are prominent among a number to whom the preservation of Spain's choreographic purity is almost a holy cause.

The dancing of Spain divides into two schools: the purely Iberian, exempt from Gipsy influence, which is known as the Classic, and the work of Gipsy origin and character, which is generically known as the *Flamenco.* The two overlap to the extent of a few dances that partake of the elements of both, and lend themselves to execution in the manner of either. On either side of this common ground the two schools are completely distinct in style, and almost equally so in gesture and posture, having in common only a limited number of steps. In general effect their individualities are absolute.

The work of the Gipsy is, above all, sinuous. His body and arms are serpentine. His hips, shoulders and chest show a mutual independence of action that would worry an anatomist, but which allows the dancer limitless freedom for indulgence in the grotesque. He delights in the most violent contrasts. A series of steps of cat-like softness will be followed by a clatter of heels that resembles Gatling-fire, the two extremes brought into direct juxtaposition. His biggest jump will be preceded by movement so subtle that it is less seen than sensed.

In all circumstances the Gipsy is an irrepressible pantomimist. Of the word and the gesture of his ordinary communication, it is highly probable that the gesture is of the greater importance. He likes to talk, and his words come at a speed that makes them indistinguishable to any but a practised ear, the confusion heightened by the free intermixture of Gipsy *argot*. But the continuous accompaniment of facial expression, movement of body and play of hands is sufficient by itself.

The dance gives full employment to the Gipsy's mimetic powers, and in fact serves primarily as an emotional expression. His dances are not composed, or "routined." He has his alphabet of steps and choreographic movements, and with these he extemporises. By some telepathy most puzzling to those who know the most about Gipsy dancing, the accompanists are not disturbed by any of the dancer's changes of mood, however sudden. The instant drop from extreme speed to the opposite never traps the guitarist into a mistake; and his air is remarkable, too, in preserving the sentiment as well as the time of the dance.

Anything like the full scope of Gipsy dancing is rarely revealed to any not of that race; because, done with abandon, it is an intimate revelation of nature. *El Gitano* is conscious of his racial and social inferiority, despite the arrogance he likes to assume. He is a vagabond living in waste places and by means, usually, of petty imposture, tolerated because of his impudent but very genuine wit. For these reasons a dance for pay becomes a scheme to extract the most money possible for the least work. And the work itself, though skilful, is accompanied by a self-consciousness directly opposed to the essentially Gipsy element of his dance.

A Spaniard who has got past the Gipsy's reserve is Eduardo Cansino, the dancer. As such it is an object for him to see their work at its best; from their all-night parties he has acquired steps. His diplomatic equipment consists, first, of an acquaintance with the Gipsy language, along with ability to make himself agreeable. Understanding of *Flamenco* dancing enables him to aid intelligently in the *jaleo,* that accompaniment of finger-snapping, hand-clapping and half-chanted, half-shouted phrases that make the Spanish dancing atmosphere what it is. (In Gipsy dancing the *jaleo* is "tricky," owing not only to suddenness of changes, but to frequent digressions into counter-time.) When asked to dance, Eduardo's hold on the company's respect is brought to a climax, as there probably is no better performer among the men of Spain. And withal he is willing to buy manzanilla as long as expediency suggests.

According to Eduardo, it is the exception when a dance performed at a Gipsy party fails to tell a story. Usually the story is improvised from a suggestion of the moment. Satire is popular; if one of the company has undergone an unpleasant experience in love, trade, or dealings with the *guardia civil,* it is capital for the dancer. Imitations of carriage and mannerisms of the persons represented are carried to that degree of realism made possible by the Gipsy's eternally alert observation and his expressive body; and he has no artistic creed to cause him to question the value of literal imitation. But the quality of greatness is not what one expects in Gipsy dancing; its contribution is the extreme of skilful, surprising grotesquery.

Notwithstanding the limitations that accompany an insistence on physical facts, the Gipsy's rendering of the great emotions is said to be impressive at the moment, even though it fails to record any lasting impression. Love, as in the dancing of almost all peoples, is a favourite motive, with its many attendants of allurement, reticence, jealousy, pursuit and surrender. But the repertoire is limited only by the Gipsy's scope of emotion—hatred, revenge, triumph and grief—his heart is probably about the same as any one's else, only less repressed by brain. So far is dancing from being merely an act of merriment that it is used in mourning the Gipsy dead.

Flamenco dances as seen in theatres and cafés are compositions made from the elements of Gipsy work; choreographic words grammatically related as is necessary, among other considerations, for accompaniment by orchestras of sober and dependable beings. The task has been admirably done; *la Farruca, el Tango,* and *el Garrotin,* the most popular *Flamenco* dances at present, preserve to admiration the Gipsy qualities. No less credit is due the composers of their accepted musical accompaniments; the indescribable Oriental relation of melody and rhythm, the Gipsy passion for surprise, they have preserved and blended in a manner charming and characteristic. It is only within the past fifty years that the process of adaptation began. Jose Otero, in his chatty *Tratado del Baile,* traces the movement to its beginning; which like many another beginning, was the result less of foresight than of desperation. The case was of a dancer whose Classic work failed to earn him a living. He strung together some Gipsy steps as a last resort and without hope, and was allowed to try them in a *café cantante* in Seville. Their success was instantaneous, and continues unabated. Even in the absence of the Gipsy's inimitable pantomime, there is comfort in seeing his dances under conditions of freedom from argument about extra charges for nothing at all, whines concerning starvation and sickness equally imaginary, care not to lose one's watch, and pressure to buy useless and foolish souvenirs at shameless prices. Parties to visit the *Triana* of Seville or the *Albaicin* of Granada are great fun, but a terrible strain on the patience of the person who accepts the responsibility for his friends' amusement.

If the *Tango* and its *Flamenco* kinsmen fail to conquer a permanent place in the Spanish repertoire, it will be through their exclusion from the respectable Spanish family. The daughter of the house does not learn dancing of the Gipsy type except in the unusual case that she is preparing for a dancer's career. The *Flamenco* has picturesqueness and "salt," but of dignity less. To the Spaniard, that which lacks dignity is vulgar, however witty or graceful. Witty or graceful things may be enjoyed, though dignity be lacking; but the doing of such things is another matter. The Gipsy's untutored point of view on obscenity is a further argument against their admission into the home. It is not a structural part of any of the *Flamenco* work. But association has

SPANISH DANCING

TYPICAL "FLAMENCO" POSES.
(From work of Señorita Elisa Cansino.)

The *Garrotin*. The *Tango*.
The *Garrotin*. The *Tango*. The *Garrotin*.

created a sentiment, and against sentiment logic is helpless.

La Farruca probably exploits more completely than any of its fellows the varied resources of the *Flamenco*. After one becomes accustomed to it sufficiently to be able to dominate one's own delight and astonishment, one may look at it as a study of contrasts, carried to the nth power. Now the performers advance with undulation so slow, so subtle, that the Saracenic coquetry of liquid arms and feline body is less seen than felt. Mystery of movement envelops their bodies like twilight. Of this perhaps eight measures, when—crash! Prestissimo! Like Gatling-fire the volley of heel-tapping. The movements have become the eye-baffling darting of swallows. No preparation for the change, no crescendo nor accelerando; in the matter of abruptness one is reminded of some of the effects familiar in the playing of Hungarian orchestras.

Another use of contrast produces a sensation not unlike the surprise you get when, in the course of drinking one of those warm concoctions of sweetened claret, you unexpectedly bite a piece of cinnamon, and during a few seconds taste vividly the contradictory flavours of both spice and sweetness. The music is moving in a flowing legato. In *counter-time* to the notes is a staccato of crisp taps—of light, "snappy" hand-claps, and dry-sounding sole-taps on the floor, two varieties of accent alternating one with the other. Success of the effect depends on the very perfection of tempo, to begin with, and after that on a command of the quality of sound in the *taps*. A good deal of attention is given to the cleanness and brilliancy of the tone of these notes, as well as the cultivation of a good sparkling "tak" in snapping the fingers. Many performers carry in each hand a series of three ringing finger-snaps, loud enough to carry sharply to the back of their smallish theatres.

It is in respect to finesse of such details that most non-Spaniards condemn themselves to the mediocre when they attempt Spanish dancing. The mere steps can be learned by any one with an intelligence and two sound legs. Many students approximate the style. But the seemingly little things often act as the big pit-falls. The castanets, for instance, expose cruelly the lack of finish of many a pretender to laurels in the Spanish field; in the hands of their master they can ring, or sing, or click, or purr, as the mood of the dance suggests. To an amateur it would be illuminating to see the care a professional exercises in mating the little instruments in pairs. They vary in pitch, and have almost personal whims. For instance, in cold weather they fail to do themselves justice unless they are carried to the performance in an inside pocket. But this is straying from the *Flamenco;* castanets are in the main an adjunct of the Classic.

Returning to the subject of contrasts, the *Flamenco*, more than any other style in the world, perhaps, insists on difference between the work of man and woman. It is seen in the greater relaxation of the woman's body, the more complete elimination of angles from her movements. The degree of rigidity that the man's body should maintain is a point of justifiable difference between artists; so with the extent to which his movements should follow the lines of curves. But that curve should be the theme controlling the woman's movement and carriage, all agree. The result is to the eye as a duet of guitar and flute is to the ear. Following the comparison further, the dance duet does not confine itself to unison—identical movements of the two performers—any more than does the duet of music; and this correlation of two harmonised parts is not the least of the causes of madness imparted to spectators of good dancing.

In all dances evolved to the plane of art, a common device is to end a phrase with a turn—a *pirouette,* or something simpler, according to the character of the work. This general rule the Spanish follow. But look how the *Farruca* makes such a turn the opportunity for one of its myriad contrasts!

The *renversé* of the ballet has a kindred turn in *la vuelta quebrada.* Both are executed with an arm always extended, so as to describe the maximum circle; of the *vuelta quebrada* the movement is low and horizontal, with everything done in such a way as to give the impression of a smooth, oily roll. The *Farruca* leads the woman up to this turn, or *vuelta,* through a series of short steps. Now visualise the man's part at the same time: as the woman enters her flowing *vuelta,* a mighty leap lands the man in the position of stooping; instantly he starts rising with a spiral movement that takes the form of a *pirouette* and so continues through the circle. The surprise the eye receives from the harmonised contrast between the extended horizontally moving sweep and the vertical spiral uplift, with its kaleidoscopic change of levels, seems never to grow less. And if the man makes it a double *pirouette* instead of a single, why, one simply shouts aloud with the joyous discovery that the law of gravitation and a lot of other cumbersome things have suddenly been abolished.

The *Tango* at the present moment familiar in North

SPANISH DANCING 133

"FLAMENCO" POSES.
The *Farruca:* devices to mark counter-time.
The *Farruca:* typical group.
The *Tango:* finish of a turn.   The *Tango:* start of a turn.
The *Farruca:* man's preparation for   The *Farruca: pito* or finger-snap-
    a *pirouette*.   ping.
(From work of Eduardo and Elisa Cansino.)

America found its way here from Argentina. In the form it takes here, its relation to the *Tango* of Spain is little more than a coincidence of names. In none of the Spanish dances does the man's arm ever go around the woman's waist—the purely Spanish, that is. Offshoots and corruptions to be found in the Latin Americas do not signify. The Spanish *Tango* is of the *Flamenco* group. It is a solo for a woman. By convention she performs it wearing a man's hat, the manipulation of which gives some grotesquely graceful occupation to her hands. Apart from this it is distinguished from the others of the group mainly by the sequence in which steps are combined; in spirit, elemental steps and poses, it conforms to the type of its family.

El Garrotin is distinguished by the importance it gives the hands. They repel, warn, invite; half the time they are held behind the back. So indirect are their hinted communications, so alien are their movements to anything in the Occidental way of thinking, that they unite with the girl's over-the-shoulder smile in an allurement no less than devilish.

Other dances of the same school are *Marianas* and *Alegrias,* long familiar. New ones introduce the names of *las Moritas* and *Bulerias*. Each has its personality, but all are composed of the Gipsy steps, performed in the sinuous manner, and rich with contrasts of fast and slow, soft and energetic movements. All are adorned with the stamping, sole-tapping, clapping and finger-snapping already described; though *Marianas,* as a quasi-Classic, may be performed with castanets. All moreover, are costumed alike, as indicated in the sketches and photographs, most of which in this chapter were made possible by the courtesy of Eduardo Cansino and his sister Elisa, of the family of one of the most capable masters in Spain. The man's suit is the habitual street dress of the Andalusian *torero*. It may represent a retiring taste by being of grey or brown cloth. But if it belong to one of those typical *Sevillanos* who believe that a man is an important decorative feature of the landscape, it may be of velvet—blue, wine-colour, purple in any of its shades, or jet-black. With the little pendant coat-button ornaments of gilt, as they may be; the silk sash, rose or scarlet, just showing under the waistcoat; with the shirt ruffled, and the collar fastened with link buttons, as it ought to be; and the whole animated with the game-cock air that the *torero* assumes as befitting a public man, it is a costume not lacking in gallantry.

For the woman, convention has strained for a substitute for the inanely garish, shapeless garments of the Gipsy sister—a good note of colour they make on the hillside, but in all truth, a poor model for dressing when placed among formalised surroundings. The conclusion is a compromise shocking, on first impression, to the ideals of the Spanish dance. But, as though to confirm the argument of the futurist painters, that colour-harmony is a matter of what you are accustomed to, you grow into an acceptance of it. Many people even like it. It has indeed this merit, that it is a realisation of the Gipsy's dream of elegance. Beginning with the *manton*—the long-fringed flowered shawl—half of these *bailarinas* of the *Flamenco* seem to patronise some special frenzied loom that supplies their class alone. The richness of design that you saw on the *manton* of the lady in the next box at last Sunday's *corrida* you find replaced here in *el teatro de variedades* by an anarchy of colour, and poppies of the size of a man's hat. The skirt is stiffened in the bell-shape surviving other days, and well adapted to composition with Spanish steps; but the colours are of the piercing brilliancy attainable only by spangles. Orange, carmine, emerald-green and cerulean-blue are the favourite palette from which the scheme is selected, with the unit of design of a size that makes more than two of them impossible on the same skirt. Nevertheless, one accepts it with custom, aided by the seduction of the dance—which has been known to secure for its performers pardon for transgressions graver, in some eyes, than crimes against colour.

Artists there are, of course, who use the colour and spangles with taste and style, just as there are those of high ability and seriousness who select the *Flamenco* on which to build reputation. For dignity, however, we turn sooner or later to the Classic.

In Andalusia, the first dance you will hear named is *las Sevillanas*—unless you happen to be in Seville, where the same dance is known as *Seguidillas*. The latter word lacks explicit significance. It applies to a form of verse, thence to analogous phrasing in musical composition, then to a structure of dance. In general it denotes a composition of three or more stanzas, or *coplas,* repeating the same music but changing the theme of the step. Various provinces and even vicinities have their special *Seguidillas*. The number of these and other dance-forms indigenous to Spain is uncounted, so far as we know; certainly any complete description of them individually would furnish material for many hundred pages of print, especially if the list should include the widely scattered derivatives. Mexico, Cuba, and various countries of South America have their local compositions; but of these many are mere degenerations of their original models, and many are compounded with steps of the Indians. Since none has contributed anything of consequence, this chapter's necessary concentration on the work of Spain itself involves little real sacrifice.

It is *Sevillanas* whose easier movements are among the first undertaken by every well-reared Andalusian

"LAS SEVILLANAS."
Grouping at pause in first *copla*. School of Don Jose Otero, of Seville.

child, whose adequate execution is half the fame of most great Spanish dancers. Of all the dances, Otero calls it "the most Spanish." Yet it gives the spectator few detached pictures to carry away in memory. Its merit is in its cumulative choreographic argument.

Very broadly speaking, the prevailing foot-work of the *Seguidillas* family is the *pas de Basque*—or, in Spanish, *paso de Vasco*. Turns, advances and retreats are almost incessant. Variety of step is secured by frequent *fouettés* and *fouetté tours* (figures 43 to 46), the leg sweep in the latter being usually "inward," the foot, with most performers (at present) raised more than waist-high. *Swinging* steps, it will be noticed; choppy elements such as *battements, entrechats* and the like are, by distinction, the elements of the sharper work of the North. *Sevillanas* makes the feet less important than the hands and arms. These, however bewildering they are made to appear, follow a simple theme of opposition, as for instance: (1) left arm horizontally extended to the side, right arm across the chest; (2) right arm extended upward, left forearm across the back. As the simplest movement of club-swinging is incomprehensible to the person to whom it never has been explained, so with the arms in *Sevillanas,* with the bewilderment multiplied by the play of line effected by the arms of a couple.

The body is held with a combination of erectness and suppleness that is Spain's own; sympathetic to every move of hand or foot, yet always controlled and always majestic. The essence of this queen of dances is not in step or movement, but in its traditional style plus a steadily increasing enrichment through the successive *coplas*—an enrichment that depends principally on the perfection of team work at a rapid tempo, and one that adds greatly to the subtle difficulties. Many performers will inform you that a sixth *copla* does not exist. Of those who can execute it adequately, the majority reserve it for competitions to present as a surprise.

The scope of moods from beginning to end of *Sevillanas* gives play to the lyric and the epic; allurement and threat; coquetry and triumph. It is a blend of the wine

SPANISH DANCING

of Andalusia with her flowers and her latent tragedy. Not that it is particularly a vehicle for pantomime. Rather its suggestions are conveyed as are the motives of flowers, or architecture—by relations and qualities of line and form that work upon the senses by alchemy no more understood than that of music. The accumulating intricacy has been so artfully designed that, as the dance progresses, its performers actually seem to free themselves from the restrictions of earth. Each new marvel tightens the knot of emotion in the throat; shouts invoking divine blessings on the mother of the *bailarina*—"*Que Dios bendiga tu madre!*"—unite with the tumult of the *jaleo*. For shouting may save one from other emotional expressions less becoming.

The music contributes to this hysteria, of course. But, with no accompaniment but their own castanets, a good team can work the magic. That might be considered a test of the quality of composition in a dance, as well as of execution.

So gracious, so stately, so rich in light and shade is *Sevillanas,* that it alone gives play to all the qualities needed to make a great artist. When, a few summers ago, Rosario Guerrero charmed New York with her pantomime of *The Rose and the Dagger,* it was the first two *coplas* of this movement-poem that charmed the dagger away from the bandit. The same steps glorified Carmencita in her day; and Otero, now popular as a singer in the Opera in Paris. All three of these goddesses read into their interpretation a powerful idea of majesty, which left it none the less seductive. Taking it at a comparatively slow tempo, the perfection of every detail had its highest value. A new generation of performers has been rather upset by a passing mode of rapid foot-work, and under its influence too many of them tend to rush the dance and so detract from its majesty. True it is that a great work of art can stand a good deal of abuse; but any menace to such a work as the one discussed, points out the need of a national academy, where

TWO GROUPS IN "LAS SEVILLANAS."

the treasures of the dancing art could be preserved from possible whims of even an artistically intelligent public, and the compliance of a non-resisting majority of artists. Unlike most great European nations, Spain has no national academy of the dance.

Fanny Ellsler electrified the America of our fathers' boyhood days with her interpretation of *la Cachucha*. Zorn's *Grammar* presents a choro-stenographic record of it, showing few elements that do not occur in *Sevillanas*. *La Cachucha* itself has disappeared from the Peninsula—practically at least, if not absolutely. Its existence is in printed records and a few old people's memories. The inference is that it was at a high pitch of popularity at the time of Ellsler's sojourn in Spain, and that *Sevillanas* subsequently absorbed it. Showing the operation of an old process: "Our buildings and our weapons of war are renewed from day to day. . . . Chairs, cupboards, tables, lamps, candlesticks are also changed. It is the same with our games and dances, our music and songs. The *Zarabanda* has gone; *Seguidillas* are in fashion; which, in their turn, will disappear to make room for newer dances." So wrote Mateo Aleman, in the sixteenth century. He might a little more exactly have said "reappear in" instead of "disappear to make room for."

Sevillanas, as was said before, is Seville's special arrangement of *Seguidillas*. *Valencianas* and *Aragonesas* are among the modifying geographic words also in use; Vuillier quotes also *Gitanas, Mollaras, Gallegas* and *Quipuzcoanas*. These terms as localising modifications of *Seguidillas* may be no longer current. But their existence is significant, as indicating a parent trunk from which many local dance forms have branched. It seems pretty safe to infer that acquaintance with the general characteristics of the *Seguidillas* type gives us an idea of the essentials of some of the dances of very early times, by whatever names they may have been known. Like *Sevillanas* and *la Cachucha, el Fandango* (which *as a name* has retired into the mountains of the North, and otherwise is preserved in the opera *La Nozze de Figaro*) is recorded as being a species of *Seguidillas*. The castanets are a link that binds the family, logically or otherwise, to earliest history.

The *Fandango*, though restrained in the theatre, seems at all times to have been danced in less formal gathering places in a manner more or less worldly. A story pertaining to it was written in the seventeenth century. The Pope (according to the story) heard that the *Fandango* was scandalous, and as a means of stopping its practice, proposed excommunication as a penalty for its performance. A consistory was debating the issue, when a cardinal proposed that the accused was entitled to an opportunity to defend itself. This seemed reasonable, and the dancers were summoned.

"Their grace and vivacity," says Davillier, "soon drove the frowns from the brows of the Fathers, whose souls were stirred by lively emotion and a strange pleasure. One by one their Eminences began to beat time with hands and feet, till suddenly their hall became a ballroom; they sprang up, dancing the steps, imitating the gestures of the dancers. After this trial, the Fandango was fully pardoned and restored to honour."

Whatever the lack of basis for the tale, it is a fact that the Church in Spain has recognised the dance as an art that, like music, lends itself to religious ritual. Seville Cathedral still has occasions for the solemn dance of *los Seises*. In 1762, dancers were taken from Valencia to help celebrate the laying of the foundation-stone of Lerida Cathedral. Instances might be multiplied at length.

The costume most picturesque and romantic that woman has at her disposal for these dances is that of the *madroñero*—the network dotted with little black balls, draped over the hips. Imagine the bodice black velvet, and the skirt golden-yellow satin, and you have a spot-and-colour translation of Andalusia. But the dress of the *madroñero* is not often to be seen; the spangled *Flamenco* costume is publicly accepted as the dress of a Spanish dancing girl.

The *manton* should be draped over the shoulders like a shawl in *la Jota Aragonesa* and other dances indigenous to central and northern provinces. It is *Flamenco* to fold it diagonally to form a triangle, and wrap it around the body in such a way that the depth of the triangle lies on the front of the body; the apex points downward, and is arranged to fall to one side of the centre. The other two ends are crossed over the back and brought forward over the shoulders; or one end may be tucked in, and the more made of the end that remains in sight.

The dance in which we see the white mantilla to which the Spanish girl owes a portion of her fame is *la Malagueña y el Torero*. Perhaps owing to the weight of the man's costume proper to the dance, it is not often performed; for the bullion-adorned dress of the *torero* is of a weight suggestive of anything but airy foot-work.

The characters of the piece—it is one of the very few Spanish mimetic dances—are represented, as might be expected, in a little flirtation. Of the three movements, the first is an animated *paseo,* or promenade, the *torero* wrapped in the *capa de gala* prescribed by ceremony as essential for *matadores* and *banderilleros* during their entrance parade into the bull-ring. The *torero* is followed by the girl, her face demure in the half-shade of the overhanging mantilla. A *manton* carried folded over her arm, suggestive of a *torero's* cape, gives to the pantomime the key of fantasy; and her weapon of coquetry is a fan.

An elaborate series of advances, turns, meetings and passings prepares the *torero* to acknowledge that he notices the girl. (Mr. Bernard Shaw was not the original discoverer of feminine initiative in man-and-woman relations.) He looks at her and is delighted.

The music changes, and the second movement, *la mimica,* begins. He will spread his *capa* for her to walk over; but first he must flourish it through a couple of the movements familiar to patrons of the *corrida.* A *veronica*—"*Olé!*" roars the crowd, whose memory instantly correlates with the writhing cape the vision of a furious bull. A *farol* throws the brilliantly coloured cloth like a huge flower high in the air: a *suerte de capa* always magnificent, one of the ever-recurring flashes of surprise that make the *corrida* irresistible despite its faults. In consecutive movement the *capa* opens and settles fanlike before the girl, the boy kneeling as she passes. Rising, he tosses his cap for her to step on. A touch of realism, this! Andalusian usage permits this compliment, with the spoken wish that God may bless the *señorita's* mother. The second *copla* draws to a close with the boy's pantomime merging into dance step as he becomes more attracted to the girl. She is now evading, alluring, and reproving, while her movements insensibly succumb more and more to the dance music which has replaced the promenade tempo of the first part. The third *copla* is the dance—*el baile; capa,* fan and *manton* are discarded for castanets. The steps are of the *Seguidillas* type; the number ends with the incredibly sudden transformation of a series of rapid turns into a group as motionless as statuary. This abrupt stop is a characteristic of Spanish dancing in general that always has been commented on, and approvingly, by its non-Spanish observers.

Las Malagueñas also employs mantilla and fan. This sprightly member of the *Seguidillas* family has no elements peculiar to itself, yet its insistent use of little steps adapts it to rapid foot-work. *Manchegas* is of the

GROUPS IN "LA MALAGUEÑA Y EL TORERO."
(From work of Eduardo and Elisa Cansino.)

same nature. The two are often performed immediately after dances of less action, for the sake of variety.

"The Fandango inflames, the Bolero intoxicates," wrote an enthusiast of other days. And in respect to the latter the truth of his observation may be proved, since the *Bolero* is still with us, and always intoxicates every one of its spectators that is not deaf and blind.

Its composition is attributed to Cerezo, a famous dancer of the early part of the eighteenth century. Material for speculation is furnished by one of its steps in particular, the *cuarta,* identical with the ballet's *entrechat-quatre.* The invention of the *entrechat* is credited to the French dancer Camargo, who was not born until after the advent of the *Bolero.* The question is: Did the *Bolero* take the *cuarta* from Camargo, or did she, a progressive in her day, merely invent the name *"entrechat"* and apply it to a "lifted" *cuarta?* Certain it is that it fits its requirements in the *Bolero* like a key in its lock. It is used in a passage dedicated to brilliancy, to which motive this twinkling, gravity-defying step is suited above almost all others. As rendered by the woman, it is dainty, as in the French ballet. But the Spanish man treats it in a manner that puts it into a category by itself, and transforms it from a little step to an evolution that seems suddenly to occupy the entire stage.

The *cuarta* at the height of the leap is only his beginning. As he descends, he kicks one foot up and backward, in a manner to give him a half-turn in the air. The leg movement opens up the lines of the elevated figure, giving it a sudden growth comparable to one of those plants that the Oriental magician develops from

SPANISH DANCING   147

MISCELLANEOUS SPANISH NOTES.

Los Panaderos: group turning.
The *Jota* of Aragon: typical group.
Las *Sevillanas:* use of primitive foot position.

The *Bolero:* a turn in the air.
Castanets: Classic, tied to finger.
Flamenco, tied to thumb.
Seises of Seville Cathedral.

seed to maturity while you wink. The expansion is augmented by the extension of the arms at the opportune moment. Altogether, the spectator is prepared to believe that all physical law has been suspended in deference to the convenience of poetic motion. Davillier's observation that "the Bolero intoxicates" is wholly inadequate.

The dance is in triple time, and arranged in three parts. The second divides the work of the two performers into solos, admitting whatever sensational steps each chooses to present, so long as they conform to the strong, aggressive style that tradition gives the dance. In this part are the *cuartas,* which good Spanish performers execute as cleanly as any French *première.* The man's work may include a series of jumps, straight up, opening the legs out to horizontal; not in itself an attractive step, but an exaggeration of the idea of the *Bolero.* Throughout, the work is vigourous and sharp, of the character created by *battements* great and small, *coupés,* and choppily executed *brisés.* The management of the castanets is a difficult addition to such vigourous foot-work, and important. To sustain, or rather constantly augment the excitement proper to the dance, the crash of the recurrent "tr-r-rá, tak-ta! tr-r-r-á, tak-ta!" must never be dulled for an instant, nor fail of perfection in rhythm. The double control is seldom acquired by any but Spaniards, if ever, and even in Spain it is none too common.

Every lover of dancing probably thinks of his favourite compositions as personalities. "Queenly *Sevillanas*" inevitably is the way of thinking of that flower of Andalusia. In similar manner memory puts together words, "the noble *Bolero."* Brusque but fine, strong

SPANISH DANCING 149

and justly proud, it sings of iron in the blood, as *Sevillanas* exhales the spicy fragrance of hot night air.

Of *los Panaderos* the introductory measures are dedicated to the elaborate salutations appropriate to the etiquette of other days. The dance in general follows the motive of light coquetry through a pantomimic first part, concluding with a dance of the *Seguidillas* type, with castanets. Interest is enriched by the dance's

TWO GROUPS IN "LOS PANADEROS."
(From work of Eduardo and Elisa Cansino.)

proper costume. The girl's *vestido de madroños* has been described in connection with another dance, and the same reserved indulgence in the ornate is seen also in the attire of the man. The velvet jacket permits subdued but opulent colour; instead of buttonholes it has a lively design of cord loops. Down the sides of the breeches runs a broad band of colour that would be too violent were it not broken up by a superimposed band of heavy black cord lace, through the open pattern of which the background silk twinkles like jewels. It is a costume to make an impression at a distance or to tickle the eye on close inspection; the tasselled leather leggings are delicately adorned with scroll-pattern traced in stitching, and other details are elaborated with the same minute care.

Of all the energetic dances of the land of the dance, the one farthest from any concession to physical infirmity is *la Jota Aragonesa*. Here is no vehicle for Andalusian languor nor yet for the ceremonies of courts. The industrious peasant of Aragon is hard of muscle and strong of heart, and so is his daughter, and their strength is their pride. For indolence they have no sympathy, be it in ermine or rags; and certainly if indolence ever forgets itself and strays into the *Jota*, it passes a bad five minutes.

It is a good, sound fruit of the soil, full of substance, and inviting to the eye as good sound fruit may be. No academy's hothouse care has been needed to develop or protect it; the hand of the peasant has cultivated without dirtying it. And that, when you look over the history of dancing in some more progressive nations, is a pretty significant thing. The people of Aragon are not novelty-hunters. Perhaps that is why they have been satisfied, while perfecting the dance of their province, not to pervert it from its proper motive—which is to express in terms of poetry both the vigour and the innocence of rustic, romping, boy-and-girl courtship.

A trace of stiffness of limb and angularity of movement, proper to the *Jota*, imbue it with a continuous hint of the rural grotesque. Yet, as the angular spire of the Gothic cathedral need be no less graceful than the rounded dome of the mosque, so the *Jota* concedes nothing in beauty to the more rolling movement of the dance of Andalusia. It is broad and big of movement; the castanets most of the time are held strongly out at arm's length. One of its many surprises is in the manner of the pauses: the movement is so fast, the pauses are so electrically abrupt, and the group (or "picture," as our stage-folk call it) in which the dancers hold themselves statue-like through a couple of measures is so suddenly formed, that a layman's effort to understand the transition would be like trying to analyse the movements of the particles in a kaleidoscope. Out of a dazzle of cross-tied white legs there *snaps* on to your retina a vision of a couple face to face, each on one knee; *one,* two, three, four—on each count the supporting knee comes up, its mate rhythmically bumps the floor. One measure; again they are in flight. Another stop, as from a collision with some invisible but immovable body—the girl is established in a seated position on the floor, madly playing her castanets, the boy flashing *pirouettes* around her. *Bien parada, palomita! pero anda!* Another cyclone, a crescendo of energy in the thump of sandalled feet and the pulse-lifting clatter of castanets, and—dead stop! She is impudently perched on his knee. Raised with the *paisanos* around you to the plane of the happy gods, you too are standing, shouting your rhythm-madness, tearing at scarf-pin, bouquet or anything to throw to the performers.

Down to the tuning of the castanets is emphasised the difference between this dance of the stalwart uplanders and the more liquid expression of Andalusia. It can be understood how, with the instruments fastened to the *thumb,* and hanging so as not to touch the palm, vibration is not interrupted after a blow from the finger;

consequently they will *ring* when touched. The successive taps of four skilful fingers on a castanet so hung will make it *sing,* as is appropriate to the flowing dance of the South. But change the tie from the thumb to the two middle fingers and you change the voice: the blow of a finger presses together the two halves of the instrument, and throws both against the palm of the hand; vibration is stopped, and the report is a dry "tak" or "tok," which is consistent with and contributory to the crisp staccato sentiment of the *Jota,* with its kicking treatment of a running *pas de bourrée,* swift *pirouettes,* and abrupt starts and stops.

There is a certain paradoxical relationship between the motives of step and music, perhaps peculiar to Spain, that asserts itself most clearly in the *Jota.* That is, the setting of brilliant dance-movement to the accompani-

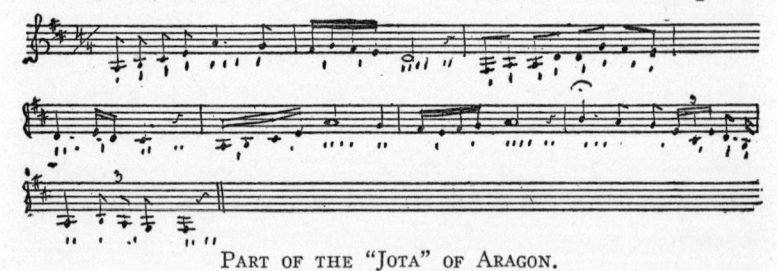

Part of the "Jota" of Aragon.
Showing rapid foot-work to slow music. Steps indicated by accents under music. The melody above quoted is that of the old *Jota*.

ment of melodies of a sadness sometimes unearthly. The juxtaposition does not always occur. When it does, as in the old *Jota* of Aragon and *las Soleares* of Andalusia, it is the very incarnation of the mysterious magic of a magic land; it is the smile forcing back the tear, words of wit spoken by the voice of sorrow. Or is the foreigner mistaken? The peasant himself sees no sorrow in the tunes, any more than in life.

Thumping the foot-beats gives an idea of the rhythm so far as related to the sound; but this fails more than to hint at the effect of the music in combination with the dance, because the dance so fills the conscious attention that the music is less heard than felt. The melody itself is unnoticed; but its underlying melancholy persistently cuts its way into the heart during the very moments that vision is most madly happy.

True to her modest and serious character, the peasant woman of Aragon puts on her *manton* like a shawl, sternly concealing her figure. Her full, rustic skirt is of dull-coloured cotton. For her no high-heeled shoes; her foot-wear—and her grandfather's—is the practical cord-soled sandal (*alporgata*) tied on with black cords, which, on their background of white stocking, have a coquettish look in spite of her. The man's dress is a representation of simple strength, saved from sombreness by well-disposed contrasting accents, few but brilliant. The lacing of the breeches slashed at the knee echoes the tie of the sandals. The waistcoat and breeches are black; the sash—worn very broad—may be either dull or bright; but the kerchief tied around the head is of colour as strong as dyes will produce. Red with a design of little black squares is characteristic ornament of the province.

Valencia, too, has its *Jota,* but of movement more fluid than that of Aragon. *La Jota Valenciana* is superficially distinguished by its employment of the tambourine; the only dance in Spain—with possible unimportant exceptions—to accompany itself with this instrument. In structure it is of the *Seguidillas* type, the coincidence of the term *Jota* being without significance.

To go into a discussion of the dances of the northern provinces—Cataluña, the Basque provinces, Galicia, Leon and others—would in most instances be to digress from the theme of Spanish dancing in any but a geographical sense. The dances of the northern region that are Spanish in type are of the *Seguidillas* family already described, and without special pertinence to the locality. Conversely, the dances that are indigenous to and characteristic of the North are not of the type generally and properly known as Spanish, but, in respect to everything but geography, pertain to the character dances of western Europe. True, the *Fandango* is seen in the Basque provinces; but it is a stray from other parts. Galicia has a pantomime of oafish courtship. A dance characteristic of Quipuzcoa was described to us by Tencita: glasses of wine were set on the floor, of the same number as the dancers, all of whom were men. At a given time every one would jump—from a considerable distance and to a good height—with the aim of missing his glass by a minimum margin. This exercise —or dance, by charity of definition—is performed after important matches of the provincial game of *pelota*. Being of the general style of racquets, control of placement of the feet follows. Many of the dances, says Tencita, are rounds. Of these the salient feature is the man's lift of his partner. Some of those iron-shouldered mountaineers, grasping the girl's waist in two big hands, lift her straight up to arm's-length. But this, to repeat, is Spanish only by grace of political boundary lines. The same feat is described in a French rustic dance of the Middle Ages. So long as the tradition of round dancing joins the performers' hands to one another, choreographic art can hardly exist.

It is doubtful if the North has carried to the superlative any of the qualities of real dancing. In pure decorative beauty; variety and force of expression; scope of motive; happy contrasts of treatment—briefly, in the art of the dance, Andalusia speaks the final word. Who wishes natural pantomime need only call a Gipsy. *Mimica* more delicate is that of *Toreo Español* or *el Vito,* both narrating the placing of *banderillas,* defence with the cape, and the final despatch of a bull. In a combination of strong movement with speed and grace, there does not exist in this world a dance-form to excel the *Jota* of Aragon.

The home of Spanish dancing is south of the latitude of Madrid, in the flowery region that the caliphs ruled. The pilgrim in search of dancing, therefore, shall not unsaddle until the nearest hilltop shows the ruins of a Moorish castle. By that token he will know that he has come to the land of grapes and fighting bulls, destitution and wit, black eyes, guitar and song, enchantment. There he may sell his horse; where falls the shadow of a castle of the Moors, on that soil blooms the dance.

CHAPTER VII

ITALIAN DANCES

PAST are the splendid pageants of the Medici, nor do the floors of Castel San Angelo remember the caress of the winged feet of choral dancers. The classic ballet, heir of the dances and masques of courts, preserves their stately charm; while their choreographic wit lives on in dances that are at once their ancestors and their survivors. An intermediate generation of dances represented the day of a society cultivated to artificiality. The dances of the people, on the contrary, are rooted in the soil and cared for by wholesome tradition. Including, as they do, many of the steps from which the ballet was derived, there is material for interesting speculation in their continued vigour.

In the *Forlana* of Venice, with its old-fashioned steps, is found a delicate mimetic synopsis of the world-old tale of the young wife, the elderly husband, and the dashing interloper; the theme immortalised by the pen of Boccaccio, in his collection of the stories that passed the time during the ten days when the court exiled itself in the hills to avoid a pestilence in Florence. The accompanying illustrations of the dance have the benefit of the knowledge of two graduates of the academy of la Scala, both children of teachers in that institution: Madame Saracco-Brignole and Stephen Mascagni. Both are enthusiastic performers of their country's character dances; Mascagni, indeed, with his wife as part-

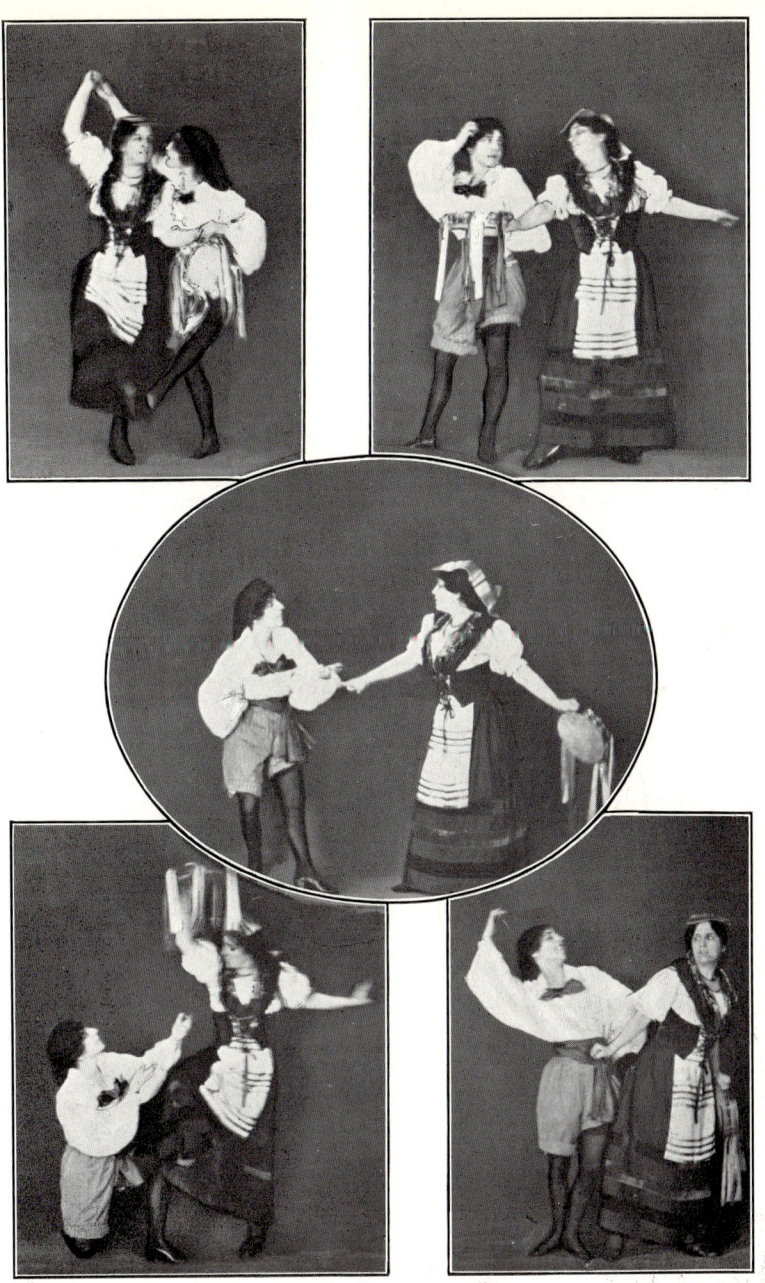

"La Tarantella"

Opening of the dance　　　　　　　　A poor collection
　　　They gamble for it: the game *La Morra*
　　She wins　　　　　　　　　　　He wins

To face page 156

"La Tarantella"

An *arabesque*

Finish of a phrase   A typical moment

Finish of a phrase

To face page 157

ner, makes the *Tarantella* an important feature of his repertoire. The trio in *la Forlana* was completed with the assistance of Mlle. Louise La Gai, as Columbina, Madame Saracco-Brignole and Sr. Mascagni representing Doctor Pantalone and Harlequin, respectively, completing the little cast.

As a stock character in other pantomimes and farces, Doctor Pantalone's characteristics, both mental and physical, are so clearly defined that he has the reality of an acquaintance. In brief, he represents self-sureness and self-importance, with a weakness of revealing complete misinformation through indulgence in a habit of correcting the statements of others. Light-headed Columbina and mischief-making Harlequin are their familiar selves. The *Forlana* is a composition essentially of tableaux, with steps of the dance serving to lead from one picture to another.

Harlequin's freedom with Columbina is resented by the elderly husband, who threatens the intruder with a cane. The frivolous young people dance away, after a mock-heroic pretence by Harlequin of protecting his inamorata from her husband. They begin a series of groups made to tantalise the dotard, whose possession of the young woman has clearly ceased to exist. Harlequin embraces her, gazes into her eyes, raises her to his shoulder, kisses her, and is otherwise familiar, while Pantalone storms and pleads. Perching aloft with her partner's support in the various ways known to dancers of an acrobatic genius, Columbina reaches out to her spouse the tip of a finger, in smiling sarcasm. Pantalone later is reduced to kissing the little foot that from time to time kicks upward as the lovers play. When at length even that is the occasion of a dignified protest from Harlequin, the defeated one withdraws from an unequal competition and gives the couple his blessing.

Pantalone, apart from his relation to the *Forlana,* is one of a group of characters attached to the various Italian states as allegorical representatives. To Sardinia, for instance, pertains a soldierly looking youth called Maschara Sarda. Bologna has its Doctor Balanzone; Florence, Stenterello; Rome, Rugantino; Naples, Pulcinella—and this is to enumerate only a few out of a number slightly in excess of the number of states. These mythical beings are neither heroes nor caricatures, nor are they supposed at all to portray the qualities typical of the population they represent. Their associations seem to be without underlying significance, but they are none the less indissoluble in the mind of the Italian. Those who have most cause to love them are the writers of popular comedies; the simple device of putting a Balanzone or a Rugantino among the characters of the play makes possible a direct expression of ideas purporting to be those of the state itself. Such lines, regardless of the literary tone of the play, are customarily delivered in the local dialect of the region represented.

It is the *Tarantella* that the world at large accepts as Italy's national dance; and rightly enough, since there is none whose popularity is more nearly general through the land. It is rather identified with Naples. There it is said to be the amusement that the younger working people think of first, when leisure allows the thought of any amusement at all; but it is very popular, too, through the South.

It is a breezy, animated dance, varied with pantomime not very profound, to be sure, but at least merry

"La Tarantella"

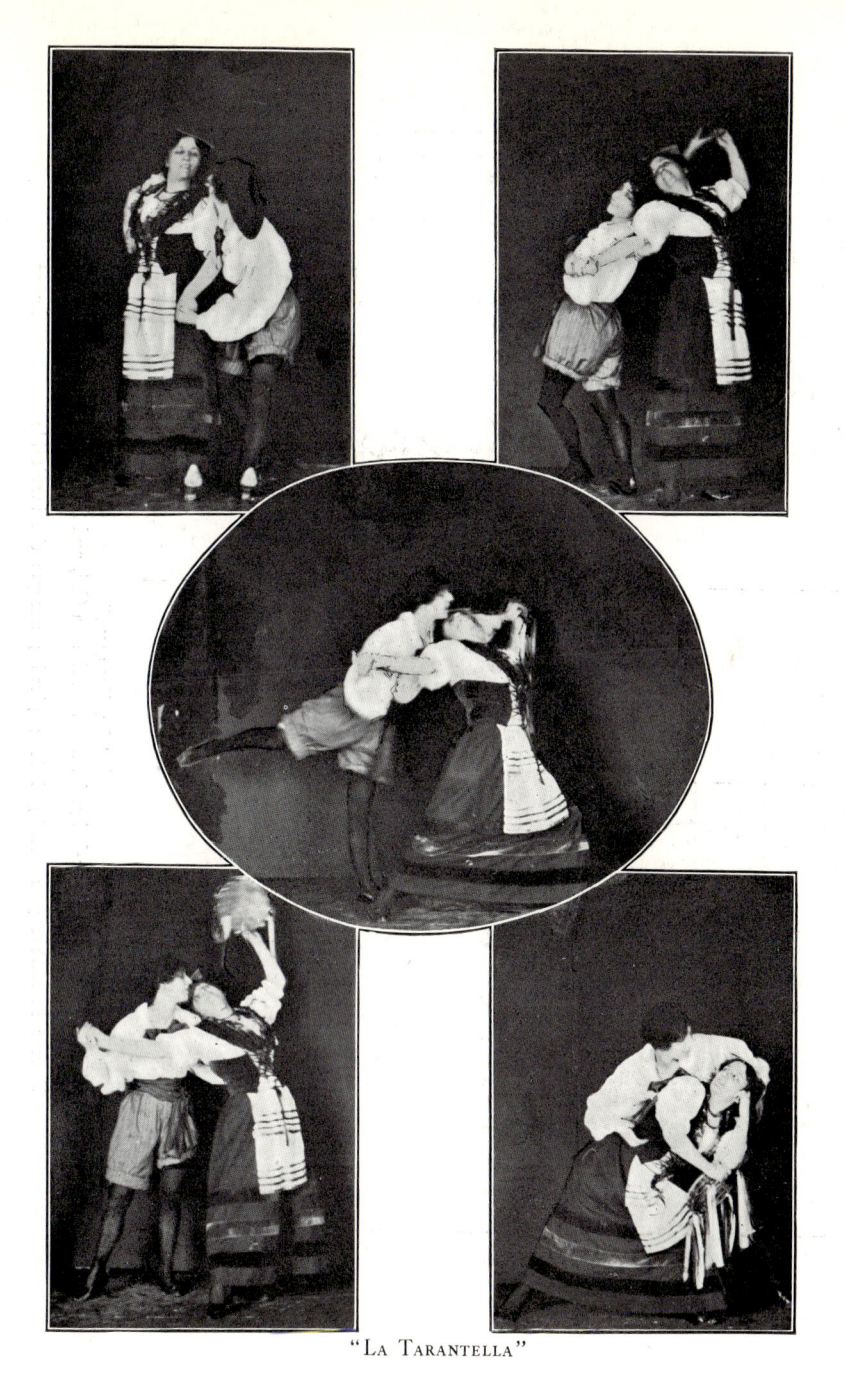

Opening of the dance A turn back-to-back
A pause after rapid foot-work
Characteristic finishes of phrases

To face page 158

"LA FORLANA"

Mme. Elise Saracco-Brignole, Mlle. Louise La Gai, and Sr. Stephen Mascagni

Doctor Pantalone patronized; defied; pleads; accepts the inevitable and is ridiculed

To face page 159

with character. The mimetic action concerns the varying luck of *la morra,* that game that consists in guessing at the number of fingers open on the opponent's suddenly revealed hand; perhaps the only gambling game for which every one is born with full equipment of implements. To a votary, every glance at his own five fingers must seem a temptation to seek a game. For whatever reason, it seems to be a necessary element in the life of the Italian labourer. The moment of the *Tarantella* given over to *la morra* is, as it were, an acknowledgment of its place among the people's recreations.

As castanets are to the dances of Spain, the tambourine is to those of Italy. Like castanets, the tambourine produces an amazing variety of tones when handled by an expert. The effect its jovial emphasis of tempo has on the enthusiasm of dancer and spectator need not be dwelt upon; again sobriety succumbs before rhythm's twofold attack on eye and ear together. Vivacity is insistent, too, in the colours of the Neapolitan costume. The tambourine is dressed in ribbons, characteristically the national red, white, and stinging green. Stripes as brilliant as caprice may suggest adorn the girl's head-dress, apron and skirt. Nor must her more substantial finery be forgotten; until a responsible age is attained by children of her own, she is guardian of an accumulating collection of necklaces and earrings, bracelets and rings that are as a family symbol of respectability. Just as in other nations the inherited table silver is brought out to grace occasions of rejoicing, the Neapolitan young woman on like occasion exhibits gold, silver and gay red coral in adornment of her person—adding much to the sparkle of the *Tarantella.*

The boy (in these and the pictures of *la Ciociara* represented by Mlle. La Gai) has a necktie as red as dyes will yield, and a long fisherman's cap of the same colour. It is Italian stage tradition, by the way, that the Neapolitan fisher boy's trouser-legs should be rolled up to slightly different heights.

The dance itself is full of pretty groups, well spiced with moods. The steps are happily varied and well composed. There are many turns, the boy frequently assisting with the familiar spiral twist of the girl's upraised hands—a device that, with any execution back of it, always produces a pleasant effect. The turns also are highly enhanced in value when, as they frequently do, they terminate so as to bring the dancers into an effective embrace. Preparation for a *pirouette* by both dancers is utilised, at one point, as a pretext for some delightfully grotesque poses.

It is a dance worthy of study and performance by artists, and of the enthusiasm of appreciators of good work. In *Corinne* occurs a passage reflecting its impression on Madame de Staël. The following selections seem most suggestive of the effect produced: ". . . beating the air with her tambourine—in all her movements showing a grace, a lissomeness, a blending of modesty and *abandon,* which gave the spectator some idea of the power exercised over the imagination by the Indian dancing-girls, when they are, so to speak, poets in the dance, expressing varied feelings by characteristic steps and picturesque attitudes. Corinne was so well acquainted with the different attitudes which painters and sculptors have depicted, that by a slight movement of her arms, holding the tambourine sometimes above her head, sometimes in front of her, while the other hand ran over the

"La Ciociara"

Opening promenade (1, 2) — End of promenade (3) — He has "made eyes" at a spectator (4) — Opening of dance (second movement) (5)

To face page 160

"La Ciociara"

Rustic affection   Again caught in perfidy

Tries to make amends

Without success   Removed from temptation

To face page 161

bells with incredible swiftness, she would recall the dancing girls of Herculaneum, and present before the eye of the painter or artist one idea after another in swift succession. It was not French dancing, so remarkable for the elegance and difficulty of its steps; it was a talent much more closely related to imagination and feeling. The mood was expressed alternately by exactness or softness of movement. Corinne, dancing, made the onlookers share her feelings, just as if she were improvising, playing the lyre, or designing figures; every motion was to her as expressive as spoken language."

The similarity between the words *Tarantella,* and "tarantula," a large and poisonous spider, causes endless speculation to the end of establishing a more than etymological relation between the two. One author seriously affirms that the dance is a standard rural remedy for the bite of the insect, the energetic movement starting a perspiration that relieves the system of poison. Various German physicians have written reports on the subject, generally ending with a statement that the said antidote for poison is of doubtful efficacy! Approaching the subject from another angle, the word *tarantismos* is discovered: a species of hysteria common in Calabria and Apulia, and (by etymology) attributed to the bites of tarantulas to be found in those parts. But along comes another learned person who finds that *tarantismos* is not due to tarantula bites, but to certain molluscs that Calabrians and Apulians customarily include in their food régime! He harks back to a certain dancing mania that was more or less epidemic in Europe during a period of the Middle Ages, a hysterical condition found curable by violent dancing. Whence he induces that the *Tarantella* derives its name from *tarantismos,* and that it originated as a cure for neurasthenia. Still another finds that the ailment causes hysterical movements, "similar to dancing!" and flatters the *Tarantella* with this spasmodic origin. Again, a grave experimenter finds that tarantulas, placed on floats in water so that they will be disinclined to run away, will move their feet in time to music. He does not ask us to infer from this that the steps of the dance were so originated and composed, but in the cause of general joyousness he might have, and that without much damage to the accumulated erudition on the subject.

All the Latin countries, no less than Scotland and Ireland, have their *Jig*. In Italy, as elsewhere, it is a composition of rapid clog and shuffle steps. More than most Occidental countries Italy has a lingering fondness for pantomime; doubtless as a heritage from the theatre of Rome, and increased through centuries of political intrigue that sometimes made the spoken word inadvisable. Like the *Forlana, la Ciociara* of Romagna is an example of choreographic pantomime carried to a high pitch of narrative quality. It represents a heavy-footed shepherd and his wife, and their unpaid efforts to collect coins for music and dancing during their visit to the village.

After a little promenade to the music of the pipe, or *piffara,* that has descended unchanged from the days of the shepherds on the slope of Mount Ida, and the tambourine of equally venerable age, the tambourine is passed before an imaginary circle of auditors. The imaginary coins failing to come forth, the couple impulsively decide to dance anyway, for their own amusement. The dance proper is of the flowing style of the *Tarantella,* but includes only the simpler steps. An important contribution to the amusing character of the performance is a bit of by-play that begins after the work has apparently terminated: the shepherd, oaf though he is, expresses an interest in a pretty face in the audience, and even a belief that his interest is reciprocated. He is roundly scolded by his wife, soothes her feelings, and at last retires under a not misplaced surveillance.

The *Saltarello,* an old and lively step-dance identified with Rome, and including several steps of the *Tarantella,* completes the list of popular dances for which Italy is famous. Other names there are in abundance, but of dances identified with their localities. *La Siciliana* is a delicate but insufficiently varied product of the island from which it has its name. Messina has a pantomimic dance known as *la Ruggera;* Florence its *Trescona,* and so on indefinitely. Of these, such as have any choreographic interest are said to owe it to the *Tarantella.* Of many the interest is chiefly historical, since they are woven into one tissue with old songs and old legends. Poetic and altogether fascinating as such compositions frequently are, however, their prevailing lack of the essential qualities of dancing makes discussion of them inappropriate to a book on that subject. On the other hand, the highly characteristic flavour of the music and the words of their accompanying songs makes them a fascinating study under the heads of folk-lore and folk-music, in which connection they are the subject of several writings of great interest.

CHAPTER VIII

EUROPEAN FOLK-DANCING IN GENERAL

TO people who toil long hours at confining work that requires care and skill, there comes at the end of the day a craving for exercise that will release the mind from the constraint of attention, that will let the muscles play with vigour and abandon. In response to this demand of nature there exists one class of folk-dancing—the *genre* of the careless, energetic romp of people bedecked in bright colours, joining hands now to form themselves in rings, or again in interweaving lines, improvising figures, heedless of step except the simplest skipping and balancing.

Acting contrariwise to the influence of daily labour involving skill and attention, is the force of habitual work that does not require enough precision to satisfy the healthy craving for fine co-ordination of muscle, nerve and mind. The latter condition, too, moves to the dance. But here, in the case of a people whose potency of skill is not spent in the day's work, the dance is likely to assume forms of such precision and elaboration that its performance requires considerable training, and such beauty that it attains to the plane of art.

These two divisions are far from exact; many influences modify them. But they serve as a beginning of the process of separating the gems of folk-dancing from the mass of that which bears a superficial sparkle but is without intrinsic choreographic value.

EUROPEAN FOLK-DANCING   165

The second supposition, of a people engaged at work not sufficiently exacting in finesse to satisfy their craving for skilled co-ordination, may be taken to indicate a merely healthy race whose daily tasks require no finer technique than the ordinary labour of a farm; in such category might be put the peasants of Aragon. The same relation would exist between a people less virile and a form of daily labour still less concerned with skill, as the Andalusians. Or again, it is valid in the case of a community engaged in crafts requiring fine workmanship, if that community be of people endowed with nervous energy in excess of the requirements of the day's work; and that is the condition in those eternally youthful nations, Scotland and Ireland.

National sense of beauty is a factor in the determination of the dances of a country. The Latins have it. The Italians and Spanish have the leisure to practice its expression. The French, on the contrary, direct their energies into work of pecuniary value, and their acceptance of the doctrine of accumulation keeps their attention where it will be paid. Pierre and Laurette frolic with the neighbours on the green, in the moonlight, in what they call a dance. It gives them exercise and many a laugh. But when they would see beauty, they patronise its specialised exponent, the ballet.

"Folk-dancing" is practically synonymous with "character dancing," or, as the word is frequently formed in literal translation of its French original, "characteristic dancing." It means what it implies, an exposition of the characteristics of the people to whom it pertains. Energy or dreaminess, fire or coolness, and a multitude of other qualities are bound to assert themselves, automatically; to any one who can even half read their language, character dances are an open book of intimate personal revelation. The portrayal of sports or trades, which is the sort of thing with which many folk-dances are concerned, does not detract from their interest as expositors of national temperament. Though it may be noted that, in general, the more a dance occupies itself with imitation, the less its value as a dance.

Not least of the elements of interest attaching to these dances is the measure they apply to national vitality or the lack of it. Through the form and execution of its dance, the nation as yet half-barbarous reveals vital potentiality; the people that has luxuriated in centuries of power displays its lassitude of nerve; and the young political organism shows marks of senility at birth. The aboriginal savage, huge-limbed, bounds through dances fitted to the limitations of muscles that cannot be controlled by brain, and the limitations of brain that cannot invent or sustain attention; his dance exposes him as of a race not in its youthful vigour, but in the degeneracy wrought less by time than by manner of living. The Indian of North America is dying of age; the Russian is in his youth.

The list of forces that make and preserve a nation's dances is incomplete without the addition of the sometimes powerful element of national pride. This undoubtedly enters into the high cultivation of the dances of Scotland. The industry, thrift and all-round practical nature of the Scotch need not be enlarged upon. Though they do not lack appreciation of beauty, they consider it a luxury for only limited indulgence, except as it is provided by nature. But the *Sword Dance* and the *Fling* of their warring ancestors are as though associated with the holy cause of freedom. On many a

Highland battlefield they have been stepped; they have wet their scurrying feet in spilled blood.

To learn Scotch dancing takes time, precious time. But it is time spent on a decent and a fitting thing; they are Scotch! Scotch as the thistle itself! From pulpits have come, at times, objections to them; from armed camps and lairds' halls of other days has come the answer, far but clear: that Scottish chiefs, godly men as well as brave, trod their *Flings* in celebration of victories dear to memory. It is enough. The cult of the dance has continued, unchecked by the inability of occasional well-meaning divines to see its significance.

Cæsar "commented" upon the fighting qualities of the *Picti,* built a wall to keep them off from the *Anglia* that he had conquered, and decided not to push his conquests farther north. The fighting spirit of those tartaned clansmen never has softened and has had much occupation throughout the subsequent centuries; and attaching to it is an epic, a saga, in the shape of the *Sword Dance.*

Around the *Sword Dance* in particular the Scotch people group associations. In earlier times its performance was customary on the eve of battle to relieve tension, to exhibit self-control, and, perhaps most important of all, to test fortune. To touch with the foot the crossed sword or scabbard between and about which the dancing warrior picked his steps was an omen of ill for the individual or his comrades. In present-day competitions, the ill luck following this error is evident; to touch the sword or scabbard with the foot eliminates the offender from the contest.

The *Highland Fling,* in distinction from the above, symbolises victory or rejoicing. With the other dances of Scotland, it has been highly formalised. Moreover, its routine, steps, and the proper execution of each are so clearly defined and generally understood that any change in them is immediately resented by any Scotch audience.

Every one has seen Scotch dances; any detailed analysis of them would be superfluous. Exhilarating as Highland whiskey, sharp as the thistle, they are carried to a high plane of art. Through them all runs a homogeneous angularity of movement that literally translates the sentiment of "Caledonia, stern and wild." To the dances of Italy and Andalusia they are as wind-blown mountain pines in contrast to orange trees fanned by Mediterranean zephyrs. The theme of the sharp angle is kept absolutely intact, unmodified by any element of sweep or curve that the eye can detect. The essential steps are two, with variations: the kicking step of the *Schottische Militaire,* of frequent mention on ballroom programmes of twenty-five years ago; and *battements,* great and small. It will be seen that these are perfectly of a kind. The surprising thing is the variety derived from combinations of these two elements with simple turns, simple jumps, and little if anything else of footwork. The result serves, from a purely analytical point of view, as an admirable demonstration of the value of a simple theme intelligently insisted on.

Spirit, of course, is another factor of great importance in making Scotch dances what they are. A Scotch dancer without spirit could not be imagined. Spanish dancers sometimes work coldly, ballet dancers often; but a Scotch dancer never. The first note of the bagpipes inflames him.

With the rigourous definition of step, technique and style that attaches to these dances, and the thoroughness of popular understanding of all that pertains to them, the Scotch public is qualified to exercise upon dancing the essential functions of a national academy. Standards are maintained by knowledge on the part of spectators. Indifference of performance or freedom with forms is quickly reproved. Nor, on the other hand, need any performer remain in ignorance as to just what details of his execution are lacking; among his friends there are plenty of capable critics. We noted the same conditions in Aragon, where the general love of the *Jota* probably would have kept its standards of execution, even without the aid of professional teachers—and certainly do protect it against the subtracting process effected by adding novelties. In Italy the *Tarantella* is cultivated in the same way, in Little Russia the *Cossack Dance,* and in Hungary the *Czardás.* And it is the force of educated public interest behind them that sustains them in a class approached, in requirements of skill, by few other character dances.

The accompanying illustrations from work by Miss Margaret Crawford and partner demonstrate the interesting fact that the Scotch, developing their school of execution along the lines dictated by their own keen discernment, arrive at a conclusion in important respects identical with the creed of the classic ballet. It is possible that the dances of mountain and heather were influenced by the *Pavane* and the *Minuet* in their day—for Queen Mary had her masques and balls and pageants, like other monarchs of her time. But even that will not account for the clean, sharp brilliancy of a Highlander's *battement* or *balloné.* In so many essentials his dances are at variance with those of the seventeenth-century courts that their excellence must be attributed to a national instinct for true quality of beauty. The splendidly erect carriage of the body, the straight knee of the supporting leg during a step, as well as the crisp, straight-knee execution of a *grand battement* (the Scotch and other dancers do not use the French designation of steps, but the general observer may well do so for the sake of clearness), might have come direct from the French Academy. This identity is in manner, it will be understood, more than in matter. Like all character dancing, the Scotch includes in its vocabulary positions and steps that the ballet ignores. Placing the hands on the hips; the heel on the ground and the toe up; and a "rocking" step, consisting of rolling from side to side on the sides of the feet—these and other devices are of the dances of outdoors. In the case of the Scotch they are so admirably incorporated into the scheme of sharp line and movement that go to make a staccato unit that—through the sheer magic worked by cohesion of theme—they avoid the plebeian appearance into which such movements fall when not artfully combined.

The *Scotch Reel* has a good deal in common with the *Fling,* and is of the same general character. It is customarily performed by two couples. Its distinguishing feature is a figure eight, traced by a little promenade, each of the performers winding in and out among the other three. Even this promenade is performed in a sharp skipping step, that the dance may lose none of its national flavour. A variation of this dance is the *Reel of Tulloch,* popular in all parts of Scotland, and distinguished principally by its history. Legend places its origin in a country church, in winter; while the congregation waited for the belated minister, they danced to keep warm, and in the course of the dancing evolved a

EUROPEAN FOLK-DANCING 171

choreographic composition that made their village famous. The *Strathspey* alluded to in literature appears also to have been a variety of the *Reel*.

The *Shean Treuse,* a rollicking dance that covers a good deal of ground, is—according to legend—the representation of a small boy's delight with his first pair of trousers. Naturally, it is based on a series of prancing steps, in each of which the leg is brought to horizontal to keep the trousers in evidence.

This concludes the list of the well-known dances of Scotland. Of the number the most representative, or one may say classic, are the *Sword Dance* and the *Fling*.

England has to her credit one dance, notwithstanding all that has been said and written to the disparagement of her originality in the arts; and, with execution to help it, a very respectable dance it is, as well as a monument to a social element that has contributed powerfully to England's rank among the nations. The dance is the *Sailor's Hornpipe*.

It is a dance of character in the truest sense, being based on the movements associated with the sailor's duties. Accompanying himself with a tuneful patter of foot-work, the performer pantomimes hauling at ropes, rowing, standing watch, and sundry other duties of the sea-dog who dealt with sails and not with coal. The hands are placed on the hips palm out, to avoid touching the clothing with the tar that—as everybody knows—always covered the palms of the deep-sea sailor. While not in any sense a great dance, it is uncommonly ingenious and amusing in its combination of patter of steps and earnest pantomime. It is literally a sailor's chantey sung in the terms of movement instead of words of mouth; even to its division into short stanzas (one for each of the duties represented) the parallel is exact. Its place in the dancing art might be defined as the same as the position of the sailor's chantey in music.

In England there has been a recent and earnest revival of the *Morris Dances,* accompanied by a good deal of writing on the subject. In England they have the importance of being English. They are "quaint," it is true. They reflect the romping, care-free spirit of Merry England; they bring to the cheek of buxom lass the blush of health; they are several centuries old; they follow the antique usage of performance to accompaniment sung by the dancers. But their composition—and its absence—commends them to the attention of the antiquarian and the sociologist, rather than that of a seeker after evolved dancing.

The word "Morris," according to the suggestion offered by certain scholars, is a corruption of "Moorish"; which theory of its derivation is not confirmed by step, movement or sentiment to be found in the dance. What does seem reasonably possible is that it is of Gipsy derivation. Gipsies are sometimes known—in Scotland at least—as "Egyptians"; so why not, by a similar abeyance of accuracy in England, as Moors?—a process of near-reasoning the value of whose conclusion is nothing at all. At any rate, the *Morris* dancers have a tradition of hanging little bells around their arms and legs, and decorating themselves with haphazard streamers of ribbon, which is Gipsy-esque. Stories are recorded to the effect that there have been performers who tuned their bells, and by the movements of the dance played tunes on them. The stories offer no definite information as to the quality of dance or music.

The *Morris* seems to have been a dance for men only,

in which respect it was unique among the old English forms unearthed in the recent revival of interest. Many of these dances certainly are interesting, if not in actual choreographic merit, in association. Their very names are rich in flavour, such as *All in a Garden Green, The Old Maid in Tears, Hempstead Heath, Greensleeves* (mentioned in *The Merry Wives of Windsor*), *Wasp's Maggott, Dull Sir John,* and others equally suggestive of rustic naturalness and fun. Their revivals by Miss Coles and Miss Chaplin include full directions for performance, which is simple. Several of them preserve the ancient usage of saluting the partner with a kiss—which is not mentioned as a warning, but as an observation merely.

England has been among the nations to preserve the institution of dancing around a pole—among the English-speaking so commonly known as the "Maypole" that its use in the celebration of anything but the coming of spring seems incongruous. Other peoples, nevertheless, incorporate it into religious celebrations and whatnot. The device of suspending ribbons from the top of the pole, and weaving them around it by means of an interlacing figure described by the dancers, seems to be universal. The steps employed are the simplest possible —those of the *Waltz, Polka,* or *Schottische,* varied perhaps with an occasional turn. It is another instance of a semiformalised romp called by the title of dance. In passing it may be noted that the Maypole has become a part of the Mayday celebration of the New York public school children—and those of other cities, for anything we know to the contrary. Some hundreds of poles distributed over a green, each with its brightly coloured group twinkling around it, tickles the eye with a feast of sparkle, at least. The same outing is the occasion of an exhibition of the character dancing that the children have learned as part of their school work during the preceding year. The exhibited skill is higher than one would expect, and remarkable, considering the difficulties in the way of imparting it. In one direction the celebration probably attains to the superlative: its participants numbering as they do well up in the thousands, and occupying about a quarter-section of ground, there is nothing in history to indicate that it does not constitute, in point of sheer size and numbers, the biggest ballet the world has ever seen.

Ireland has a group of dances exclusively her own, unique in structure, and developed to the utmost limit of their line of excellence. Their distinguishing property is complicated rhythmic music of the feet. The *Jig*, the *Reel* and the *Hornpipe* of Ireland are at once the most difficult and the most highly elaborated dances of the clog and shuffle type that can be found. In them are passages in which the feet tap the floor seventy-five times in a quarter of a minute.

They have, too, the art that interprets the character of their people. But it is not the Irishman of the comic supplement that they reveal. Rather, by means of their own vocabulary of suggestion, the eloquence of which begins where words fail, they present the acute Hibernian wit that animates the brain of Irishmen like Shaw. Intricate combinations of keen, exact steps, the Irish dances are a series of subtle epigrams directed to the eye. And like the epigrams that proceed from true wit, they are expressed so modestly that their significance may be quite lost on an intelligence not in sympathy with the manner of thought that lies back of them. To the end

IRISH DANCES
Mr. Thomas Hill and Mr. Patrick Walsh

The *Jig* (1, 3, 4) — The *Hornpipe* (2, 5) — The *Reel* (6, 7, 8)

To face page 174

A "Four-hand Reel"

Preparation for woman's turn under arms (1) — Characteristic style (2) — A turning group figure (3)

of convincing us onlookers that this everyday world is made up of nothing but happiness, the music of tapping shoe flatters our senses without shame, chloroforms reason and shows us the truth—that our minds at least will float in the air like dancers' bodies, if we but abandon them to the rhythmic charm that coaxes them to forget their sluggishness. Irish dancing has too often been the victim of caricature. In all truth, its refined intricacy makes it cousin rather to the *Book of Kells*, whose ancient decoration of rich yet simple interlacement gives it place among the masterpieces of the book-designer's art.

The intent of the art of Irish dancing is the sooner understood by a word of negative description to begin with: namely, it is at the opposite pole from dancing of posture, broad movement, or pantomime. All its resources, on the contrary, are concentrated in making music of the feet. Happy music it is, with lightness of execution as a part of it. That no incident may distract attention from foot-work, the body is held almost undeviatingly erect, and the arms passive at the sides; and this is in accordance with unquestioned usage.

Among the dancers represented in the accompanying photographs is Mr. Thomas Hill, four times winner of the championship of Ireland. "The thing of greatest importance in Irish dancing," Mr. Hill says, "is the music of the shoes. In the eleven years that I have been dancing, the greater part of my attention has been spent on the development and control of the variety of tones that can be produced by taps of heels and soles on the floor and against each other. Style is necessary, of course, as in any other dancing, and so is exactness in 'tricky' time. But control of a good variety of sounds, which is the most difficult part of Irish dancing, is the most important because it is the most Irish."

Once in a great while coincidence puts one in the way of hearing the work of a virtuoso on the snare-drum. Within a minute the effect is found to be nothing less than hypnotic. Every one within hearing is patting time, swaying with the time, restraining the most urgent impulse to do something that will bring every fibre of his body into unison with that inebriating rhythm. Now, the feet of a fine Irish dancer are drumsticks as amenable to control as the drummer's; notes long and short, dull and sharp—he has all the drum's variety. No resource of syncopation, emphasis, or change is unknown to the Irish dances; the rhythm gets into the blood—with double the seductiveness of sound alone, since every tap on the tympanum is reinforced by the same metric beating on the vision. Joined to the resulting exhilaration is the peculiar excitement always felt in the presence of suspended gravitation; for no less than suspended gravitation it is when the foot of a man taps the ground like the paw of a kitten, and the body floats in the air like a bird that has paused but will not alight. The good Saint Basil was not only eloquent when he asked what could be more blessed than to imitate on earth the dancing of the angels. His question carries with it the important indication that he had seen an *Irish Reel* in his day. Because, among all the dances that are stepped on this mortal earth, what other is so light that the saint could see in it the pastime of angels?

For the sake of accuracy, let it not be thought that the steps of the *Reel* and the *Jig,* and the *Hornpipe* as well, were not old while Christianity was new. Mr. Patrick J. Long, himself at once a dancer of pronounced

EUROPEAN FOLK-DANCING

ability and a well-read scholar on Irish history, writes for this chapter: "In the days of Druidism, the Irish nation celebrated an annual feast lasting six days; three days before the first of November, and three days after. Coming after the season of harvest, it probably was like a Thanksgiving. The celebration was called in Gaelic a *Feis* (pronounced 'fesh'). Now it was the custom, at the time of the *Feis* for the nobles of Ireland, and their ladies, and bards and harpists from far and near, to gather at the castle of the king; and there for six days there were competitions in all kinds of music and dancing.

"The dance that was popular with the nobles and their ladies was called the *Rinnce Fadha* (pronounced 'reenka faudha'). This we know was a dance for several couples. It was a favourite of King Leoghaire (pronounced 'Leery'), who ruled Ireland when St. Patrick came to convert the people from paganism. From it was derived in a later century the form of the *Sir Roger de Coverley;* from the *Sir Roger* came the *Virginia Reel* of America.

"The dances of Ireland are variations on the *Reel, Jig* and *Hornpipe*. The *Reel* is probably the most classic; it is executed in a gliding movement, and is speedy and noiseless. The *Jig* and the *Hornpipe* have a good deal in common. Both use clogging and shuffling; that is, taps of heel or sole on the floor, and light scrapes of the sole. Of the two the *Hornpipe* contains the more clogging. But it is richer than the *Clog Dance* that it resembles more or less. It is less mechanical, more varied and has prettier foot-work.

"The *Reel* and the *Jig* are danced as solos by man or woman, by two men, two women, a couple, two men and a woman, two, three, four or eight couples. In 'set dances,' as they are called when performed by a 'set' of couples, the steps are simpler than in solo work; and the time also is simpler in the music of set dances than in the airs used to accompany solos and the work of teams of two. There are *Hop Jigs, Slip Jigs, Single* and *Triple Jigs* in 9-8 time. Another peculiarity of Irish dancing, due to the character of the music, is in the irregularities of repetition of the work of one leg with the other leg. The right leg may do the principal work through eight bars; the same work is naturally to be repeated then with the left leg; but often the composition of the music gives the left leg only six bars. This is good because unexpected, but it adds a great deal to the difficulty of learning Irish dancing."

The above-named dances represent the utmost development of clogging, which is tapping of heels, and shuffling, or scraping of the sole on the floor. Footwork, especially that of short and rapid steps, is the element impossible to show in pictorial form. Accompanying photographs, therefore, give little idea of the charm of the art of Mr. Hill, Mr. Long, Mr. Walsh, Miss Murray and Miss Reardon, from whom they were taken.

Thanks to the American branch of the Gaelic League and its activity in the cause of Ireland's arts, Irish dancing is in a flourishing condition in this country. In intelligent public interest, standards of excellence and number of capable performers, America now leads even Ireland. Mr. Hill attributes this to a combination of well-directed enthusiasm, and the practice of holding four important competitions each year. These are divided among as many cities. Capable management at-

THE "IRISH JIG"
Miss Murray, Miss Reardon, Mr. Hill, Mr. Walsh — Single figure,
Mr. Patrick J. Long

tracts competitors of good class and large numbers, and they are classified in such a way that there is hope for all. Liberality in prizes is an added stimulus. All told, Mr. Hill says that one *feis* of the four annually held in this country accomplishes as much in the interest of dancing as is done in Ireland in a year.

Dublin and Cork each has its annual *feis,* with an interval of half-a-year between the two. Each has the dancing championship competition among its features; Mr. Hill's title was won in 1909, '10 and '11 at Cork, also in 1911 at Dublin. As the Gaelic League has prominent among its purposes the restoration to popular use of the Gaelic language, dancing is only one of several artistic contests. Singing, elocution, and conversation, all in the ancient Irish tongue, have their respective laurel-seeking votaries. Superiority in the playing of violin and flute is rewarded, as in playing the war pipes and union pipes. (War pipes, as may not be universally known, are the Scotch form of bagpipes, played by lung power; the wind for union pipes, in distinction, is supplied by bellows held under the arm.) And until within a couple of years *lilting* has been competed in—the old singing without words, "tra-la-la-dee" sort of thing. The irreverent called it "pussy-singing." Athletic games are included for the sake of variety. Prizes in all events are usually medals.

The *feis* in America follows the same model. Dancing enjoys a gratifying popularity. Good work always incites the spectators to shout their enthusiasm. With a prevailing eagerness to learn to judge it more exactly, and a highly respectable knowledge of it at the present moment, there exists also that most wholesome adjunct to interest, a division of beliefs as to school. The Cork technique is comparatively short in step, and very precise; Limerick favours a rather looser type of movement. And there comes in the world-old argument between the Academic and (by whatever name it matters not) the Impressionistic creeds. Each claims to represent the true Hibernianism.

Sweden, during a period beginning a few years ago, has taken up an enthusiastic revival of the dances of the Scandinavian world. The movement began with the foundation by the late Dr. Hazélius of the Museum of the North, and is carried on by his son.

The Museum was planned to bring together a representation of Scandinavia of old, in such a complete way as to show not only products and methods of manufacture, but modes of life and social customs. The result is unique among undertakings of the kind. In a park called the Skansen are preserved the Scandinavian flora and fauna, in appropriate surroundings. Farms are cultivated in the manner of the various provinces, and on the farms are their appropriate buildings, characteristic in every detail. To complete the re-creation of antiquity, churches and all the other structures pertinent to community life are included.

The numerous people required to animate such an establishment, including as it does accommodations for visitors, are the expositors of the national dances. Farmers, shoemakers, waiters in the cafés, are required to learn and practise them, and present them publicly three times a week. It goes without saying that they dress at all times in the costume of the locality of which they are representatives.

The influences of the Skansen have been of a sort to gratify its founder. Society now, as a custom, dresses itself for garden parties in the picturesque gaiety and brilliant colour of old Scandinavia, and dances the *Skralât* and *Kadriljs* of the peasants. A saying has sprung up that "dancing is a form of patriotism." The sentiment has impressed itself no less upon the working people than upon the rich. Children receive dancing instruction gratis in the Skansen, and knowledge has spread into all parts of Sweden. Now, instead of the *Polka,* which fifty years ago swept over Scandinavia and fastened itself on the land with a hold that smothered every other dance, are to be seen the merry steps and forms that are distinctively of the Norseland, accompanied by the old music. A princess of the royal house sanctions the revival of Scandinavianism (if the word be permitted) to the extent of dressing herself and the servants at her summer-place according to the new-old modes. She is popular and the movement is strengthened accordingly.

The dances are simple in step, though often complicated in figure; lively and gay in manner, and rich in pantomime. Accepted standards of execution require decided grace and a good style. Gustavus III, when he visited France, is said to have been deeply impressed by the exquisite dancing of Marie Antoinette and her court. The element of beauty to be seen in Swedish dancing is supposed to be due in part, at least, to that royal visit.

One of the most pleasing dance-arrangements is inspired by the work of the weaver, with the happy changes of effect constantly wrought by the action of the loom. The *Vafva Vadna* this dance is called. It is highly complicated, the stretched threads are simulated in the lines of performers, through whom flashes back and forth the girl who represents the movements of the shuttle. Rich variety is gained by involved intercrossings of the lines of boys and girls.

The taming of womankind is the motive of the pantomimic *Daldans*. Over the head of the meekly kneeling woman the man swings his foot, as a symbol; in another figure the woman's coquetry reduces the man to helplessness. The *Vingakersdans* pantomimes the competition of two women for the same man. The favoured one seats herself a moment on the man's knee, and finishes the number by waltzing with him; while the defeated charmer bites her nails with vexation.

These are characteristic specimens of a very numerous group. Their revival seems to progress more rapidly in the villages than in the big cities—interesting as a case of the country leading the cities in a movement of modernism. Many of the pantomimes are based on work from which the rural population is less remote than are those who dwell in cities. The movements of making a shoe are known to every villager; he has watched the cobbler many a time, and known him usually as the local philosopher. Upon the village, therefore, no touch of character in the *Cobblers' Dance* would be lost. The humours of harvesting might in like manner fail to reach a city audience without the aid of spoken word; harvest, with other elemental work, provides many of the Scandinavian dance motives.

Holland and Belgium are alike unproductive of dancing of much choreographic value. The strength of the people is not accompanied by either the lightness or agility found in dancing nations. As a coincidence, it is notable that dancing does not flourish in regions of wooden shoes. The Dutch have a species of sailors' dance called the *Mâtelot,* performed by groups of men and women; but it is a romp and little or nothing more. This is characteristic of the dances of the Netherlands, as is confirmed by *genre* pictures from the time of Teniers down to the present.

The *Waltz,* it should be said at this point, is universal. If ever it is asserted that the people of a locality do not dance, an exception may be made to cover the *Waltz,* so long as the locality referred to is in the Occident. The seeming caution with which peasants perform their *Waltzes* practically removes them from the category of dancing, though not from that of humour.

France, the Eden of the Grand Ballet, the home of a race of lovers of beauty, might be expected to abound in rich character dances; but the exact reverse is true. The people of the country are, first of all, workers; the dances that enliven their fêtes are the careless celebration of children released from confining tasks. The principal cities have their opera ballets; through them is supplied the national demand for choreographic beauty.

The old name of *la Bourrée* survives in Auvergne. In its present form it bears no resemblance to the old *Bourrée* of eighteenth-century courts, but is one of those informal frolics of an indefinite number of couples, hand-clapping, finger-snapping, and energetic bounding, mingled with shouts of joy.

The *Farandole* is popular in the South of France. Under its name a chain of boys and girls, united by handkerchiefs that they hold, "serpentines" and zigzags in directions dictated by the caprice of their leader, perhaps traversing the length of the streets of a village. From time to time the leading couple will halt and form their arms into an arch for those following to pass under; or again stop the procession in such a way as to wind up the line into a compact mass. Again the game partakes of the nature of "follow the leader," the whole party imitating the leader in any antic he may perform.

The ancient *Contredanses*—which word England changed to *Country Dances,* of frequent mention in story —were the roots of modern *Quadrilles.* These, however, are polished out of any semblance to character dances; they are of the ballroom and infinitely removed from the soil.

Germany, with its fondness for legend and care in its preservation, would be a fertile field for search on the part of a compiler of ancient observances more or less allied to dancing. A specimen of the latter is the *Perchtentanz* of Salzburg. Perchta is another name for Freya, Woden's consort and the mother of the Northmen's gods. She is powerful even in these modern times, and malicious unless propitiated by proper formulæ of actions and words. Placing a spoonful of food from each dish of the Christmas dinner for her on the fence outside the house is one of the tributes. She has spirit-followers: some kindly, called *"schön Perchten,"* others wild and fierce, known as *"schiachen Perchten."* The latter alight on houses and scream mischievously, lure men into danger and punish undiscovered crimes.

At irregular intervals is performed the *Perchtentanz;* not apparently as an act of propitiation, but presumably having that motive as its origin. Good and evil *Perchten* both are represented. On an accompanying page of European miscellany is a drawing of one of the "beautiful." The huge plaques are covered with sparkling trinkets and adorned with braid, ribbon and embroidery. Stuffed birds are also popular for their decorations; a dozen of them may be affixed to the lower plaque, a

EUROPEAN FOLK-DANCING 185

FROM VARIOUS FOLK-DANCES.

Scandinavian. Russian.
Hungarian. Scandinavian.
From the *Perchtentanz* of Salzburg. Bavarian.
Russian Court (Princess Chirinski-Chichmatoff.)

smaller number to the upper; an ambitious crown to the whole is sometimes seen in the form of a peacock with spread wings. The structure is supported by a rod running down the bearer's back, and fastened to him by belts. Its weight prohibits any movement to which the word "dancing" applies except as a convenience; but a series of slow and necessarily careful evolutions performed by the wearers of these displays is called a dance, nevertheless. Meantime the "fierce Perchten," made up with masks as demoniac as possible, run about among the legs of the crowd and do their best to startle people. The spirit accompanying the celebration is levity, modified only by the sincere admiration considered due the serious decorations. They represent a great deal of work and considerable money.

In various parts of Savoy is performed on St. Roch's Day what is called the *Bacchu-ber*. On a platform erected in front of a church, and decorated with garlands and fir-trees, a group of men dance with short swords; passing under bridges of swords, forming chains by grasping one another's weapons, and so on. That its origin is pre-Christian seems a reasonable conjecture; but nothing specific is known about it.

Munich celebrates with dancing an episode connected with an epidemic of cholera: the guild of coopers decided that the care the people were taking against exposure was defeating its purpose, since it was keeping them indoors to the detriment of health. They therefore went out and enjoyed themselves as usual, for the sake of example. Others did the same, and the plague ceased. Periodically the brave coopers are honoured, therefore, by dances of large companies of people, who carry garlanded arches and execute triumphal figures.

The foregoing instances are no more than a specimen of the varieties of tradition that dancing may commemorate. Europe collectively doubtless will produce thousands of such dances, when the task of collecting them is entered upon with the necessary combination of leisure and zeal.

Bavaria's *Schuhplatteltanz* is altogether delightful in itself, without aid from history or tradition to supplement its interest. It is full of a quaint Tyrolean grace mingled with happy and delicate grotesquery. Women it causes to spin as though they were some quaint species of combination doll and top; the atmosphere that surrounds a marvellous and pretty mechanical toy is preserved in a delicate unreality in the pantomime and in the treatment throughout.

It is accompanied by zithers, instruments which themselves sing of a world suspended somewhere in the air. In silvery, floating tones they play less a waltz than the dream of a waltz, in sounds as unmaterial as the illusive voice of an Æolian harp.

A little opening promenade; a few bars of the couple's waltzing together—in steps infinitesimal, prim with conscious propriety. The man raises the girl's hand and starts her spinning. She neither retards nor helps, being a little figure of no weight, moved solely by power from without itself. Her skirt stands out as straight and steady as though it were cardboard; her partner must lean far over now, not to touch it and spoil the spin. Now she is whirling perfectly; with a parting impulse to her arm, he releases her. On she turns, at a speed steady as clockwork, revolving, as a top will, slowly around a large circle.

Her partner follows, beating time in a way that bewilders eye and ear alike; for his hands pat shoes and leather breeches with a swiftness incredible and ecstatic. Of this perhaps sixteen bars when, as though his partner were beginning to "run down," he starts blowing her along with vigorous puffs. Nevertheless, she is slowing down; the skirt is settling. He reaches over it, gets his hands on her waist. To the last the spinning illusion is preserved by an appearance of her rotary motion being stopped only by the pressure of the man's hand as a brake.

The foregoing interpretation is suggested by the delicate work of Herr and Frau Nagel, and the company with which they are associated. It is a dance whose fancy easily could disappear under its mechanics, if performed without imagination.

Having caught his partner after her spin, waltzed again with her for a few bars, and lifted her up at arm's length in sheer playfulness, the man joins arms with her in such fashion as to form almost a duplicate of the "mirror" figure of the *Minuet*. The courtliness of the cavalier in the *Minuet* is matched by adroitness on the part of the *schuhplatteltanzer;* he contrives to draw his partner's head nearer and nearer to his, as they walk around in a lessening circle. Finally, when the circle of the promenade can become no smaller, and the faces have come close to the imaginary mirror framed by the arms, he suddenly but daintily kisses her lips.

Germany is the home of the *Waltz,* of which it has evolved several varieties. The *Rheinlander Waltz* is perhaps the most popular. In one form or another it has spread through the Balkan countries; not, however, with any apparent detriment to the native dances, because of these dances' natural crudeness. Servia, Montenegro and the neighbouring monarchies celebrate weddings and christenings and enliven picnics with a "round" called in Servian language the *Kolo*, that employs the simple old figures of the bridge of arms and the like, but which, as to step, is quite formless. Colour in the costumes goes far to provide spectacular interest to these exuberant frolics. The linen gowns of the women are embroidered in big—and good—designs of two distinct reds, scarlet and rose; emerald-green and a warm yellow-green; the most brilliant of yellows; wine-colour and blue. As is frequently found in a region that has kept a scheme of design through a sufficient number of generations to allow the formation of traditions based on long experiment, the seemingly impossible is accomplished by the peasant women of the Balkans: the colours whose enumeration on the same page would seem outrageous are, in practical application, brought into harmony. It is a question of proportionate size of spots of colour, and their juxtaposition. The results of using the same colours in new designs is to be seen in the expressions of sundry new schools of painting that refuse to acknowledge limitations.

Men's sleeves and waistcoats are frequently embroidered in the same way as the jacket and sleeves of the women, as exemplified in the accompanying photographs of Madame Koritiç. Loose linen trousers, which are sometimes worn, may be likewise decorated. In the sunlight and in appropriate surroundings, a performance of the *Kolo* should be a sight to dispel trouble, whatever its deficiencies from the point of view of dancing.

Greece, too, diverts itself with rustic rounds, as **form-**

less as in other lands. Of the Hellas that gave the Occident its civilisation there remain some architectural ruins, to which latter-day inhabitants of the land may have given some care; and certain statues, preserved in the museums of other lands. For Hellenic ideals and Attic salt, search the hat-boy at the entrance to the restaurant. The Greek of to-day is a composite of Turk and Slav; his dances have neither the grace of the one nor the fire of the other. The discovery in Greece of survivors of ancient dances—which discovery is occasionally asserted—may have a basis in fact; but more likely its foundation is in a similarity between an ancient and a modern word. But enough of disappointments and of great things lost.

Hungary, Russia and Poland have a family of strictly national dances that not only take a position among the world's best character dances; without departing from their true premise as expressions of racial temperament, some of them attain to the dignity of great romantic art, combined with optical beauty of the highest order. A *Czardás* in one of the Pavlowa programmes (season 1913-14) showed qualities of choreographic composition that were equalled, in that entertainment, only by the ballet arrangements of the most capable composers whose works were represented. The juxtaposition of ballet and character numbers, performed with the same skill and accompanied by the same orchestra, furnished an uncommonly good measure of the folk-dances' actual merit.

The *Czardás*,* the *Mazurka* and the *Cossack Dance* of Russia and the *Obertass* of Poland form a group that occupy in the dance the place that Liszt's "Hungarian Rhapsody" fills in music: they are the candid revela-

* Hungarian.

THE "KOLO" OF SERVIA
Madame Koritic

Start of a turn   Progress of a turn
           A bridge of arms
An emphasis   A lift

To face page 190

POSES FROM SLAVONIC DANCES
Miss Lydia Lopoukowa

Coquetry   Petulance
        Indifference
Emphasis   Jocular defiance

tion of the heart of a people simple, sympathetic, unrestrainedly romantic, violently impulsive. Each represents an exciting diversity of ammunition, fired in one rousing volley; an expression to which one may become accustomed, but which always remains unfamiliar, and which always produces an intoxicating shock. The abrupt changes of movement from slow to fast, from furious speed to a dead standstill; the recurrent crescendo from short, close movement to broad sweeps, open *jeté* turns, and the lowest of "dips"; the diverse effects gained by play of rhythm—such effects are indescribable in word or picture. Fortunately, however, characteristic poses are within the range of the snapshot; so also, to an extent, is the expression of human moods—if portrayed by rare pantomimic ability.

Possession of such ability, backed by the unfettered imagination of the Tartar and accompanied by superlative artistry, describes Miss Lydia Lopoukowa. To her great kindness this book is indebted for the accompanying photographs representing characteristic poses and moods of northern Slavonic dancing. Taken from the work of such an artist, the pictures represent an idealisation, or perfection, of their subjects. They show movements of the dances themselves, in their spirit, without the usual limitations imposed by physique. The clean-cut definition of pose; the co-ordination of pose and features in all the expressions of allurement, appeal, petulance, esctasy—these represent a standard at which the merely mortal dancer aims, but a conjunction of conditions that one may hope to see accomplished few times in the course of one life.

Yet, as noted before, the dances are so composed that,

performed with a degree of skill not uncommon in their native land, they are rich and surprising. In steps, the Russian, Austrian and Polish group have most of their material in common: naturally, since they are united by ties of race. The salient point by which each dance is distinguished, in the eye of the spectator, is one big step.

The *Czardás* employs a long glided step that is all its own. The active foot is started well to the rear, and glided forward; the glide is accompanied by a very low *plié* of the supporting knee; as the active foot comes into advanced position, the dancer sharply straightens up, rises to the ball of the supporting foot, and continues the advancing foot forward and upward in a rapid kick. The masculine version drops the body lower, and kicks higher, than the feminine; but even the latter's change of elevation remains fixed in the memory.

In the *Obertass*, the man goes into the low stooping position, in connection with executing a very individual *rond de jambe*. At the moment, he is face to face with his partner, his hands on the sides of her waist, her hands on his shoulders; after a swift step-turn in the usual direction, he takes a long step backward (she forward), and, keeping his right leg extended before him, stoops until he is squatting on his left heel; the right leg, held straight, is swept rapidly around to the rear; meanwhile the couple continues to turn. The man's momentum turns him until he faces in the same direction with his partner. He springs up on her right side, and goes with her into a short, fast polka-step. During the turn, the woman keeps hold of the man to prevent centrifugal force from flinging him into space.

In the *Mazurka* (not the ballroom version) the same

POSES FROM SLAVONIC DANCES
Miss Lydia Lopoukowa

Negation (1) — Fear (2) — Supplication (3) — An emphasis (4)

To face page 192

Poses from Slavonic Dances
Miss Lydia Lopoukowa

Characteristic gesture (1) — Characteristic step (2) — Characteristic gesture (3) — Characteristic step (4) — Same, another view (5) — Ecstasy (6) — The claim of beauty (7)

step, modified as to elevation, is performed by both man and woman, alternately, during certain passages.

The *Szolo*, a Hungarian dance introduced into America by Mr. and Mrs. Hartmann, gives the woman a unique turn in the air. The woman standing at her partner's right, the two join their crossed hands above her head, she reaching up, he downward. She is turned by being swung through the air—in a horizontal position—finishing on her partner's left side. The arms, of course, have "unwound" from their first position, and re-crossed in its converse position. This movement, masterfully executed, is one of the devices by which the dance contradicts gravity. Ill done, of course, it would be as painful for spectator as performer.

But these dances are not often ill done—at least by the people to whom they belong. We are credibly informed that the problems of involved steps and tricky tempo, exacting requirements of agility and expression, are met with a laugh; that, while great virtuosity is naturally rare, real elegance of execution is the rule. Which leads back, of course, to national choreographic traditions and ideals. The artistic level they occupy in Russia (and presumably Hungary and Poland) is indicated in a few lines of a letter to the authors from Princess Chirinski-Chichmatoff, of Moscow. Apart from its value as quite the finest statement of the meaning of character dancing that is to be found in the literature of choreography, the paragraph has the interest of showing one of the reasons why the folk-dancing of northeastern Europe is good:

In every dance the principal things are the harmony (1) of movements with the rhythm of the music, (2) of movements with the subject that the music represents, and (3) of the sentiments with the pantomime, to give a certain impression; and finally this, that it should be a dance which has exclusively the national character, with the movements natural [familiers] *to a certain people and to a certain epoch. In the dance the artist ought to show all the richness of his soul; ought to instil into his movements all of that which the sculptor puts into his marble; while above the idea and the mood ought to be felt the beauty and freedom of movements and lines.*

Quite a difference between that and some other national ideas of character dancing!

Describing her national dance (i. e., the *Cossack Dance* and its derivatives) she writes:

"The Russian dance is composed in two parts, Adagio and Allegro. In each part we see the traits most natural to the people, and which were formed in historic times, under other conditions.

"1. Adagio: length, freedom, tranquillity of movement with much dignity and grace, and with a little softness and simplicity; all relating to the traits that were formed during the period when all Russian women passed the whole time in their *térémas* (house of Russian style), retired from the world, working and singing, thinking melancholy thoughts about life but never seeing it in reality, never leaving the house nor being seen except on the rare occasion of visits.

"2. Allegro: expresses, with the gay and popular songs, the vivacity, the carelessness, the humour and the pleasantry that were born in a people still a little barbarous and simple, whose sadness and gaiety were somewhat naïve. All the traits natural to the Russian people are portrayed in their national dance and in the simple music created from the most popular and beloved songs."

Within the form so sketched there is room for a wide variety of interpretation. The peasant expresses the motives of happiness and vivacity in movements that translate the joy of an almost wild man. An advance while maintaining a low squatting position, the spring for each step coming from a leg bent double, is a grotesquery trying to the strength of the toughest thighs. Still more difficult and as grotesque is a movement of squatting on one heel, and rapidly tracing circles with the extended leg held straight, as though it were the arm of a compass. The feminine version of the movements is less violent; but the Allegro portion of the woman's work is nevertheless tremendously animated in the rustic version of this dance.

As the court of seventeenth-century France took the dances of the peasant and modified them into adornments of ceremonious occasions, so polite society has done in Russia. The *Court Dance* is the result. Refinement has not robbed it of the national qualities described by Princess Chirinski; her own performance of it demonstrates, in almost spiritual terms, the "dignity and grace," the "little softness and simplicity," the "sadness and gaiety" that she puts into words. Through her performance, too, runs an undercurrent of the indefinable—a hint of latent mystery that is not European. It is a quality not infrequently sensed in the work of artists of Tartar blood; it is a trace of the Orient.

CHAPTER IX

ORIENTAL DANCING

FROM a race of artists Mohammed took away the freedom to paint or model representations of living things. Yet the prohibition was a seed from which sprang a garden of expression more graphic than paint, a school of symbolism perhaps the most highly wrought the world has seen.

Artist the Arab is, whether measured by tests of his command over abstract symbol or—in such media as his religion permits—vivid portrayal of nature. Of concrete things and occurrences he has the alert observation of a reporter. Upon what he sees he ponders; intensely religious, he sees the hand of Allah in many things, draws morals, and seeks meanings.

His nomad forefathers mastered the geography of the stars, in search of a celestial message. Though the message be still unread, mathematical problems that vex the learned in academies amused the Arab when the race was young. Written numerals he invented, occult relations he sees in their functions. And, underlying all, he has a passion for intellectual order.

Geometry is the educated Arab's plaything; from long practice he can project its figures upon the wall of imagination, free of the need of pencil. Owing to this practice, perhaps, his thoughts express themselves in the form of images. His literature is crowded with them, vivid sketches thrown before the mind's eye; each a

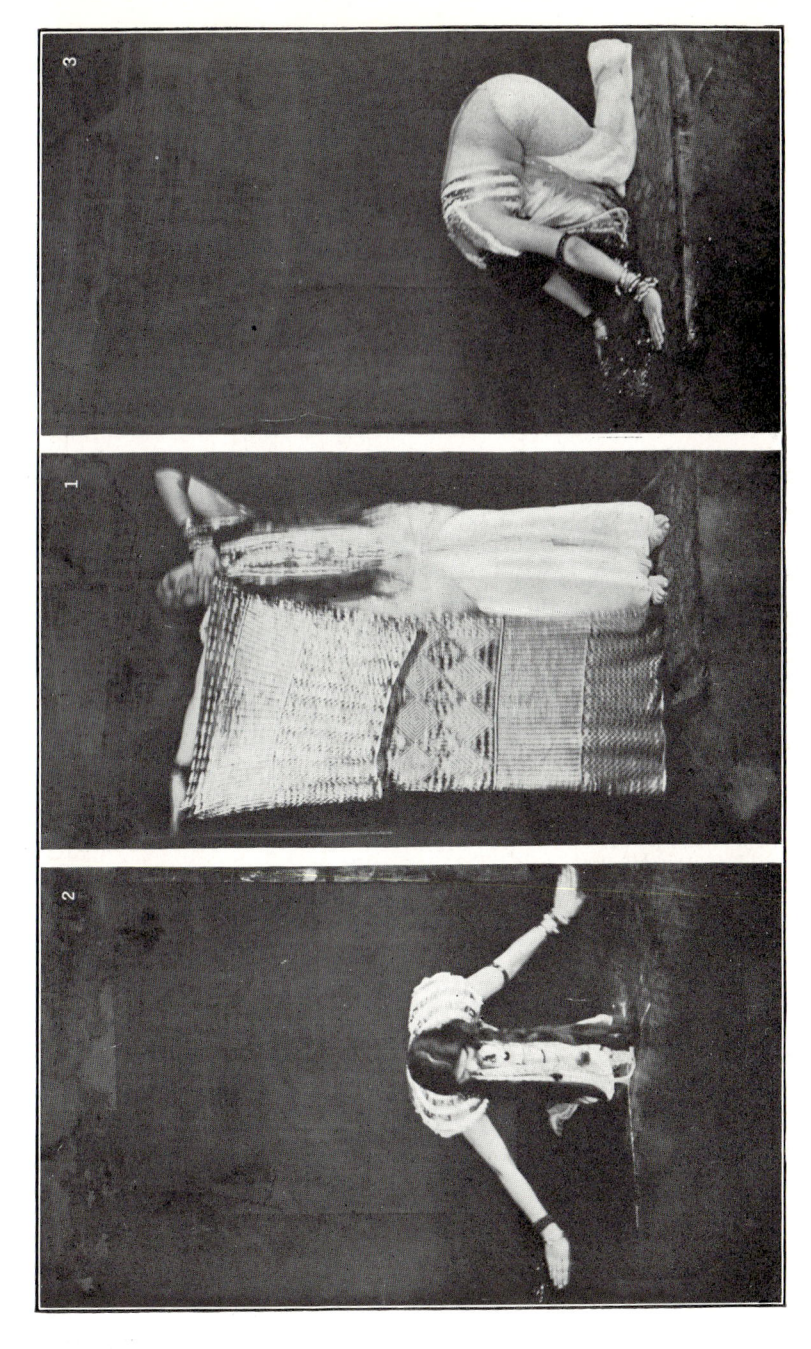

Arabian "Dance of Greeting"
By Zourna

Called upon to dance, she reveals herself (1) — Salutation (2) — Profile view of same (3)

To face page 106.

Arabian "Dance of Greeting" (*Continued*)

"For you I will dance" (4) — "From here you will put away care" (5, 8) — "Here you may sleep" (6) — "Here am I" (7)

ORIENTAL DANCING

symbol more eloquent than description, a metaphor more compelling than logic.

As astronomy was born of the search for meanings in the stars, so the search for mystic functions among the figures of geometry evolved a school of decoration that drowns the eye in pleasure, baffles the mind to explain. From square and compass spring the best of the interlaced ornament of the palace of Alhambra—the ornament that raises material things to a plane almost exempt from material limitations. And not the designer alone gleaned from the geomancer's play with line. Experiments profitless to the magician yielded of their magic to the architect, to the end that he was able to make of a gateway a song of thanksgiving, of a square tower a hymn of aspiration—and these, if it suited him, by the magic of proportion alone, without the aid of any adornment whatever.

Such a race, if it could have painted and drawn, would have produced artists superlative in more than one direction. Clear observation and the wit to discern significances would have made satirists and commentators of the most subtle kind. In picture, the Arab metaphor would have been better expressed, even, than in words, which often seem a weak translation of a graphic symbol in the Arab story-teller's mind. As to decoration, it seems inevitable that with knowledge of the figure and freedom to use it, the Moors that adorned Alhambra's inner walls could have painted such designs as are not even dreamed of; for their designing—so far as its field extended—was to Occidental designing in general as evolved musical composition is to arrangement by guess-work.

All these things the Arab must have done as a painter.

Yet despite the injunction depriving him of life as material for picture and sculpture, and indeed because of it, he has evolved an art in which painting and sculpture unite to express the human emotions through the medium of the human form. That art, of course, is dancing. He has dignified it with his accumulated knowledge of decoration, imbued it with the mystic symbolism of his speculative mind. In light mood it narrates the passing occurrence or the amusing anecdote. And not the least of the wonders of the Arab dancing is the emphasis it places upon the beauty of womankind. Instead of movement, as in most European dancing, its essential interest is in a series of pictures, charged with significance and rich in harmony of line. The eye has time to dwell upon a posture, to revel in the sensuous grace into which it casts body and limb. To complete the task of sculptural composition, the Arabic dancer studies to a rare completeness the art of eliminating the many natural crudities of position that prevent arms, legs and body from showing to the utmost advantage their physical perfection. Though the material body does not—in the work of a genuine artist—distract attention from sculptural nobility of pose, neither is physical attractiveness lost sight of in the beauties of the abstract.

That the treasure-house of Arabian choreography never has been really opened to Occidental eyes is probably due, as much as to anything else, to the Arab's inability to contribute any explanation to a thing which, by his way of thinking, explains itself. He has seen no dancing except that of his own race. To him Arabian dancing is not Arabian; it is just dancing. In his eyes the mimetic symbols are as descriptive as spoken

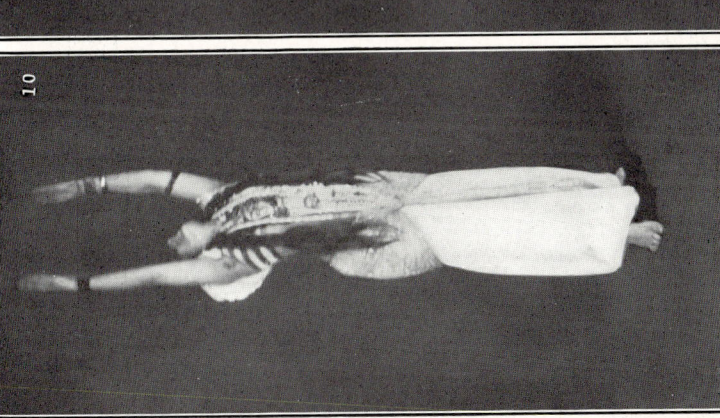

Arabian "Dance of Greeting" (*Continued*)

"And should you go afar" (9) — "May you enjoy Allah's blessing of rain" (10) — "And the earth's fullness" (11)

To face page 198

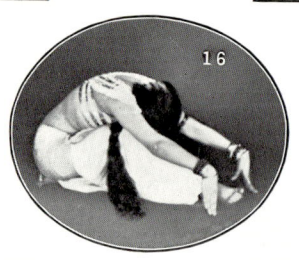

ARABIAN "DANCE OF GREETING" (*Continued*)

"May winds refresh you" (12) —   "Wherever you go" (13) —
"And your slave" (16)
"Here is your house" (14) —   "Here is peace" (15)

words. Except he could see them with Occidental eyes, he would see nothing about them to explain.

Europe has seen the Arabic work, and enjoyed it for its ocular beauty. Gérome, Constant, Bargue and others have painted its sinuous elegance with admirable results. But no insight into its motives has become general, nor has any key to its meaning heretofore been printed, so far as can be ascertained, in any European language.

America still further than Europe has been excluded from satisfactory acquaintance with the Oriental, because it has been so rarely presented here except in a manner to defame it. At the World's Fair in Chicago, where we saw it first, its sinuous body-movement caused a shock. Along that line opportunist managers saw profit. Sex—an institution whose existence is frankly admitted by every civilisation except our own—was, under managerial inspiration, insisted upon to the exclusion of every other motive of the dance; and insisted upon in such a manner as to make it repulsive. Ruth St. Denis has gone far in removing the resulting stigma from the art of India and Egypt. That the prejudice is not going to persist in the face of a national commonsense and love of beauty is further indicated in the reception met by the work of Fatma a couple of seasons ago in *The Garden of Allah;* a Moroccan woman, doing work unreservedly typical of her country, always received with delight by the audience, and never regarded from the wrong point of view.

The mission of calling Western attention to that which lies below the surface of Arabic dancing, however, appears to have remained for Zourna, the Tunisian. To her it is possible, by virtue of a point of view resulting from a dual education, Mohammedan and European.

Zourna is the daughter of an Arab father and a French mother, who lived in Tunis. In childhood she was taught the Arab girl's accomplishments, dancing included; but an occasional visit to France enabled her at all times to see her African way of living somewhat as it would appear to the European. In the natural course of events she married; destined, however, to a short time of enjoyment of the dreamy dancing of the sheltered harem. The death of her husband and loss of fortune drove her to dance in cafés. That genus of work she had time to learn well before Fate again intervened. A chain of circumstances brought her an opportunity to study ballet in the French Academy. It was not her medium of expression, but it gave her a clear measure of the difference between the Oriental and Occidental philosophies of the dance.

Of formulated dances the Arab has few, and those no more set than are the words of our stories: the point must not be missed, but we may choose our own vocabulary. In terms of the dance, the Arab entertainer tells stories; in the case of known and popular stories she follows the accepted narrative, but improvises the movements and poses that express it, exactly as though they were spoken words instead of pantomime. Somewhat less freedom necessarily obtains in the narration of dance-poems than in the recital of trifling incident; but within the necessary limits, originality is prized. In the mimetic vocabulary are certain phrases that are depended upon to convey their definite meanings. New word-equivalents, however, are always in order, if they

ARABIAN "DANCE OF MOURNING"
By Zourna

The body approaches (1) — The body passes (2) — "I hold my sorrow to myself" (3)

To face page 200

ARABIAN "Dance of Mourning" (*Continued*)
"He has gone out of the house and up to Heaven" (4) — "Farewell" (5)

can stand the searching test of eyes educated in beauty and minds trained to exact thinking.

Nearly unlimited as it is in scope, delightful as it unfailingly is to those who know it, Arabic dancing suits occasions of a variety of which the dances of Europe never dreamed. In the café it diverts and sometimes demoralises. In his house the master watches the dancing of his slaves, dreaming under the narcotic spell of rhythm. On those rare occasions when the demands of diplomacy or business compel him to bring a guest into his house, the dancing of slaves is depended upon to entertain. His wives dance before him to please his eye, and to cajole him into conformity with their desires.

Even the news of the day is danced, since the doctrines of Mohammed depress the printing of almost everything except the Koran. Reports of current events reach the male population in the market and the café. At home men talk little of outside affairs, and women do not get out except to visit others of their kind, as isolated from the world as themselves. But they get all the news that is likely to interest them, none the less; at least the happenings in the world of Mohammedanism.

As venders of information of passing events, there are women that wander in pairs from city to city, from harem to harem, like bards of the early North. As women they are admitted to women's apartments. There, while one rhythmically pantomimes deeds of war to the cloistered ones that never saw a soldier, or graphically imitates the punishment of a malefactor in the market-place, her companion chants, with falsetto whines, a descriptive and rhythmic accompaniment.

Thus is the harem protected against the risk of narrowness.

In the daily life of the harem, dancing is one of the favoured pastimes. Women dance to amuse themselves and to entertain one another. In the dance, as in music and embroidery, there is endless interest, and a spirit of emulation usually friendly.

One of the comparatively formalised mimetic expressions is the *Dance of Greeting,* the function of which is to honour a guest when occasion brings him into the house. Let it be imagined that coffee and cigarettes have been served to two grave gentlemen; that one has expressed bewilderment at the magnificence of the establishment, and his opinion that too great honour has been done him in permitting him to enter it; that the host has duly made reply that his grandchildren will tell with pride of the day when this poor house was so far honoured that such a one set his foot within it. After which a sherbet, more coffee and cigarettes. When the time seems propitious, the host suggests to the guest that if in his great kindness he will look at her, he—the host—would like permission to order a slave to try to entertain with a dance.

The musicians, squatting against the wall, begin the wailing of the flute, the hypnotic throb of "darabukkeh." She who is designated to dance the *Greeting* enters holding before her a long scarf that half conceals her; the expression on her face is surprise, as though honour had fallen to her beyond her merits or expectation. Upon reaching her place she extends her arms forward, then slowly moves them, and with them the scarf, to one side, until she is revealed. When a nod confirms the command to dance, she quickly drops the scarf to the

ARABIAN "DANCE OF MOURNING" (*Continued*)

"He slept in my arms" (6) — "The house is empty" (7) — "Woe is in my heart" (8)

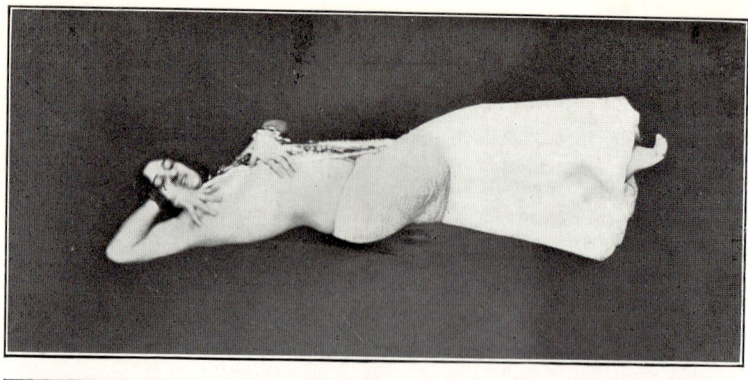

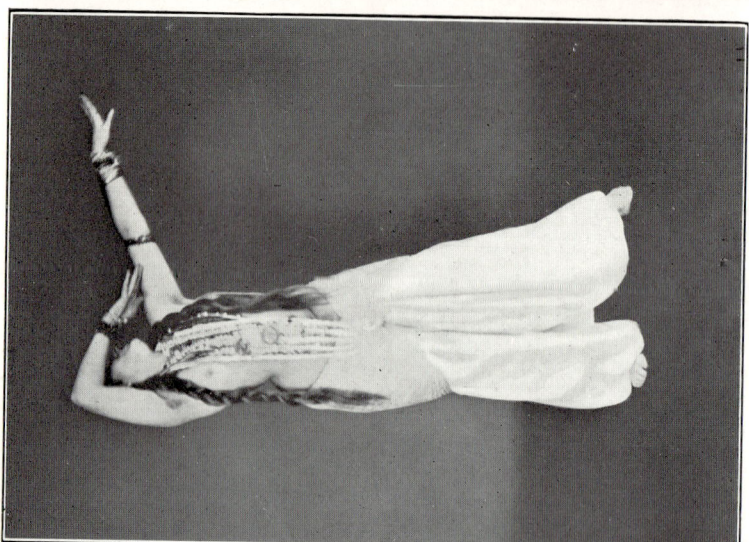

Arab Slave Girl's Dance
By Zourna
A non-narrative dance, for the exhibition of personal attractions

floor, advances to a place before the guest and near him, and honours him with a slave's salutation. Then arising she proceeds to her silent greeting.

"You are implanted in your house," says a movement [see photographs]. "Here is food, here may you sleep well. When you go forth, go you East, West, North, South [indicating quarter-circles by pointing the toe], yet you are here. May Allah's blessings descend upon you. May the breezes blow upon you, may the rain refresh you, may abundance be showered upon you; yet may you remember that here you are in your house, and that here is your slave."

That is the lifeless skeleton of the story, without grace, or the animation of movement, or the embellishment of expression. To try to force words into an equivalent of the semi-ritualistic splendour of the dance would be attempting to build a Moorish palace of dry grains of sand.

In Occidental entertainment, when a performer has gained the sanctuary of the platform, he is practically immune from interruption until his "number" is finished—unless exception be made of "amateur night" in vaudeville houses, where offenders are forcibly removed with a hook, or suddenly enveloped in darkness. With that probably unique exception, however, the audience confronted by an indifferent performer can only summon patience. The Orient offers no such security, to the dancer at least. At the first sign of failure to interest, a signal, perhaps no more noticeable than the raise of an eyelid, commands the dancer to cease. Not later, but instantly.

To interrupt a dance of movement without regard to its argument would be worse than interrupting a story.

It would not only undo the preceding work; it would be very likely to arrest the artist in a transitional position, in itself weak. At all events, such an interruption would painfully mar an entertainment programme. But the Arabian dance is not a dance of movement; it is a dance of pictures, to which movement is wholly subordinate. Each bar of the music accompanies a picture complete in itself. Within the measure of each bar the dancer has time for the movements leading from one picture to the next, and to hold the picture for the instant necessary to give emphasis. At whatever moment she may be stopped, therefore, she is within less than a second of a pose so balanced and sculptural that it appears as a natural termination of the dance. The Oriental's general indifference to the forces of accumulation and climax are consistent with such a capricious ending. In his dance, each phrase is complete in itself; it may be likened to one of those serial stories in our magazines, in which each instalment of the story is self-sufficient.

To the Occidental unused to Oriental art, the absence of crescendo and climax, and the substituted iteration carried on endlessly, is uninteresting. Nevertheless, a few days of life among Oriental conditions suffice to throw many a scoffer into attunement with the Oriental art idea. Which is to soothe, not to stimulate. Moorish ornament is an indefinitely repeated series of marvellously designed units, each complete in itself, yet inextricably interwoven with its neighbours. In music the beats continue unchanging through bar after bar, phrase after phrase. The rhythmic repetition of the tile-designs on the wall, the decorative repetition of the beats of music, produce a spell of dreamy visioning comparable only to the effect of some potent but harmless narcotic.

To the foregoing generality exception must again be made of the dancing in cafés. While it conforms to the structure of a picture-complete-in-each-bar, its treatment is more or less at variance with the idea of soothing. But the symbolism is likely to lack nothing of picturesqueness. The *Handkerchief Dance* is characteristic of the type.

Of the two handkerchiefs used in this dance one represents the girl herself, the other her soon-to-be-selected lover. She first takes a corner of each handkerchief into her teeth, warming them into life. She lays them parallel on the floor and indifferently dances around and between them, to state her power to cross the line and return free from entanglements of lover's claims. Into the waistband of her trousers she tucks opposite corners of both handkerchiefs so that they hang as panniers: the hands pushed through show the panniers empty; she would receive gifts. To show, too, that she can give, a flourishing gesture releases a corner of each, to spill the imagined contents. Interest progresses until as a climax she kisses one of the fluttering cloths, slowly passes it downward over heart and body, and throws it in a wad to the elected one. The token is his passport to her; and its return at any later time is announcement that she no longer interests him.

One dance the Arabs have that is not associated with the idea of symbolism, but is rather a vehicle for the display of technical skill for skill's own sake. It is the *Flour Dance*. On the floor a design is drawn in an even layer of flour—a favourite figure is the square imposed on a circle, familiar in Saracenic ornament. The dancer's first journey over the figure establishes a series of footprints; a successful performance consists in planting the feet in the same tracks during subsequent rounds. Difficulties can be added by crossings of the feet, turns and other involutions, and multiplied by increasing speed. This dance was mentioned in connection with the ancient Greek *Dance of the Spilled Meal,* of which it may reasonably be supposed to be either a direct descendant or a surviving ancestor.

There are a number of little dances popular in light entertainment. In one, a woman in the act of eavesdropping is startled by a lizard dropping on her back. Her efforts to get rid of it attract her husband from his [imagined] conversation on the other side of the curtain. She must now explain why she was standing at the curtain, and above all she must appear calm. The comedy opportunity lies in her efforts not to squirm away from the [imagined] lizard.

Another of these one-character sketches tells of the lazy washerwoman. She enters steadying on her head an imaginary basket of linen. Arriving at the edge of the stream she puts down the basket, kneels, and indolently begins mauling and scrubbing the garments over the half-submerged rocks. (And she turns the move- ments into poetry!) But her attention wanders from uncongenial work. Whose hasn't? one sympathetically asks oneself as one watches. She looks up the stream, and down; her eye sees beauties, and her mind finds subjects to wonder about. She falls a-dreaming, and then asleep—still kneeling.

When she wakens, the other women have finished their work and gone, and it is late. Not stopping to wring out the clothes that she hurriedly collects from the

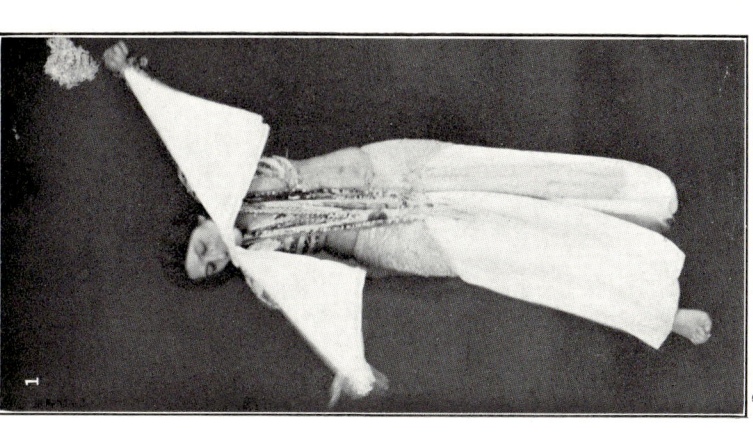

"Handkerchief Dance" of the Cafés
By Zourna

The handkerchiefs symbolizing the lovers are animated with the breath of life, but kept dissociated (1) — Brought into semi-associaton (2) — Separated and dropped (3)

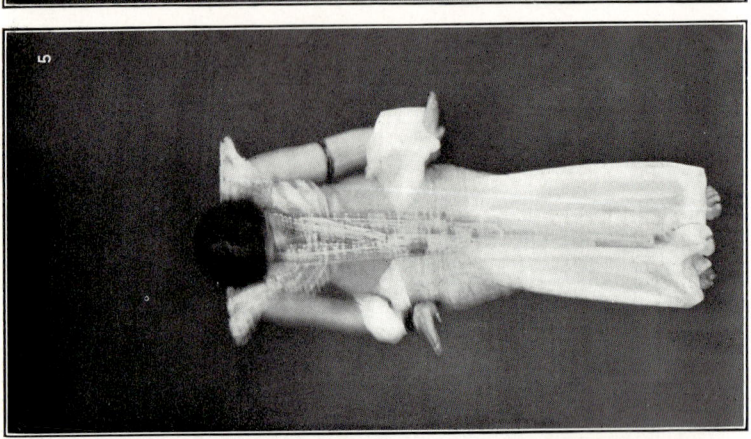

"Handkerchief Dance" (*Continued*)

She can dance about, between or away from them, indifferently (4) — Made into panniers, the panniers express her willingness to receive, turned inside out, her willingness to give (5) — One of the two handkerchiefs is thrown to the selected lover (6)

pool, she throws them into the basket. Humour is put into the artist's mimicry of the poor woman's efforts to avoid the dripping water, while carrying the weight of a basket of wet clothes balanced on her head. Embodying as it does both dream-sentiment and comedy, the little pantomime is a pretty vehicle for versatility.

A serious story is that of the Mohammedan woman who, against her father's wishes, has married a Jew. The representation opens with the woman's entrance to the room where her father lies dying. Her hair falls loose in token of mourning or penitence. She kneels beside the death-bed, and strips off her many jewels. Her vow to re-enter the fold of Islam she shows by drawing a strand of her hair across her mouth, suggesting the face-covering of the women of Mohammedan faith. The father offers his hand to be kissed. Grateful, she slowly rises, crosses the room, closes and bolts the door, in token of shutting out all but the paternal faith.

The dance of mourning for the dead is a fixed composition only to the extent of including certain accepted postures; their sequence is not prescribed. "Here he lies dead; Allah takes him. I am as a fallen tree; I am alone. He held me in his arms; we played together; and he was my protector." In such manner runs the widow's lament for her departed husband. Pulsing through all is the solemn beat of "darabukkeh" undertoning the wails of mourners.

The Bedoui of the desert celebrate marriage, peace-compacts, declarations of war and other happy occasions with a gun-dance, which is known as a *Fantasia* or *Fantaisie*. It in no way conforms to the fundamentals of Arabic dancing, and in fact it is a dance in name only. But it is joyous exceedingly. Approximately rhythmic rifle-firing is continuous from beginning to end. Performers both mounted and afoot leap and whirl in maniac confusion, shooting up, down and all around in merry abandon. Dust, howls and powder-smoke attack ears, eyes and throat in unison, and the only unhappy ones in the gay assemblage are those that Allah wills to have been shot, stepped on by horses, or both.

Tangier is the setting of an occasional savage celebration of religious fanaticism; and these celebrations, too, fall into a category of quasi-dancing. They are demonstrations of a sect styled the Hamadsha. To a deafening accompaniment of fifes and drums, a few leaders start a crude hopping dance in the market-place. The number of participants grows rapidly; excitement increases with the number, until, at a point of frenzy, the leaping fanatics begin hacking their heads with axes. The example is so contagious that small boys dash into the mêlée and snatch axes from the hands of men, to inflict the same castigation. Christian spectators frequently faint at the spectacle, but fascination holds them at their windows until they are overcome. During the four hours or more that the blood-spilling continues, as well as during a period before and after, the street is a dangerous place for the unbeliever.

Ostrander, the traveller, while in Constantinople, found himself unaccountably in the midst of a celebration differing in character from those of the Hamadsha of Tangier only in the respect of being held at night. The resemblance in all essentials indicates the existence of Mohammedan undercurrents completely unknown to the Western world.

Egypt, notwithstanding centuries of Arab domination, preserves—or re-creates—in her dancing the style shown in the carvings of the Pharaoh dynasties. In contrast to the softly curving Arab movements, the Egyptian's definitely incline to straight lines. Gestures change their direction in angles, rather than curves. Poses of perfect symmetry are sought. Even when symmetry is absent, the serpentine, plastic character of Arab movement is pertinently avoided. The sentiment of architecture is cultivated; the head is not turned on the shoulders, nor the torso on the hips, except as such relaxation is required in the interest of pantomime. In movement and position the Egyptian seeks verticals, horizontals and right angles. To the beauty of the work the severely geometrical treatment adds an architectural quality almost startling in its surety and majesty.

Egyptian form "toes out" the artist's feet, so that they are seen without perspective when the performer is facing the spectator.

Whether the dances of the Valley of the Nile established the conventions of early relief carvings, or whether, on the other hand, the carvings determined the character of the dances, is a question neither possible nor necessary to decide. Both arts certainly were the expression of rigid religious ceremonialism, and likely are twins. To-day the records in granite are the subject of conscious study on the part of dancers. In the past, too, they undoubtedly have been chart and compass to the sculpture of ephemeral flesh and blood, that unguided might have perished in any one of the thousands of generations of its existence.

In type of subject and motive the dances of Egypt

resemble those of the Barbary States, as above described. Mourning, homage and incident are narrated in about the same vocabulary, the dissimilarity of technique being comparable to a dialectic difference of pronunciation of a language. On their commercial side the two are identical. In tourist-ridden cafés of Cairo and Port Said, as in those of Tangier and Algiers, girls dance what the tourist expects and wishes. In the Coptic town of Esneh, dwelling in the ruined temples, is a community of people known as Almées. They are literally a tribe of dancers, removed by a khedive in former times from Cairo on grounds of impropriety. Dancing as they do in the temples of five thousand years ago, they form a curious link with antiquity. Their work, however, is said to be shaped to the tourist demand.

Such dances, however, despite the insistence with which they are pushed upon the attention of tourists, are not of the kind with which the name of Egypt deserves to be associated. The mystic still dwells along the shores of the Nile; but its votaries do not commercialise it, nor is it a commodity that lends itself to sale and purchase, even were there a disposition so to degrade it. One of the dances illustrated by Zourna symbolises in terms as delicate as the most ethereal imaginings, the awakening of the soul.

The body's initial lack of the spiritual spark is represented by the crossed hands, as bodies are carved on sepulchres. An imperceptible glide through a series of poses so subtly distinguished from one another that movement, from one moment to the next, is unseen, creates an atmosphere mysterious and almost chill in its twilight gloom. Gropingly the arms rise to the po-

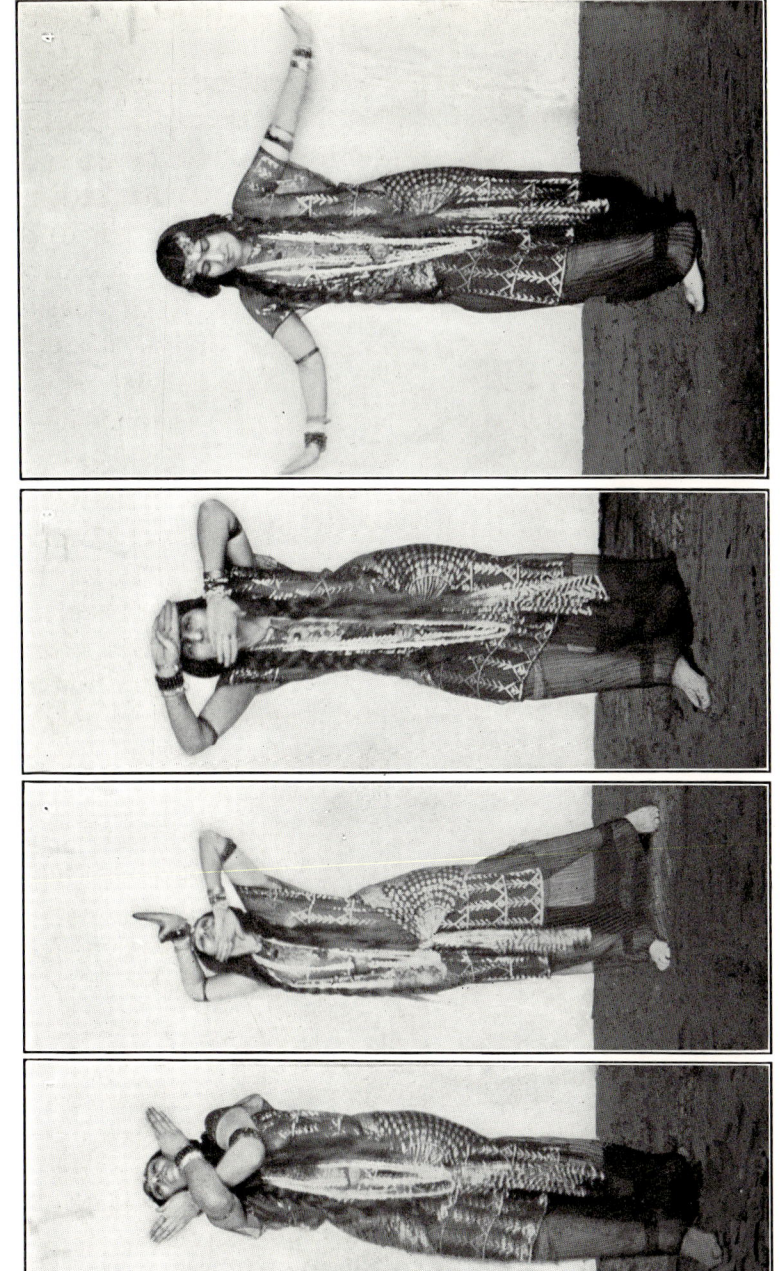

"Dance of the Soul's Journey"
By Zourna

The soulless body (1) — Asks for the light of life (2) — Vision dawns (3) — Inexpert in life, she walks gropingly (4)

"Dance of the Soul's Journey" (*Continued*)
She draws aside the veil of the future (5) — Life is seen full and plenteous (6)

sition that symbolises prayer for the divine light—the hand below the chin emphasising the upturn of the face, the upper hand suggesting the flame. With awe the new intelligence gazes upon the world, open-eyed; then it must draw aside the veil of the future. Fulness of life is seen awaiting, which the dancer expresses by a gesture representing roundness, the accepted Oriental representation of completeness and richness. But wait! she will grow old, and with bent back will walk stumbling at the heels of a camel. But a defiance to age and the future! Now she is young; her body is straight and her limbs round. A defiant expression of the joy of life follows, yet undertoned withal with unforgettable sadness; movements of happiness, a face of tragedy.

The sombre majesty of the pictures, especially those of the search into the future; the reverence-compelling mystery of the somnambulistic movements—a hundred things about this dance raise it to the very uppermost plane of its kind of art. So far beyond mere skill are its movements, so completely alien to anything in Occidental knowledge, that to Occidental eyes they are as unearthly as they are imposing. Reason fails, chloroformed by beauty; the real becomes the unreal, the unreal the real. Imagination is released from the tentacles of fact and time. The future? It could be seen for the trouble of turning the head to look; but what profit foreknowledge either of cuts or caresses? Curiosity is for the very young. Better and wiser the lot of ignorance. . . .

Hypnotism of a kind? Granted. Finely rendered, this dance represents the utmost development of the coordination of rhythm, sentiment, and appropriateness of movement. That combination in its turn is undoubtedly the essence of the Oriental magic that, since the world was young, has enabled men to dream dreams and see visions. Among the newer civilisations the emotional power of rhythm is as unknown as it is untried.

The Egyptian's passion for decoration is served by the dance, no less ably than is his love of the metaphysical. In the homes of the rich there is said to be a form of decorative choreography, like a ballet in structure, that duplicates and animates a painted or sculptured frieze on the walls of the room. The dancers enter one at a time, taking their positions in turn under the figures of the frieze, copying each in pose as they come into place under it. The intervals between poses are of course enriched by carefully related movements, so that the line of dancers, advancing together from figure to figure, shall move as a harmonised unit. The scheme creates a manifold interest: the line of dancers represents an animated version of the frieze; though it is seen to move, its figures remain in a sense unchanged; yet to watch any one performer is to see her change constantly. The human line and the mural frieze collectively form a background for the work of a leading dancer, who flits from place and duplicates the poses of such figures as she may choose.

In another entertainment, descriptions tell of huge vases carried in and placed back of the dancing space, as though they were decorative adjuncts forgotten until the last moment. They are placed, and the servants retire, just before the first dancer opens the programme. A spectator unfamiliar with the diversion would notice that the vases were elaborately ornamented with carved figures. These one by one relax their archaic severity

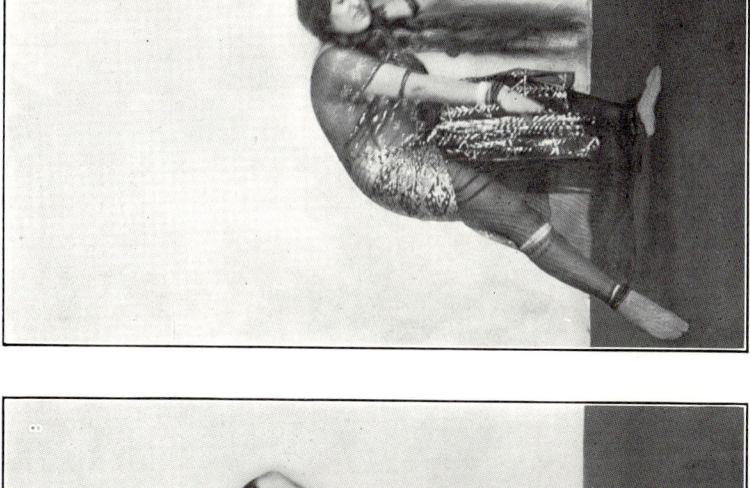

"Dance of the Soul's Journey" (*Continued*)

But old age will come (7) — Grief will visit (8) — She shall walk with her nose close to the camel's foot (9)

To face page 212

"Dance of the Soul's Journey" (*Continued*)

Yet now, from the crown of her head (10) — To the soles of her feet she is perfect (11)

To face page 213

of pose and very slowly come to life. Keeping the colour of the stone and without wholly losing its unbending character, each dances her allotted number and returns to her pose on the vase.

The foregoing is by no means a complete list of Egypt's dances of decorative interest or occult significance. Dance representations of subjects of everyday interest are also popular; there is one that sketches a series of incidents connected with a hunt with a falcon. But, as stated in another place, the choreographic taste of Egypt has many points of similarity with that of the Arabs of all the southern coast of the Mediterranean. Egyptian technique is distinct, its interpretation of the abstract is marvellously developed, its union of the dance with architecture is its own. But its taste in pantomimes of light motive is already characterised without the addition of further examples.

Following Oriental dancing eastward toward India, its probable birthplace, it is found to preserve with approximate consistency certain general characteristics. The combined pantomimic and decorative use of the arms, subject to regional ideas as to what comprises decorative quality, runs through it all. The apparent freedom of chest, abdomen and hips from any restricting inter-relationships, is an attribute of it emphasised in some localities more than others; it decreases toward the north, generally speaking. The women of Turkey compare with those of the Barbary States in phenomenal flexibility and control of the abdominal muscle—resulting in capability for a species of contortion not at all agreeable when exaggerated.

A principle of all Oriental dancing is its frank acknowledgment of avoirdupois. It employs none of the devices by which lightness is achieved, choosing as its aim, rather, the representation of a plastic quality that exploits rather than denies the meatiness of flesh texture. The heel is not often raised high from the ground, and indeed the foot is often planted flat. A mannerism intensely characteristic of the Oriental use of the foot is a trick of quickly changing its direction after it is set on the floor but before the weight of the body is shifted to it; the twist may leave the heel stationary as a pivot, or the ball. The effect is as though the dancer were making a feint to deceive the spectator as to the direction of the next turn, and doubtless such contribution to interest is the intent. It at least adds intricacy, and directs attention to a pretty foot. Of the latter adornment, whether covered with little Turkish slipper with turned-up toe, or bare, possessors are impartially proud.

Mystery of movement in certain parts is a further characteristic distinguishing the Oriental work from anything to be found in the Occident, with the exception of certain tricks of the Spanish Gipsy—tricks which, after all, furnish no exception, since they are Moorish absolutely. The Oriental covers little space in her work. A space large enough to kneel on would admit all that her art requires. She has no leaps to make, nor open leg-movements. Much of the time she has both feet on the floor, is active chiefly in arms and body. Much more of the time her feet are engaged in steps hardly noticeable.

The foregoing observations on Oriental work apply more particularly to the low latitudes than to lands farther removed from the equator. China and Japan have a choreography like that of the Southern regions in some respects; but their custom of bundling the dancer

ORIENTAL DANCING 215

MISCELLANEOUS ORIENTAL NOTES.
Dancing girls of Biskra.
Turkish Sword Dance.
Egyptian bas-relief, Metropolitan Museum, N. Y.
Japanese Dance of War.   Japanese Flower Dance.
The Hula-Hula Dance, Hawaiian Islands.

up in clothes is the cause also of differences so pronounced that they had best be considered as of a different category. Purely as a convenience, therefore, let it be understood that Japanese and Chinese dancing shall be referred to by those names; and that the word Oriental shall be understood to signify the dances of the sinuous-body type, to which pertain those of the Arabs of North Africa and elsewhere, the Persians, Turks and some others.

To the dancing of men, where any is done, generalities as to the style of Oriental dancing fail to fit in many cases. Exceptions are not numerous, however; because, if for no other reason, far the greater part of Oriental dancing is done by women. Of the few exceptions some are dances of religion, others of war.

An intoxicating *Sword Dance* is practiced in Turkey. Like almost everything else that is danced (or sung or acted) its merit of course depends in great degree on the quality of its interpretation. Well done, this Turkish *Sword Dance* shows itself a composition of rare individuality and a fine, wild beauty; for good measure, it is a sword combat of a reality that threatens the spectator with heart failure. The two combatants advance and retreat, accenting the music with clashes of sword on shield; the interest is that of a barbarously beautiful dance as long as they continue to face each other. Notwithstanding rapidity, the chances are against a mishap. But when of a sudden both launch themselves on a series of lightning *rond de jambe pirouettes,* the scimitars sweeping around fast enough to cut a man in two if he should fail to parry, the affair becomes a sporting event, and that of a kind to harrow the nerves.

Turkey also is the place, or one of the places, where

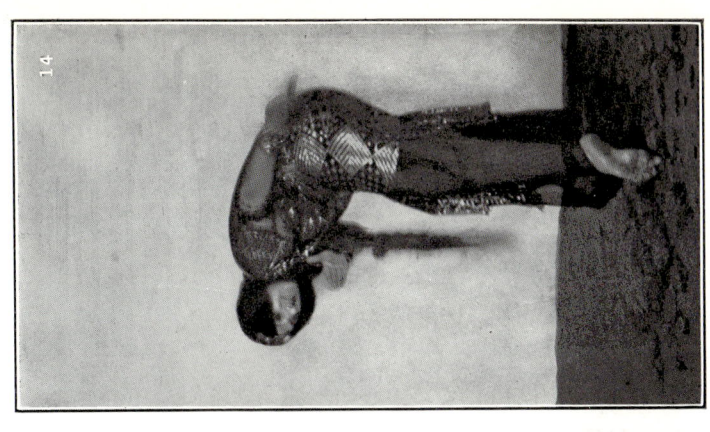

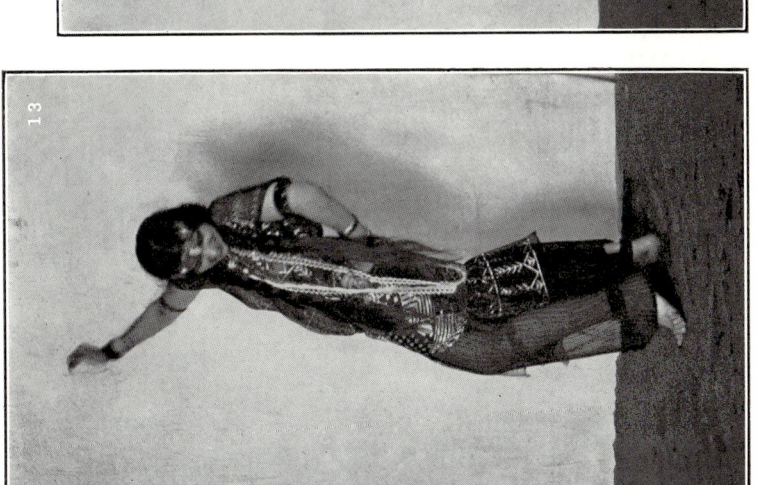

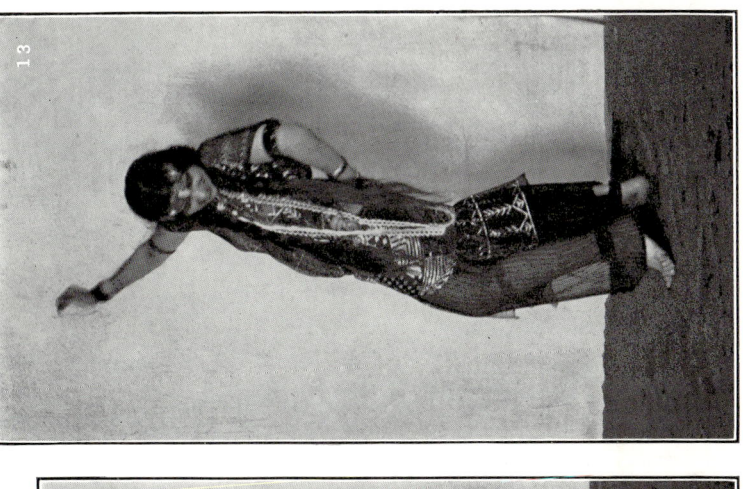

"Dance of the Soul's Journey" (*Continued*)
Rejoices in the perfect body (12) — And in all good things (13) — Runs from the scene (14)

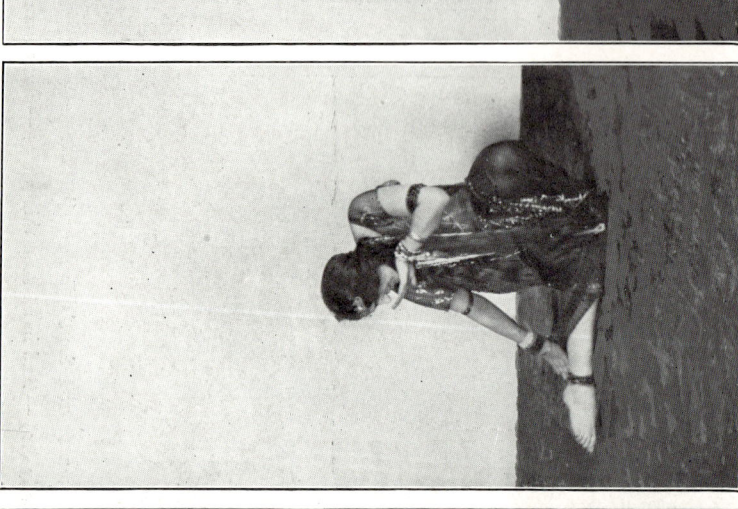

Characteristic Pantomime in Dancing of Modern Egypt
By Zourna

Express sorrow (1, 3) — Represents a prayer directed downward and back; *i.e.*, to spirits of evil (2)

To face page 217

Whirling Dervishes are educated for their curious calling. Mr. H. C. Ostrander is authority for the statement that an apprenticeship of a thousand days is considered a necessary preparation for proper performance of this apparently simple act of devotion. Since nothing whatever is attempted in step beyond that which the ballet-dancers call "Italian turns," it must be supposed that the art of the Whirling Dervish has qualities that do not appear on the surface. It is taught in monasteries scattered through the mountainous regions.

The Caucasus, that land less known than fabled, has dances of a fame as persistent as it is vague. Its map is dotted with names immortalised in the *Arabian Nights.* It is the setting of *Scheherazade* and *Sumurun;* a region whose inhabitants declare their intention never to become Occidentalised, and whom no power is likely to push in any direction. Being under the Czar's dominion, most of its few visitors are Russians; they alone among Occidentals possess any definite knowledge of its choreography. Princess Chirinski-Chichmatoff, at present making it an object of special study, writes the following in reply to an inquiry from the authors:

"*Lezginkà,* the Oriental Dance of the Caucasus, was born in the mountains of a beautiful country whose nature is wild and grandiose; among a people courageous and energetic, who have preserved much of the savagery and temperament of the Oriental races.

"The men of these people . . . have the custom of never parting from the poniard. They pass the greater part of their time horseback, always prepared to meet an enemy and to defend the happiness and honour of the family. To this day they retain the custom of answering for every spilling of blood with a revenge; each victim has his victim. There still exists the custom of abducting the fiancée from the paternal house and carrying her away to one's own. The women have all the timidity of beings who live under the strongest of despotism. They have preserved all the softness and grace of daughters of the Orient, with body accustomed to careful attention and not to any physical work; who seek only to rest, to look at themselves, and to enjoy the gifts by which they are favoured by nature and usage. Under this exterior the woman keeps covered many passions which sleep until the first moment of provocation, when they break forth like the eruption of a volcano—surrounding her with fire that sweeps with it any imprudent one that happens to be near. Passion is the principal theme in the life of an Oriental woman, and that sentiment she can vary like a virtuoso. . . .

"You see her quiet, beautiful, relaxed, in the calm of a great fatigue, with softness enveloping face and movements. Suddenly one detects an unusual sound, a look cast, a movement—she is fired, she becomes fierce and wild like all the Nature around her. You see before you a tigress, beautiful, live and strong, ready to spring on the prey, playing and attracting, making mischief and exhausting herself at the same time. After which her movements become few, slow, tired and melancholy.

"Thus is Oriental dancing built on contrasts; sentiments and moods change unexpectedly. Gentle, relaxed and melancholy, of a sudden it is brusque, animated, fiery. It has much coquetry, passion, and often tragedy."

In India dancing is sharply divided into the classes of sacred and profane. In the latter division are to be

FROM THE DANCES OF THE FALCON
By Zourna

Shock as the bird strikes his quarry (1) — Rejoicing as he overcomes it (2)

DANCING GIRLS OF ALGIERS

To face page 219

RELIEFS ON TOWER OF THE TEMPLE OF MADURA (INDIA).

found dances of ceremony, pantomimic representations of wide variety, and eccentricities that almost trespass on the domain of sleight-of-hand. The best known is a *Dance of Eggs*. The performer, as she starts whirling, takes eggs one by one from a basket that she carries, and sets them into slip-nooses at the several ends of cords that hang from her belt. Centrifugal motion pulls each cord taut as soon as it receives the weight of an egg. Finally all the cords, numbering from a dozen to twenty, are extended, each bearing its insecurely fastened egg. The dance is completed by collecting the eggs and returning them unbroken to the basket.

Another diversion is the *Cobra Dance* popularised in America by Miss Ruth St. Denis—assisted by numerous imitators. One hand is held in a shape to suggest the form of a cobra's head, and huge jewels add a striking resemblance to the creature's eyes. The performer of the cobra representation sits cross-legged. The hand suggesting the snake's head glides over the body, with frequent sudden pauses to reconnoitre; the arm following it—in the case of Miss St. Denis so amazingly supple and so skilfully made to seem jointless that it suggests the snake's body almost to reality—takes the appropriate sinuous movements around shoulders and neck. The free hand completes that which at times is almost an illusion by stroking and semi-guiding the head. Miss St. Denis herself watches the hand with just the alertness and caution to convey an impression of latent danger of which she, the snake charmer, is not afraid, but which she must anticipate with keen attention. Withal she never for an instant slips from her high key of grace, rhythm and style.

It is to Miss St. Denis that America and western

PERSIAN DANCE, PRINCESS CHIRINSKI–CHICHMATOFF

REPRESENTATIVE ORIENTAL POSES
Miss Ruth St. Denis

Votive offering (3 poses) — Decorative motives (3 poses) — Disclosure of person (1 pose)

To face page 22

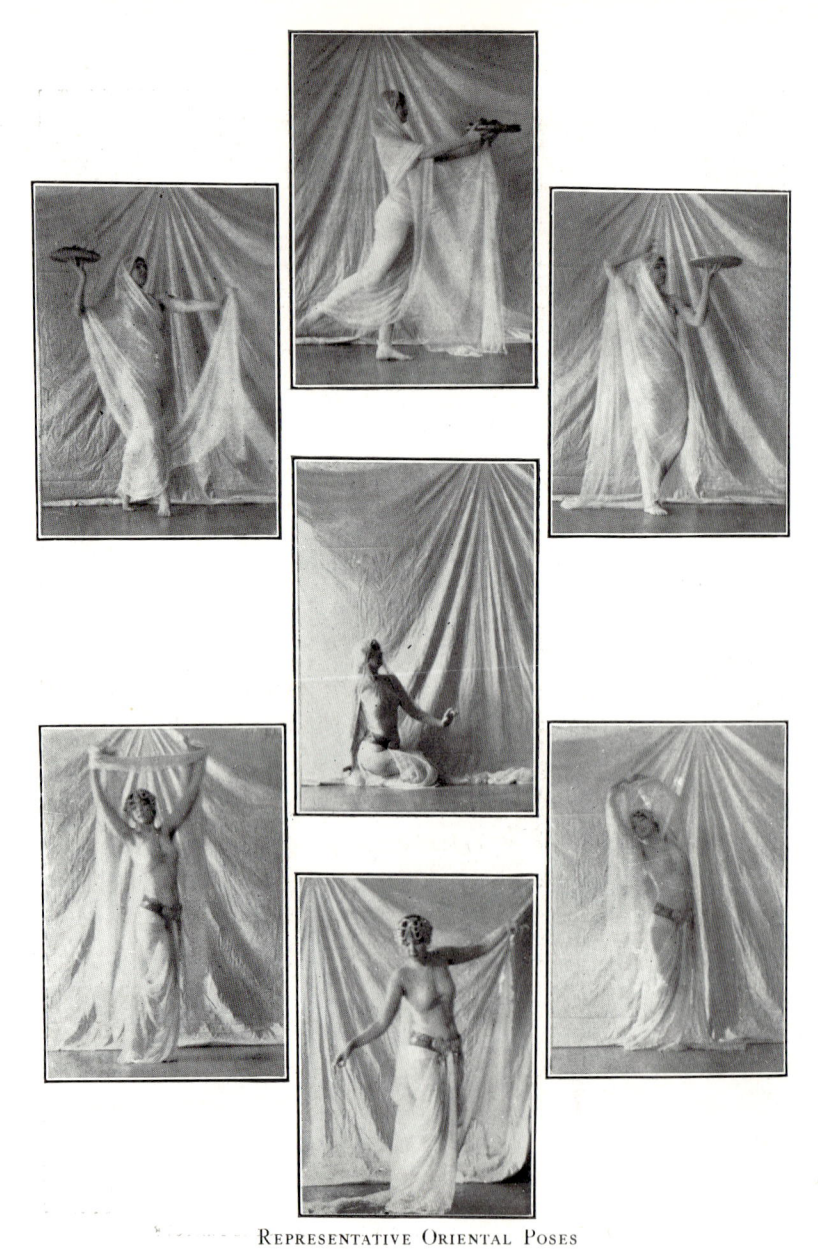

Europe owe the greater part of their impressions of the dancing of the Far East. She has given the subject years of study; with the object, far more comprehensive than an imitation or reproduction of specific dances, of interpreting the Oriental spirit. To this end Miss St. Denis uses the structural facts of the various dances as a basis for an embodiment of their character in such form that it shall be comprehensible to Western eyes and among Western surroundings. The loss inseparable from the adaptation of such a creation to the conventions of the stage, she compensates—perhaps more than compensates—by a concerted use of lights, colour and music, co-operating to produce a sense of dreamy wonder, and to unite in the expression of a certain significance.

Her *Nautch Dance,* with its whirling fountain of golden tissue, she sets in the palace of a rajah, where it serves a social purpose similar to that of the *Dance of Greeting* already described. The *Spirit of Incense* is an interpretation of the contemplative spirit that accompanies Buddhistic thought and worship. *The Temple*—with which Miss St. Denis remains an inseparable part, in the mind of every one who has seen it—throws the spectator into an attitude of something like awe at the rise of the curtain, so perfectly considered is an indefinable relationship of magnificence and semi-gloom in the setting. An idol occupies a shrine in the centre of the stage. After a stately ritual executed by priests, the idol (Radha) descends and performs a *Dance of the Five Senses,* glorifying physical enjoyment. Interwoven with increasing manifestations of pleasure in the senses is a counter-expression of increasing despair. The opposed sentiments reach their climaxes simultaneously. Radha resumes her shrine, and the attitude of endless contemplation, in token that peace of spirit lies only in denial of sensual claims.

The technical character with which Miss St. Denis invests the Indian representations is, first, the elimination of any movement that might detract from a feeling of continuity. Every action proceeds in waves; a ripple slowly undulates down the body, and even seems to continue on its way into the earth; like a wave running the length of a cord, a ripple glides from body through the extended arms and fingers, to go on indefinitely through the air. Rapid movements are employed only enough to meet the demands of variety. Long gesture, long line, deliberate action and even colour quality are held in an indescribable rapport with the insistent tempo with which the whole is bound together; there is no escape from acceptance of the resultant multiple rhythm; it is inevitable. A simple, rapid movement, therefore, introduced with due consideration of all the parts of the complex, magic mechanism, has the dramatic power literally to startle.

The success of the composition as a whole, in its purpose of conveying an impression of the very essence of an aspect of India, is asserted most emphatically by those to whom that mysterious land is best known. To regard the production as an exposition of Indian dancing would be quite beside the point. The dances, though wholly consistent with their originals in point of character, are only a part of a whole. Nor do they pretend to exploit the complete range of Indian choreography; Miss St. Denis herself would be the first to disclaim any such intention. As she explains her work, she uses the dancing of a people as a basis on which to

JAVANESE DANCER, MODERN

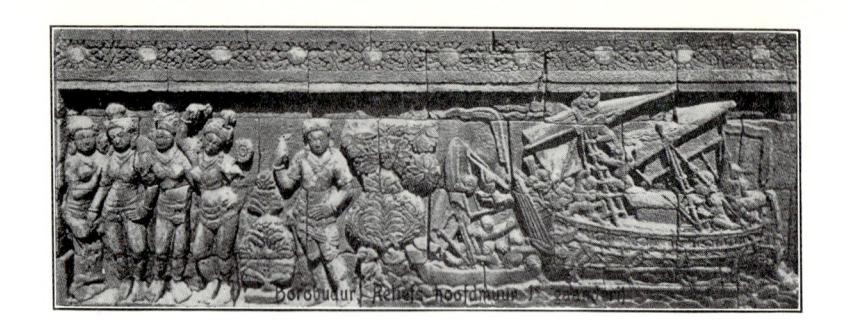

Relief Carvings, Temple of Borobodul, Java
Dance of Greeting [?] (1) — Dance of Worship (2) — An Arrow Dance (3)

To face page 223

ORIENTAL DANCING

compose a translation of that people's point of view and habit of thought.

To exactly the same process Bizet subjected the music of Spain to produce the score of *Carmen;* Le Sage to construct *Gil Blas.* Than the latter there is nothing in Spain that could more quickly acquaint a foreigner with certain aspects of "Españolism."

A link with antiquity is furnished by multitudinous carvings of dancers on Hindu and Buddhistic temples in India and Java. The temple in Java, some of whose sculpture is here reproduced, was recently rediscovered after several centuries of burial in a jungle. It is known to be at least eight hundred years old. A comparison between the style of the dancers there represented, that of the little Javanese present-day dancer shown in a photograph, and that which is indicated in line drawings (from photographs of temples in India) hints at indefinite age back of Oriental dancing as we know it, as to style, technique and spirit. The photographs, including those from which the line drawings were made, are from the collection of Mr. H. C. Ostrander.

With variations, the India type of movement and pantomime, with the practice of striking a significant pose at regular intervals, continues eastward as far as the Hawaiian Islands. The *Hula-Hula* of the graceful Hawaiians has been well exemplified recently in an interpolation in *The Bird of Paradise.* Essentially, the *Hula-Hula* is a dance of coquetry; its thematic position, which recurs like a refrain, is that shown in one of the accompanying drawings.

Any effort to trace the path of Oriental dancing farther east than the Hawaiian Islands leads to the shoals of unsubstantial speculation. Aztec ruins are said (on authority not vouched for) to bear carvings that show the early existence of the India type of dancing in Mexico. There are said to be traces of India influences in the dancing of Mexican Indians of to-day. But the interest of such fact—even if it is a fact—is more closely related to ethnology than choreography; because it is pretty certain that any trace of India dancing that may exist will be an almost unrecognisable corruption. The study of dances on grounds of oddity, ethnological curiosity or legendary association leads away from the study of dancing for its own sake, and that of its inherent beauty. It is in the endeavour to keep within the lines of reasonably pure choreography that this book has been restrained from digressions into the quasi-dancing of American Indians, African negroes, various South Sea Islanders and many other interesting folk.

Dancing has an immense importance in religious worship of most of the many denominations of India. Priestesses are trained to it; *corps de ballet* into which they are organised are maintained in the temples under a system like that of ancient Egypt. Their rites are unknown—or practically so—to those outside of their own faith. In other cults the rites are performed, in part, by laymen. The latter ceremonies include a not-to-be-described orgy periodically celebrated in certain Hindu temples, by women, with the motives of propitiating Vishnu.

China has a school of rhythmic pantomime, the movement of which hardly justifies its consideration as a branch of real dancing—so far as known to the authors. An annual religious spectacle is to be noted: in it are employed animals' heads, recalling the *Snake Dance* of the Hopi Indians.

Japan, by means of sundry additions to the older Chinese school of mimetic posturing, has converted it into an organism to which the name of dancing is quite appropriate, and which constitutes by far the greater portion of her national choreography.

It appears that the dances of occasional merry-makers, priestesses, and the much-misunderstood Geishas have a common characteristic of slow, even movement, small steps, and a highly abstract pantomime. Of a style distinct from these are certain dances of men, including a stirring dance of warriors; in which group is seen vigourous action, a good proportion of open movement, and genuine steps. The accepted classification of the Japanese, as *Nô,* or sacred dancing, and profane, doubtless has its merits; but the division previously indicated, distinguishing between dances of posture and those of movement, which is the one established by the eye, is at least convenient.

With choral posture and gesture the Japanese celebrate auspicious conditions of nature or happy events in the family. The coming of spring; the cherry blossoms; the season of fishing with cormorants; flowers in general; rice-harvest—in honour of a thousand occurrences may be imagined groups of gaily coloured kimonos enveloping little figures, softly and rhythmically swaying over the green, from each kimono protruding a fan or a bouquet held in a cloth-enshrouded hand. In the tea-house the Geisha (who is a skilled professional entertainer, no more and no less) pantomimes, in delicate symbol, the falling of the petals of flowers, the hearing of distant music—any motive is suitable, apparently, so long as it is pretty, dainty, fanciful. Movement conforms to the same manner of thinking; much of it barely disturbs the silken folds of the kimono. A thousand meanings are hidden in little turns and twists of the fan; but, when explained, the connection of act and meaning is often so tenuous that it seems less mysterious, or suggestive, than merely vague. Nevertheless, taking it on its own premise as a demonstration of Japanese-doll prettiness, which is not concerned with any but the lightest emotions, this type of dancing is pleasing. Its virtue is its gossamer frailty.

The dances of war fall into a distinct class. Some of the drawings of Hokkai represent them: combats between swordsmen, or between a swordsman and a spearman. The dances themselves are charged with a vigourous spirit and executed with big, noble movement of flourished weapons. The poses follow the indefinable angularity which, through the very consistency of its use, is an agreeable element in the more virile school of Japanese drawing; and the spicy effect of sharpness so produced combines to admiration with the crab-like design of old Japanese armour.

Other men's dances, equally vigourous, are recorded in drawings. But any exact study of these or any other dances of Japan is almost hopelessly handicapped by a scarcity of individuals who possess the desirable combination of definite knowledge and personal reliability.

The Japanese theatrical dancing, so called, leads into a labyrinth of pantomime both subtle and involved, and movement so slight that a troop of dancers can continue in action four consecutive hours, without relays. That is almost too much for real dancing, under existing hu-

"Nautch Dance"
Miss Ruth St. Denis

JAPANESE DANCE
Miss Ruth St. Denis

To face page 227

man limitations of heart and muscle. The ballet dancer is entitled to a rest after a solo of four minutes; to the ballet, therefore, it would be well to return, for the certainty that the discussion is safe again on the solid ground of reality.

CHAPTER X

THE BALLET IN ITS DARK AGE

WHEN a plant has passed a climax of luxuriant blossoming, a heedless owner is likely to leave it to the mercies of weather and worms, while he turns his interest to other plants whose season of bloom is just beginning.

Taglioni and Ellsler faded about the middle of the nineteenth century. Cerito, Grahn and Grisi were, at best, unable to surpass them. Jenny Lind set people talking about singers, and spending their time listening to songs. Dancers, desperately straining to recatch the lost interest, multiplied *entrechats* and *pirouettes,* jumped higher and more bravely than ever. Straining for technical feats, they forgot motive; the public called the ballet meaningless, its work a stupid form of acrobatics, its smile a grimace. A genius could have made such words seem the words of fools; in the default of a genius, the words were accepted as of more or less true judgment.

The years that followed produced a certain amount of dancing that was good, notably some of the operatic ballets of Europe, and a few ballet spectacles of the seventies and eighties; more that could not exactly be called bad; and, lastly and principally, a series of monstrosities that were nearly infinite in both number and ugliness.

In trying to find something that would suit the new

BALLET IN ITS DARK AGE

and unsettled state of the public taste, managers apparently tried any concoction that could be devised by stage, paint-bridge, property room or box-office. Montmartre dance-halls evolved the *Can-can;* half of Paris caught its fever; England, and thence America, were engulfed in the lingerie of high kickers. Not dancers, just high kickers.

"One, two, three, KICK!" was their vocabulary—or is, for they are not all dead yet.

In England several managers at various times offered good productions, with casts of capable artists. Of such productions the most fortunate made small profits; the majority lost whatever money was put into them. Managers said the public did not want good work—a deduction apparently justifiable. They devised the elaborate scenic production—Aladdin's-cave sort of thing, with millions of jewels the size of roc's eggs, delirious with yards and furlongs of red, yellow and green foil-paper, acres of chrome-yellow, and "magic transformation scenes"; with one hundred people on the stage, one hundred, obviously making two hundred legs, every one of which was considered thrilling and dangerous in those days. Of all those legs displayed in all their amplitude, usually not one pair could dance a step; but they did not need to dance.

That was the form of art called the extravaganza. It was a naughty thing to patronise. Its inanities, without its "stupendous" cost of production, survive in the present-day burlesque.

In the morbid conditions of Montmartre there came into favour a species of acrobats whose aim was to produce the illusion that their legs and spines were out of joint, if not broken. Although of an ugliness demoniac, their work was called dancing. "Wiry Sal" in England and "Ruth the Twister" in America were the illuminating pseudonyms associated with the specialty. Perhaps a specimen of the kind might still be unearthed in a dime museum.

Enter Lottie Collins, she of "ta-ra-ra-boom-de-ay." To high kicking and contortion, and the *Skirt Dance* vogue of the moment, she added action so violent that it seemed a menace to life itself. The combination of attractions was irresistible; Europe and America made her rich. Her master-stroke was bending back until her body was horizontal, and violently straightening up to emphasise the "boom" of her song. For no less than a dancer she was a singer! The two talents were employed together. And hordes of little plagiarists of her act, as of every other "hit," brought delight to the many and despair to the few.

Lottie Collinsism left no territory to be explored in its direction. So an eager world turned to the inanity of sweetness.

The dear little girl had been discovered. Evil among days! Preferably she was dimpled. She wore a blond wig with curls falling artlessly over her shoulders. Her eyebrows were painted in a smoothly curved arch extending around on to the sides of her face, and her eyes were shaded with the luxuriant lashes begot of heavy "beading"; they, too, were carried out an indefinite distance to the sides. She dressed as a child of twelve, with a sash that conveyed the idea of being dressed for Sunday-school; imagination always supplied a cent gripped in her fist. She wore "cunning" little low-heeled shoes, with straps. It was not amiss that she have some sort of sunbonnet, of lace, slipped carelessly off her flaxen head and hanging down her back. Rouge, with a bloom of rice powder, gave her a perfect peaches-and-cream complexion. Grease paint widened and shortened her lips, curved them into an infantile cupid's bow. And from that cupid's bow emerged, in piercing calliope tones, inflectionless recitals of her devotion to her dear old mother. At the end of each stanza she had a little dance—usually a slow polka-step, *one, two, three* and *kick!* (An irreproachably discreet little kick, to the side.) Repeat four times each side, and on to the next stanza—which instead of "mother" and "other," will avail itself of the felicitous rhyme of "roam" and "home," or "heart" and "part."

Lest the enumeration of the foregoing horrors should be criticised as out of place in a discussion of dancing, be it recorded at this point that the said horrors went under the name of dancing within easy remembrance of people now living, that there are still people living who call them dancing, and—for artistic sins of the world as yet unexpiated—they still influence the dancing situation in these United States.

The Black Crook is a name that stands for superlatives. It was the most lavish spectacle America ever had seen. It made such a "hit" as rarely has been duplicated since. Its dancing features, which were of the first order, made more of an impression than had any dancing in this country since Ellsler's tour, in 1840, '41 and '42. Its origin was in part due to the sometimes favourable factor of accident.

"In consequence of the destruction by fire of the Academy of Music, this city," writes J. Allston Brown in his *History of the New York Stage,* "Jarrett and

Palmer, who were to have produced *La Biche au Bois* there, had on their hands a number of artists brought from Europe. They made an arrangement with William Wheatley to utilise the ballet troupe, the chief scenic effects, of which they had models, and the transformation scene." From those beginnings grew *The Black Crook*. With Marie Bonfanti, Rita Sangalli, Betty Rigl and Rose Delval as principal dancers, it opened at Niblo's Garden in September, 1866. The run closed in January, 1868, after 475 performances. A return to Niblo's in December, 1870, yielded 122 performances. December of the following year added 57 to the score. A revival in August, 1872, brought into the company the Kiralfy family, dancers, among whom were the brothers destined to fame as managers and producers. This 1872 revival ran twelve weeks. In 1874, Kiralfy Brothers appear as lessees of the Grand Opera House. They initiated their term with *The Black Crook*, with Bonfanti as *première*.

Of American appreciation of good dancing pantomime, during that period, at least, there is no question. It must be borne in mind that the New York performances above mentioned represent only a fraction of the production's total business. The tours that largely occupied the intervals met the same success. The box-office measure of public enthusiasm is incomplete, moreover, without mention of *Humpty Dumpty,* also a spectacular pantomime with good dancing. Of its first run (in New York, and largely coinciding with the first run of *The Black Crook* in point of time) the gross receipts were $1,406,000. It was commensurately profitable as a "road" attraction. Pertinent to the quality of its dancing, we have a few words of its manager, Clifton W. Tayleure, as quoted by Brown: ". . . principal dancers were not easily to be found. A quarrel between Vestvalli and Sangalli enabled me to secure the latter. Betty and Emily Rigl, who had previously seceded from Niblo's, were also secured."

Notwithstanding desertions, *The Black Crook* maintained its high standards. Its ballet has never since been equalled in America, according to Mme. Bonfanti, in the classic style of work.

For its managers, at least, dancing had earned fortunes. To the Kiralfys it was evident, too, that the kind of dancing America wanted was good dancing. To produce their *Excelsior* in 1882 they brought from Paris Sr. Ettore Coppini, now ballet-master of the Metropolitan Opera; and George Saracco, now ballet-master of the Brussels Opera, as a leading dancer. Nor did Jarrett and Palmer modify their faith in quality. Their *White Fawn,* with an excellent ballet, was little less successful than *The Black Crook*.

The fame of such works is food for parasites; creatures incapable of discerning the quality of successful works, and upon whom the goodness of the successful dancing had made no impression. *Black Crook* and *White Fawn* companies overran the country like a flood of counterfeit money—one part fine, ninety-nine parts base. Plausible advertising protected the deception, but only for a time. It was not long before lovers of good dancing began to realise that they were being defrauded.

In a similar contingency, the supporting public of a baseball club loses no time in applying to that club's manager whatever pressure may be necessary as a means to correcting shortcomings, as far as within him lies. The source of their ability to do this is twofold:

they can analyse the game, and they have a vocabulary in which to express themselves. Baseball had not so many enthusiasts in those days as dancing had. But the appreciators of dancing lacked analytical knowledge of the art, and the language in which to discuss it. Promoters of counterfeits were not taken to task, therefore, as would have been to their own good. Instead, the names of *Black Crook, White Fawn,* dancing and pantomime became synonyms for theatrical imposition, and America laid aside interest in them and all their appurtenances.

Of all the consequences of the above incidents, perhaps the most unfortunate was a generally accepted managerial deduction that America does not like dancing after all. Though the Russian ballet has shaken that belief, the belief is not dead yet.

There is a saying that no man is indispensable; that, after his removal, there is always another to take his place. The saying is not true.

Pantomime—not dancing to be sure, but so closely related to it that the prosperity of either usually means that of both—at one time had the alliance of Augustin Daly. He believed in it as a great art, and contemplated increasingly ambitious productions. To those closely associated with him he declared himself willing to lose money on it for three years, and more if necessary; he was confident that eventually it would attain to great popularity in this country. But after producing *L'Enfant Prodigue* and *Pygmalion and Galatea,* death stepped in and took away from the stage one of the best influences it ever had, and from dancing a possible friendship of the kind it sorely needed.

BALLET IN ITS DARK AGE

In the eighties there was in Chicago a child who had considerable fame as a temperance lecturer. Her name was Loie Fuller. She was moved to take dancing lessons; but (according to biographers) gave them up after a few lessons, on account of difficulty. After a certain amount of voice culture, she qualified as an actress with a singing part. During an engagement in this capacity she received, from a friend in India, a present of a long scarf of extremely thin silk. While playing with it, delighting in its power to float in the air almost like a vapour, Miss Fuller received the idea that was to bring her before the world, the *Serpentine Dance*. The dance was there in its essence, needing only arrangement and polish, and surety of keeping a great volume of cloth afloat without entanglement. Steps were of no consequence, nor quality of movement in arms or body. The cloth was the thing, and Miss Fuller lost no time on non-essentials.

The success of the *Serpentine* was not one of those victories gained after long experimenting for a perfect expression, patiently educating the public, and years of disappointments. It was instantaneous and complete; a few weeks sufficed to make Loie Fuller a national figure. A period of tremendous popularity followed, popularity amounting to a fashion. And still another impulse was to come, second only in importance to the use of the gauze itself.

In Paris Miss Fuller had a sketch in which she, a solitary figure, stood on a height at dawn, silhouetted against the sky. The rising sun was arranged to illuminate, one after another, the prominences in the landscape falling away into the distance. The figure, on being touched by the rays, represented its awakening by the fluttering, raising and full play of its hundred yards or so of drapery.

It happened that an audience mistook the intent of the effect, and greeted it as a dance of fire. The upward rush of the cloth, obviously, had suggested flame. "La Loïe" lost not a moment in seeing the possibilities, nor an hour in setting to work on their development. Stage electric lighting was new; so new that it acknowledged no limitations. Electricians were enthusiastic over new problems, because new problems were being solved by new and sometimes sensational inventions. To lighting Miss Fuller turned to make the effect of the fire dance unmistakable and startling. With the result that the colours and movement of flame were almost counterfeited. Variously coloured glasses lent their tints to the rays of spot lights; set into discs made to revolve in front of the lamp, they simulated the upward rush that helps make flame exciting. As a precaution against theft of ideas, the essential parts of the electric arrangements are said to have been trusted exclusively to Miss Fuller's brothers.

La Danse de Feu, consistently prepared as such, created an enthusiasm in Paris probably equal to the "hit" of the *Serpentine* in America. Indeed Miss Fuller was practically adopted into the French nation, where she was affectionately and widely known as "La Loïe." French is the language in which she wrote her memoirs. (*Mes Memoires,* Loie Fuller.)

Her work, always startling, never failed of being agreeable also. By a loose application of the word it was justified in being called dancing. Strictly speaking it was not, from the point of view of step, movement or posture. Interest in steps the work frankly disclaimed by its own terms; an easy movement from place to place, with reference always to the drapery, was all that was undertaken in the department of foot-work. The arms were equally subordinated to the drapery; their movements, as interpretation or decoration, meant nothing. The performer held in each hand a short pole as aid to manipulation of the cloth, in which her arms were buried most of the time. They committed no awkwardness, nor did they contribute to the effect except as they furnished motive power. As to the drapery, any idea of making it a vehicle of controlled lines would obviously have been out of the question. Colour without form was the result; and form, when all is said and done, is the essence not only of dancing, but of any art that would attempt to convey a message to the senses as well as pleasure to the eye.

Imitators affected Miss Fuller very little. So closely were her means guarded—it is said that no one of her designers and sewing-women knew more than a part of the construction of her draperies—that attempts to reproduce her work were generally laborious compromises with failure. But the musical comedy stage underwent an inundation of illuminated dry-goods. With the mechanical problem simplified by the distribution of the hundred yards of drapery among forty people, there followed a sea of cavorting rainbows and prisms that lacked even a semi-careful selection of colours.

The World's Fair in Chicago brought to America a variety of dancers, most of them good. The novelty element was the work of the Orient. The Oriental point of view differs from that of England and America; it accepts as natural the existence of sex. In all its expressions, whether literary, sculptural, pictorial, or choreographic, the subject of sex is neither avoided nor emphasised. It takes its place among the actuating dramatic motives exactly as it has done in the expressions of all civilisations of all times, except those of our Anglo-Saxon civilisation since about 1620, in which it is evaded, and of certain decadent civilisations, where it is an obsession.

The World's Fair crowd was so amazed by the Oriental disregard of Puritan tradition that it could see nothing in dances of India and North Africa except obscenity. Instead of trying to acquaint the public with the wealth of poetic symbolism of the dances, and their unlimited scope of meaning, every manager on the Midway at once adopted the motto of the majority of his profession: "Give the public what it wants." That at least is the inference from conditions. Before the fair was a month old there was hardly an Oriental dancing attraction on the grounds that did not claim, in the sly-dog language of naughty suggestion, to surpass all competitors in lewdness. And it verily seemed as though most of them were justified in their claims.

They all made money. And they created against Oriental dancing a prejudice just beginning to melt now at the end of twenty years; the majority of the public is still convinced that no Oriental dancing is anything but a pretext for offensiveness. For any physical quality truly is offensive the moment it is unduly insisted upon. And with few exceptions the managers of the unhappy Arabs dancing in this country have inspired their charges to exaggerate one quality to the almost complete exclusion of every other one.

The ghastly reaction of such a state of affairs is on

dancing in general. In this present year, 1913, one of the most prominent and successful managers in America said: "There are two ways to succeed with dancers. If they have a sensational acrobatic novelty that never has been seen before, *that* will make money. Otherwise you've got to take their clothes off, if you want anybody to look at 'em. Duncan? St. Denis? What does the American public care about art? They have succeeded because they took their clothes off."

It sounds unreal, it is so demonstrably silly. But it was what that manager said. In his profession there are several who hold contrary beliefs; but the one quoted is of the opinion common among the present custodians of the dancing art in America. In their offices is determined what character of dancing shall occupy the stage; to their beliefs the lover of good dancing must give heed.

Any refutation of the above cynicism as affecting Miss Duncan and Miss St. Denis is superfluous. Their work has at all times been charged with a big, romantic or mystic meaning. Imitators, basing their activities on the manager's creed above quoted, have furnished an illuminating experiment to determine exactly what interest the public finds in the work of the two artists named. Invariable failure has accompanied their approximate nudity, despite the fact that many of them are pretty in face and figure.

Great dancers have come, been seen, but—until the coming of the Russians—have achieved few victories of lasting value. Genée is an exception; to delight in her work is to be added a real influence in favour of real art. Carmencita, Otero and Rosario Guerrero, all great artists of expression conveyed through the medium of the dances of Spain, have had good seasons in this country. Even though their influence on taste did not seem far-reaching, it must be believed that they helped prepare the way for great things that were to come.

But the real force of the coming change, the change that was to take its place among the important revolutions in the history of all art was quietly preparing itself in an American village.

CHAPTER XI

THE ROMANTIC REVOLUTION

THERE are few people who are complete in any one direction. The statesman hesitates at a measure that will wreck his political organisation, unless he is a complete statesman. The yachtsman will lose a race to pick up a man overboard, unless he is an unscrupulous or complete racing fiend. A corporation manager who disregards every consideration except his end may be a law-breaker, but before that he is a complete business man. Cromwell and Luther were complete reformers. Most people in the arts are incomplete artists, because they hesitate to depart from accepted means of expression. They cripple impulse with logic, and accommodate their course more or less to other people's opinions. Noverre was a complete stage director. Isadora Duncan is a complete disciple of beauty.

Beauty in all its natural manifestations is her religion. Waves and clouds and running water, the nude body and its natural movements are the tokens by which it is revealed to her. Its high priests, by her creed, were the Greeks of old. And, conversely, all other priests are false. In the soul afire with a cause there is no room for adjustment of points of view; such adjustments bear the form of compromise. That which is not right is wrong—not even partly right, but hopelessly, damnably wrong. A state of mind exactly as it should be in a person with an idea, and exactly as it must be if he is going to carry the idea to fruition.

Miss Duncan is not in attunement with the ballet, and never was. She is a worshipper of nature; not as translated into abstract terms, but as nature is, as revealed in the waves and clouds and running water. If she were a leader in a logical controversy instead of one of taste, it would be in order to question how she tolerates modern music, instead of insisting on a reversion to the music of the winds in the trees; for certainly the piano is no less a man-made convention than the dancer's position *sur la pointe,* and orchestration is far from the sounds of nature. But the controversy is not an affair of logic, and it follows that any question prompted by logical considerations becomes illogical, automatically. The point at issue is that Miss Duncan, complete disciple of beauty, is a complete opponent of beauty expressed otherwise than in the way revealed to her. Again, lest this analysis bear any resemblance to criticism, let it be affirmed that her attitude is exactly as it should be in relation to her destiny.

At an early age she was fascinated by the representations of dancing to be found on Greek ceramics, and in Tanagra and other figures. A work of art means many things to many people. What Miss Duncan saw in the early representations was a direct and perfect expression of nature. Among other elements, she noted in them a full acknowledgment of the law of gravity, which is an obviously natural quality. Now, Miss Duncan's essay *The Dance* shows in her mind not the first stirrings of a question as to whether gravity may not be an unfortunate mortal limitation. On the contrary, it is natural, therefore right. Therefore the ballet, in

Isadora Duncan

Photograph by Claude Harris

GREEK INTERPRETATIVE DANCE
Mme. Pavlowa

To face page 243

denying gravity, is wrong. The Greeks usually danced without shoes; bare went the feet of Miss Duncan.

Let it not be supposed that her ideal contemplated an imitation of natural actions, or had any relation to realism. *Natural qualities, not actions,* she proposed to *interpret, not imitate, by means of natural movements.* That is at least the inference pointed by the essay referred to, confirmed by her work. "Natural movements" would be defined, if the same process of inference may be followed, as movements whose execution are possible by a normal body without special training. From this it does not follow that uncultivated movements would be acceptable by the terms of the proposition. To raise an arm is a natural movement, hence acceptable to this code. To learn to raise it gracefully, a Duncanite would need to put in just as much time and thought as a ballet student, standards of grace being equal. It does, however, follow that any gravity-defying step would be unacceptable by the terms of the proposition. Without special training it cannot be executed, badly, or at all; which, from the Duncan point of view, would throw it into the class of unnatural movements.

To fix the meaning of the idea of interpreting natural qualities, nothing better can be done than to quote a paragraph of Miss Duncan's own words: "These flowers before me contain the dream of a dance; it could be named: 'The light falling on white flowers.' A dance that would be a subtle translation of the light and the whiteness—so pure, so strong, that people would say, 'It is a soul we see moving, a soul that has reached the light and found the whiteness. We are glad it should move so.' Through its human medium we have a satisfying sense of the movement of light and glad things. Through this human medium, the movement of all nature runs also through us, is transmitted to us from the dancer. We feel the movement of light intermingled with the thought of whiteness. It is a prayer, this dance, each movement reaches in long undulations to the heavens and becomes a part of the eternal rhythm of the spheres."

Fifteen years ago a creed of interpreting qualities in the manner above indicated, by means of dancing, was quite as alien to the United States as was the Greek costume that left the legs uncovered and the feet unshod. The costume probably was as surprising on the stage then as it would be in a ballroom now. And right there comes in the complete artist. Miss Duncan knew she was right, and she went ahead. Perhaps she anticipated the snickers with which a new idea is usually greeted; more likely she was sublimely heedless of immediate effects.

It was in 1899, or thereabout, that she gave a recital in the little theatre of a dramatic school in Chicago, before an audience principally of dramatic students,

IMPRESSIONS OF ISADORA DUNCAN.

painters and sculptors. After the performance, which took place in the morning, the painters and sculptors unconsciously grouped themselves into informal committees to exchange verdicts. The general conclusion —arrived at after hours of acrimonious argument, in most cases—was that the young woman had an idea, but that clairvoyancy was required to understand it. At that time, it should be added, Miss Duncan was far from mature in grace, surety or any other of the technical qualities; and her art, naïve though it be, has its technical requirements just as surely as any other art.

It is now necessary to transfer attention to certain people whose path and Miss Duncan's were beginning to converge.

In Russia the ballet is as definitely a ward of the government as the army is. No more carefully are candidates for a national military academy selected than are applicants for admission to the Imperial Ballet Academy.

Those admitted are cared for as though each were an heir to the throne, given an all-round art education that could not be duplicated anywhere else in the world, and rigourously drilled in dancing six days a week for seven or eight years. As they qualify for it, they appear on occasion in the *corps de ballet* of the Imperial Opera, dear to the hearts of nobility and a theatre-going public. By the terms of agreement with the government, they are assured employment at specified pay for a specified number of years in the ballet, after which they retire on a pension. The pay is not high, but with it is an assured career and an honourable one, and a likelihood of considerable emolument through instruction, imperial gifts and government favours. Withal a thing not lightly to be thrown away.

Like their contemporaries in Paris and Vienna, the people of St. Petersburg and Moscow (homes of the two Imperial Opera Houses and of the two arms of the Academy) were dissatisfied with their ballet. Beyond the vague charge of lack of interest they could not analyse their complaint. They were puzzled. Training more careful than that given in their Academy could not be. Nor was any school of the dance superior to the composite French-Italian on which the Russian ballet was based. Each detailed objection was answered; yet a decided majority agreed that something was wrong.

Miss Duncan, rightly believing that Europe was more attentive than America to a new idea, had left her native land after a period of neither success nor failure in any pronounced degree. She had interested Paris, startled Berlin, and set Vienna into a turmoil of wrangling. St. Petersburg waited, with interest aroused by echoes from Vienna.

Before the end of the St. Petersburg performance, M. Mikail Fokine, a director in the Academy, had not only declared Miss Duncan a goddess, as he had a perfect right to; he, with others, had invited her to give a special performance in the Academy, and that was against the rules.

The special performance was given; the Romantic Rebellion dates from that hour. In no time at all the secessionists were a body including some of the ablest of both masters and pupils.

With Miss Duncan's technical limitations or virtuosity they were not concerned. What she brought

MLLE. LOPOUKOWA   MLLE. NIJINSKA
MLLE. PAVLOWA

With the famous instructor, Sr. E. Ceccetti. From an amateur photograph taken
in their student period

MLLE. LYDIA KYASHT AND M. LYTAZKIN
"Harlequin and Blue-bird"

THE ROMANTIC REVOLUTION 247

them was the vision of the ballet now known to the world as Russian. To lost pensions and the certain displeasure of a firm-handed government they gave no heed. They were complete idealists, bent on a big purpose. Of the stories of that secession that we have had from various participants, not one shows the faintest reflection that any of the band thought of the possible sacrifice of his career. They were not estimating material prospects. They simply saw the vision of something that looked better to them than the art they had known; into the path indicated by that vision they turned without vacillation, and without emotion save enthusiasm.

With the fact that they were the advance guard of a movement that was about to assume a significance equal to that of the Barbizon School in painting and of Victor Hugo in literature, these Russians—boys and girls in age, most of them—were as supremely unconcerned as were Adam and Eve with the destiny of the race of which they were founders. To a group of incomplete artists the epic romance of the thing would have appealed, and there would have resulted columns and reams of print to tell about the inspiration, and all the rest of it. In the consciousness of these Russians —and make no mistake, most of them are alert, intellectually vigourous people—there was no concern about their own value as figures in a romance. They were filled with the excitement accompanying the possibility of radically improving their work.

Spontaneously the pieces of the new structure came together. To M. Fokine the group looked as head. In him they had a choreographer of the highest order, with the imagination of an epic poet. Nijinski and

Bolm were prominent men of the group; heading the list of women were Mlles. Pavlowa, Lopoukowa, and Karsavina. As a matter of exact history, Mr. Joseph Mandelkern points out to us that the enlistment of Mordkin, Volinine and other important recruits occurred somewhat later; being in the Moscow arm of the school, their first receipt of the romantic impulse was connected with Miss Duncan's appearance in Moscow, which occurred after the St. Petersburg engagement. The secession at Moscow was largely a repetition of the occurrences at St. Petersburg.

The new cause gained, without delay, the alliance of the musical composers, Glazounov, Rimski-Korsakov. Tcherepnin, and others of stature little less.

Among the forces most important in contribution to the new-born art, moreover, was Léon Bakst, the decorator. M. Bakst, for a number of years, had enjoyed a high and steadily improving position in his craft; he had been variously honoured, he had executed responsible commissions to the satisfaction of every one—with the possible exception of himself. In a comparatively recent interview he is quoted as saying —in effect—that he believed that the function of a painter was to express emotion rather than to record fact. Taking as an instance an architectural sketch before him, he said that if a change of certain classic architectural proportions would add impressiveness, he would not hesitate to make the necessary changes. In other words, he regarded fact as material and not as an object to be recorded for its own sake. So it may be inferred that his success in rather conservative decoration, notwithstanding that it did not lack the note of individuality, was not satisfying to him.

THE ROMANTIC REVOLUTION 249

For material for new compositions in which the new creed could be exploited, ballet-master, musician and painter turned unanimously to the legendary lore of Russia and Persia, the intervening land of the Caucasus, and the near-by realm of Egypt. Strange new plots they found; plots of savagery, passion, and mystery. While dancers translated lofty motives into choral and solo steps, musicians worked with mad zeal to render them into tone and tempo. New music was composed, old was seized with avid hand and pounded into its appointed place in the new romantic structure. Bakst—and other painters allied with him—revelled, now in a deep and ominous palette that should spell mystery, again in ardent and seemingly impossible harmonies that sang wild opulence.

In short, the secessionists had attained to a point that marked nothing less, and something more, than a recreation of the mimetic drama of the best days of Athens. They had achieved that at which the early patrons of opera had consciously but unsuccessfully aimed. The Russian achievement is not to be measured except by a glance back into history.

In the great spaces of the Greek outdoor theatres, actors found their voices inadequate. In consequence, we must accept as essentially true the belief that dramatic representation underwent a more or less definite division into two forms. One body, complying with the world-old demand for explanatory statement to accompany dramatic action, adopted a device to magnify the voice; that device was a small megaphone, concealed by means of a mask. To the unimaginative audience, the resulting falsification of the voice was not objectionable. That species of audience, to this day, is deaf and blind to the message of quality or to delight in it. Its interest centres on narrative and it welcomes diagrammatic aid to its understanding of that narrative. The mask, therefore, was rather satisfying than otherwise to the patrons of the drama that it typified. In labelling character, it was a boon to the intellectually toothless; to whom, moreover, its immobility of expression would not be offensive. That the spoken drama was the popular form, the mimo-drama the aristocrat, seems an unavoidable inference.

To artists and audience versed in the language of symbol, as opposed to imitation; of suggestion, as opposed to diagram; of abstraction, as opposed to material fact—to such performers and connoisseurs the vastness of stage and auditorium presented no inconvenience whatever. To both performer and auditor, the eloquence of pose, step and gesture was sufficient. Indeed, we may suppose that they regarded the spoken word as limiting, rather than amplifying, the meaning of the action it accompanied. The high-heeled *cothurnus* the pantomimist avoided, for the sake of perfect freedom of foot. To him was open the full resource of facial expression, posture and dance. All of these means, in whole or in part, were denied the wearer of mask and *cothurnus*.

Rome, consistent with its own level of artistic mentality, chose the less imaginative of the Greek forms. It follows that Greek popular drama is identical with the so-called classic Roman drama.

When the originators of opera set themselves, in the seventeenth century, to the task of re-creating a classic form, it is a matter of record that they turned to Rome for their model.

Thus, in availing themselves of advances in the arts of music, scenery and costume, both opera and ballet have strayed from pure classic tradition. And there is no harm in that, *per se*. But a point to be most strongly emphasised is this: that the Russian ballet has re-created, in its essence, the best of classic drama.

Employment of the full eloquence of step, pose and facial expression, without the restriction that the spoken word imposes upon meaning—that is the paramount distinction of the Russian ballet's dramatic form. Hardly second in importance is its independence of elaborate stage mechanism as a means to effects. The first opera busied itself with mechanical contrivances to an extent that was commented upon—with amusement—by writers in its time. How far its originators were justified in believing that they had re-created a great classic form needs no further comment. That the Russians, searching for the great fundamentals of art, devised a form practically coincidental with that accepted by the best intelligence of the best period of Athens, is a chapter of dramatic history whose importance is not likely to be exaggerated.

We left the secessionists, on an earlier page, in the position of having defied a strong-handed government. In this crisis, M. Sergius Diagilew enters the narrative, not as an artist, but as one of art's indispensable allies. He it was who, some years before, had arranged the exhibitions that first acquainted western Europe and America with modern Russian painting. When the rift occurred in the Ballet Academy, M. Diagilew, by virtue of experience and sympathies, was the one man to perform certain needed diplomatic services in the interest of the rebels. Their situation lacked little of being politically serious. M. Diagilew performed the felicitous miracle of turning a fault into a virtue.

To proper government authorities he outlined a plan which in itself deserves a place in diplomatic history. "Contract-breakers these people are," he admitted, "and on a par with deserters from the army. But instead of punishing them, I have another suggestion.

"They have created a new and great art. Their combined work represents a greater expression than any living man has seen, perhaps the finest thing of its kind that ever has existed in the world.

"Europe respects Russia for her force, not for her thought. Its common belief is that Russia is a nation of savages, because it has seen no purely Russian art that it would call great.

"My proposal is that these people be reinstated in the Opera and the Academy, that they be granted a long leave of absence, and that I be commissioned to arrange for them a season in Paris, as an exhibition of representative Russian art, sanctioned by the Russian government."

The capital necessary for a full equipment of costumes and scenery was provided by Baron Ginsberg. And there followed the first season of *le Ballet Russe* at the Châtelet Théâtre, in 1909. Paris, like every other progressive city in the world, was surfeited with plays that would better have been enclosed between the covers of books on law, sociology or medicine. Its ballet, though fighting valiantly against the effect that time works on old governments, old religions, old institutions, had settled into the ways of habit, and could no longer fire the mind or the imagination. As to all that miscellany of "musical comedies" that, with their con-

MLLE. LYDIA LOPOUKOWA, M. MIKAIL MORDKIN, IN A BACCHANAL

To face page 252

MLLE. LYDIA LOPOUKOWA

To face page 253

comitant novelties, were wallowing in a gaudy slough of despond ten years ago, Parisians had come to regard them as a highly improbable means even of amusement, leaving edification quite out of account.

The success of the Russians was assured from the first curtain. Here was something that conveyed a message of noble beauty, executed with the skill of the craftsman possessed of all that education can give, fired with enthusiastic genius. Above all, it was a thing that released thought from earth-bound conditions and, with the persuasion of its multiple beauty, invited it to roam the unlimited domain of poetry and magic.

Full appreciation required time, naturally. Here was a creation new in freedom of movement and pantomimic vocabulary: dressed in costumes never seen before; backed by scenery in colours never dreamed of, with a species of line-composition like an alien language; and accompanied by music of a type unfamiliar, to many individuals unknown. Wagnerian music to the unaccustomed ear is confusing as well as overpowering. The Russian ballet presented its equivalent in three different forms acting simultaneously.

The Russian ballet season is now one of the institutions of the French capital. The Russian government annually grants several months' leave of absence to the necessary number of artists, and Paris for several months crowds their performances. The annual increase in quantity and depth of thought bestowed upon them, as measured in magazine writings, indicates that public satisfaction with the organisation and its work has not yet found its limits.

The seasons of 1909-10 and 1910-11 found a small but admirable Russian ballet in the Metropolitan Opera of

New York. Pavlowa, Lopoukowa, Mordkin, Volinine and Geltzer were of the number. They presented many *divertissements* in opera performances as well as a number of ballet pantomimes. As to their impression on the public, it is most briefly to be expressed by calling attention to the fact that the dancing enthusiasm now strongly rooted in America dates directly back to these Russian ballet seasons in the Metropolitan Opera. Naturally, the public's lack of knowledge of the language of pantomime and choreography stood in the way of such an immediate "hit" as the same company had made in Paris. But in spite of incomplete understanding, New York was charmed from the first, and appreciation grew rapidly through the two seasons.

The contract was not renewed, nor has the Metropolitan Opera undertaken anything great in choreography since that time, in which it is probably right. Notwithstanding the popularity of the Russians, they did not increase box-office receipts commensurately with the heavy cost of salaries, transportation and incidental expenses.

It is natural, when service is needed, to turn to those whose fitness for such service has been proven. But the opera company, by its service to music, has earned exemption from added responsibilities to art. Since its organisation, the stockholders' dividends have had the form of deficit statements every year until two years ago. Every year the stockholders wrote their checks to aggregate a quarter of a million dollars or more that opera cost in excess of its receipts. The past two years have turned the balance into the other column. If they chose to, the same set of gentlemen could, in a few years, put

THE ROMANTIC REVOLUTION 255

the ballet-drama on the same footing; but the sacrifice of money and effort is more than the public has a right to ask. Against appalling odds, the Metropolitan took up the cause of popularising opera. That the task proves other than a labour of love is due neither to skimping nor to lowering of standards, but to quite the contrary policy. The undertaking has succeeded; those connected with it are entitled to a period of enjoyment of their rewards. The American Academy of Dancing, when it is organised, is not morally their responsibility. For its own good, moreover, it had best be an independent organisation, with music definitely relegated to the secondary importance. As an auxiliary to music, the dance has not progressed as it should; only as the sole occupant of one of the pedestals to which the great arts are entitled will it receive the attentive care that it deserves and needs. But this is anticipation of the matter of another chapter.

Since the Metropolitan engagement, Russian ballets have seldom been seen in America except under misrepresentative conditions. Not through intentions to misrepresent, but through tactical errors easily understood in the light of subsequent knowledge, they have been too often advertised in such terms as to prepare their audiences for sensationalism rather than art.

A company including some of the best dancers that Russia has produced was headed by a vaudeville performer whose prominence proceeded from genius in imitations, and whose choreographic aspirations were based on two years (the programme confessed the period) of ballet study. It was believed that her name would be of service to the box-office; it was demonstrated that, by the standards of the supporting company, she was not a dancer. So she did not dance. Obviously, the function of subordinates is to be subordinate; so, perforce, they did not dance, either. People who came expecting to see great things inevitably felt that the Russian ballet was, to say the least, an overrated institution. A consequence even more unfortunate is that many managers draw, from this hapless alliance and its consequences, the deduction that Americans do not like high-class dancing.

NOTE.—See post-script to the second edition, p. 322.

MME. PAVLOWA IN A BACCHANAL

To face page 257

CHAPTER XII

THE RUSSIAN ACADEMY AND ITS WORKINGS

A STUDENT in the Russian Academy does not risk discovering, after some years of study, that he cannot stand the physical training, nor does he learn, when it is too late to turn back, that his road to high places is blocked by defect of health, structure, or proportion. As a candidate for admission he undergoes an examination by a board of physicians, painters and sculptors. If he enters, it is after their approval, the examiners measuring the candidate by the standards of their respective arts. He knows, and his parents know, that he is starting, free from handicap, on the road to an at least respectable position in a respectable profession, with which he will be associated and by which he will be supported through life. His studies will be guided by the best instruction that can be secured; if he has genius it will receive the most favourable of cultivation. At all times his life will be surrounded by conditions as favourable to physical health as they can be made by science and free expenditure.

His payment for these advantages is complete renunciation of every interest apart from those of the Academy's curriculum. To one not passionately fond of his art, the enforced devotion to work would spell loss of liberty. As a matter of fact, however, this does not often seem to be felt as a privation. The interests of the school are so varied, and the dance is possessed of such endless allurement, that life within the academic walls is generally felt to be complete in itself. In other words, the contract binding the pupil is not usually felt as a tether, notwithstanding that its operation covers the most restless years in a boy's or girl's life.

Seven or eight is the age for entrance, and the contract binds the pupil for nine years of training—which may be reduced to eight if proficiency warrants. At the expiration of this time the government has all rights to the dancer's services, at a moderate salary, varying according to the rank for which he qualifies in the ballet organisation. From the graduates of the Academy are recruited the ballets of the two Imperial Opera Houses: the Marianski Theatre in St. Petersburg, and the Opera House in Moscow. In both houses, ballet pantomimes are presented twice a week, approximately.

Graduates with an aptitude for teaching are so employed. All of which must cost the government a great deal less than would the alternative of hiring *corps de ballet, premiers* and *premières,* and ballet-masters from Paris and Milan. In fact, until half a century ago, foreign talent was depended on for the important work. From its continued use, it may be inferred that the present system is the more satisfactory.

Naturally, a member of the Imperial ballet must have government consent to leave his country; departing without such consent, he automatically forfeits his pension. A few individuals have chosen the high salaries to which their work entitles them in other parts of the world, and deliberately stayed away at the expiration of a leave of absence. To the great majority, however, the pension and artistic conditions attaching to their home organisation have been the greater inducement.

MLLE. LYDIA LOPOUKOWA

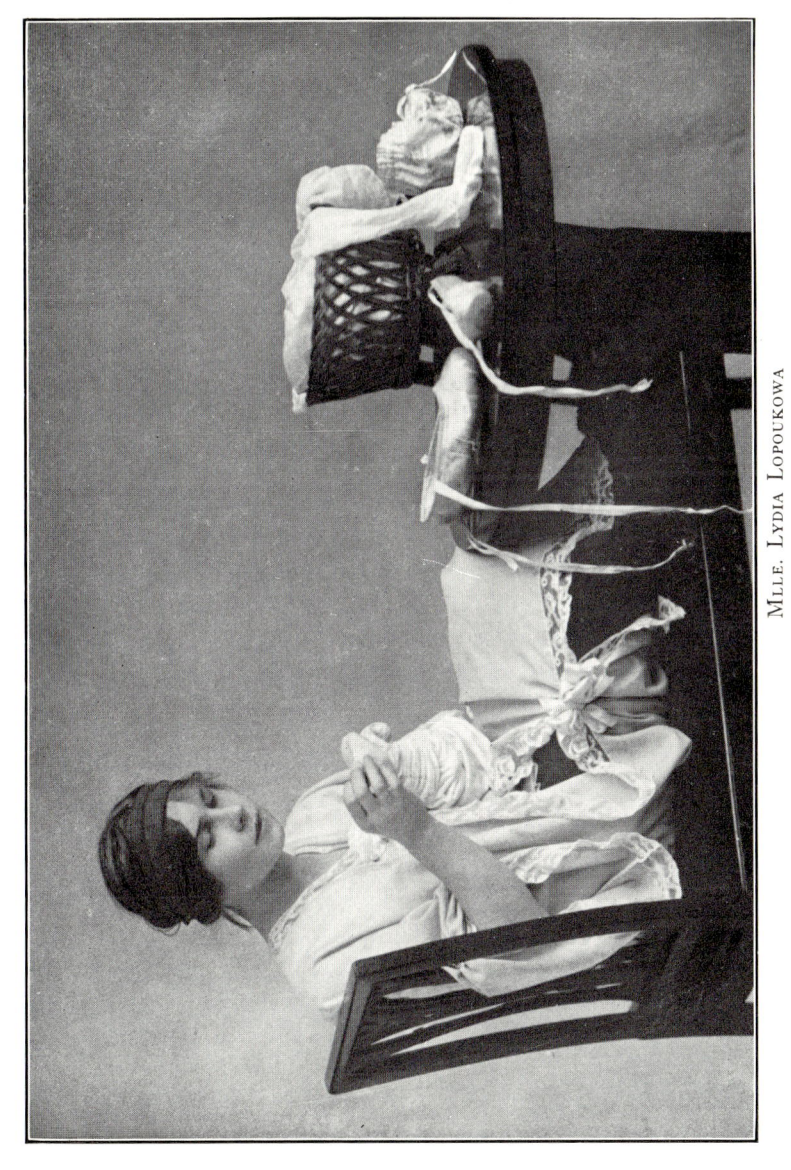

An aid to secure footing, the toes of ballet slippers are usually darned

To face page 258

LOPOUKOWA AND NIJINSKI IN "LES SYLPHIDES"
From a dry-point by Troy Kinney

Between performances and their preparation, and teaching, it will be seen that the members of the ballet never need pass an unoccupied hour. They are insured against such deterioration as might result from lack of constant work. On the other hand, they are protected against the danger of overwork. Think of the difference between such conditions and those created by competition! Between engagements, the generality of ballet people under the latter conditions study and train, if at all, at their own expense; and competent coaching costs money. During engagements, the number of supreme efforts of which they are capable each week is considered only by those in whom are combined good fortune and conscience; others arrange their work to economise strength, or else break down.

Of the curriculum of the school we have been told in some detail by Miss Lydia Lopoukowa. During the first year, which is a period of probation, pupils are allowed to visit their parents on Sundays. After that they remain in the direct charge of instructors, in the school, in the opera-houses, and in carriages going and coming; visiting with parents or others is confined to stated times, and is done in the school. If this arrangement seems severe, the answers are to be found in results: if any students of any art attain to full artistic development and perfection of artistry in an equal length of time without similar concentration, enforced either by self or by regulation, then the detachment effected by the Russian Academy is carried to an unnecessary degree.

The curriculum may, for convenience, be divided into two departments, pertaining respectively to technical and general education. The latter is the equivalent of the

Continental European *gymnasium*, which carries the student to a point somewhat more advanced than that which he reaches in the American public high school.

On the technical side, the training begins with the breadth of a general conservatory's course in the arts. As the pupil's aptitude and tastes begin to crystallise, his instruction becomes increasingly specialised. The first year's work covers, besides dancing, a beginning in music, acting, and a certain amount of drawing. The music includes theory and piano. Acting embraces the beginnings of pantomime, along with enunciation, expression and the rest of it.

The dancing tuition is based absolutely on the French-Italian ballet. The undisputed success of the romantic movement, and the prevailing sympathy with its motive, have not shaken faith in the classic as a necessary framework for the support of expression and adornment. An orthodox and unreconstructed Italian ballet-master remains in charge of this department; his influence is not modified until after the pupil has acquired the equilibrium, in short the discipline that is a tradition of the classic school alone. Parallel with this training, however, is instruction and drill in plastic gymnastics, which concerns itself with training the body in grace and expression. The separation of the two courses naturally enables the pupil to keep classic precision clear in his mind; while, having at the same time mastered the more fluid treatment of the plastic gymnastics, he is ready to unite the two understandingly when the proper time arrives, and to combine with their graces the eloquence of pantomime.

Music has sometimes been found to be the natural *métier* of students whose original intention was dancing.

In other instances the embryonic dancer has revealed a genius for acting. In such cases the pupil is encouraged to follow the line of natural aptitude. The ranks of both opera and drama in Russia include women whose ultimate vocations were discovered after they had become proficient dancers. While such cases are not common, neither are they rare; which is rather illuminating as to the quality of the musical instruction.

An acquaintance with musical theory is insisted upon as a part of the dancer's equipment, though there be no probability of his ever applying his knowledge in any of the usual ways. Music and dancing are so interwoven that the latter's full meaning can hardly be expressed, or understood, without musical knowledge as an aid. Moreover, of every class of youngsters a certain number are destined to be choreographic composers; to these a knowledge of orchestral possibilities and limitations is indispensable. Indeed it is an asset of the utmost practical utility to any dancer; any rehearsal demonstrates its value. In respect to this department and its lifelong value to those who have had its training, graduates of other academies unite in approval of the Russian.

The course in drawing and painting seems to aim at critical appreciation of beauty, as expressed in the abstract qualities of grace in line and harmony in colour; this in distinction to the regulation art school discipline in proportion and anatomy of the figure. The practical value of such training, in sharpening the power of constructive criticism of dancing, is obvious.

To the accomplishment of all this work—and more that need not be detailed—the pupils are not driven; they are led. Everything is fun. Play is made contributory to the general purpose of training artists. As an escape from realities into that world of make-believe that children crave, pantomimes are practiced evenings after dinner; self-expression is encouraged on these occasions, criticism no more than hinted. As a playground for the girls, a large garden is provided. But the boys, to relax from the restraint of a daily two-hour lesson in French ballet, delight in class fencing lessons. The health of all is under unobtrusive but constant supervision. In each of the girls' dormitories a nurse is on watch every night, alert for the first unfavourable symptom—and ready, too, we may be sure, with sympathy for any little attack of loneliness. Miss Lopoukowa's remembrances are not of any rigours of work, but rather of a protecting gentleness.

Diet is studied; the children are trained into hygienic positions in sleep! Hair, teeth, skin, heart, lungs, digestion and nerves are cared for by the most capable of specialists. By no means last in importance to a dancer are his feet; the Academy has its chiropodist always in attendance not only to rectify trouble, but to prevent it.

As the academic years draw toward their close, the pupil receives instruction in supplementary branches necessary to the finished artist. Character dances are not only performed; they are studied in relation to the temperaments of their respective nations. Make-up receives its due attention; with paint and false hair young Russians practice transforming themselves into Japanese, Egyptians, Italians. When they leave the Academy, they know their trade.

Somehow such an institution seems too good to last; yet its excellence is far from being the product of any momentary enthusiasm. Its beginning was made in the first half of the eighteenth century. Ballets had been

THE RUSSIAN ACADEMY 263

presented before the Imperial Court as early as 1675. Peter the Great had insisted on Western dancing as one of the means to his end of bringing Russia abreast of the times. Indeed he is supposed to have learned it and taught it himself, as he did shipbuilding. In 1735 the Empress Anne engaged a Neapolitan composer and musical director and a French ballet-master, and bade them present a ballet every week. Cadets from the military academy were at first impressed into service; which may be contributory to the military exactness of the organisation of the Ballet Academy.

As ballet material, the cadets were gradually (according to Flitch) replaced by boys and girls of the poorer classes, whom the ballet-master trained free of charge. The assignment of quarters to them in the palace, the appointment of a coachman's widow to take care of them, an appropriation of extra pay to the ballet-master for teaching, may be said to mark the beginnings of the Academy. Its existence has been uninterrupted, and, under the almost idolatrous Russian love of ballet representations, its growth has been steady. A composite French-Italian technique was adopted, as before stated, and kept unmodified until the recent romantic movement had proven its worth. Italian principal dancers were employed until, a generation ago, the need of them was ended by the Imperial Academy's arrival at a condition of adequacy.

The difference between the romantic ballet and the classic could not be described in an infinity of words, but it can be summarised in a few, and its character suggested in a few sketches. Briefly, the difference consists in liberty to depart from classic restriction of pose and movement, wherever such emancipation will contribute to expression. This freedom inevitably clashes with ballet tenets that have been unquestioned for a hundred and fifty years. The classic keeps the shoulders down; the romantic does not hesitate to raise them, one or both, to portray fear, disdain, or what-not. In the eyes of the classicists, straightness of body (its detractors call it rigidity) is of absolute importance; romanticists, in their Oriental representations, for instance, do not hesitate to exploit the body's sinuosity to the utmost. Yet, in their apparent disregard of choreographic law, they have preserved rigourously the underlying truth of choreographic structure. Than their brilliant steps those of no dancer are cleaner or more perfect; in equilibrium, in exactness, in all that makes for style and finish, they have no superiors. Nevertheless some of the classic ballet people, especially the Milan element, still protest that the romantic idea, with all its appurtenances, is a heresy. M. Legatt, of the St. Petersburg Academy, is said to group all the new elements into one category: Duncanism!

As the painter Bakst (and with him may be mentioned Boris Anisfeldt and others of the same artistic creed), while preserving recognisable national character in his scenes and costumes, does not scruple to subordinate historical facts to his motives, so does the romantic balletmaster disregard the natural limitations of folk-dances that he may choose to employ in his composition. If it suited the dramatic intention of M. Fokine to bring an Arabian dancer on to the point, or to introduce into her work a pure *pirouette,* it is fairly safe to assume that he would do so, despite the fact that Arabic dancing itself knows no such devices. It is to be added that although he should make such amendment to an

REPRESENTATIVE RUSSIAN BALLET POSES AND GROUPS.
Two groups at top from *Thamar*, M. Bolm and Mme. Karsavina, Mlle. Nijinska; MM. Govriloff and Kotchetovski; M. Seilig and Mlle. Stachko, all in *Thamar*. Figure with peacock, Mme. Astafieva in *Le Dieu Bleu*.
(Courtesy of *Comoedia Illustré*.)

Arabic dance as known to its own people, his product would express as forcibly the quality of Orientalism as would any dance to be found in Bagdad. The essential difference would be that the composition of M. Fokine would serve the immediate intention of grief, rage, or whatever might be the desired emotion, as well as emphasising Oriental quality.

It will be seen that the means of expression above indicated relieves the ballet pantomime of any limits of scope. The classic, generally speaking, is by its nature confined to fairy fantasies, the play of elves and spirits, Pierrot and Columbine. All that is dainty it renders to perfection. The new school, on the contrary, can treat with complete dramatic impressiveness all the mystic, epic and sometimes terrible imaginings of the Tartar mind. To its advantage it has among its disciples a full supply of dancing men; lack of them has crippled the classic expressions for many years. The woman doing a boy's part becomes ridiculous as soon as dramatic action departs from the lyrical mood. For this reason, perhaps, both opera ballets and academies of Europe outside of Russia have long lost the custom of staging pantomimes of greater consequence than operatic *divertissement*. Whereas the Marianski Theatre and the Moscow Opera dedicate two nights a week to ballet pantomimes exclusively, and have done so for many years.

The mimetic dramas that have sprung into life with and as part of the new school draw material from legends dark and savage, lyrical and dreamlike. *Cleopâtre* is a story of love and a cruel caprice of an idle queen of fabled Egypt. *Prince Igor* presents a background of the ever-threatening Mongol, a myriad savage horde encamped outside the eastern gate of Europe.

REPRESENTATIVE RUSSIAN BALLET POSES AND GROUPS.
Prince Igor (M. Bolm).   *Thamar* (Mlle. Tchernicheva).
L'Oiseau de Feu (Mme. Karsavina).   *Thamar* (Mlle. Hoklova).
L'Oiseau de Feu (M. Boulgakow, M. Fokine).
Le Dieu Bleu (M. Nijinski).
(Courtesy of *Comoedia Illustré*.)

Scheherazade is tropic passion marching undeviatingly into tragedy. In contrast to these are such ethereal creations as *Le Spectre de la Rose, Le Carnaval, Les Sylphides, Le Lac des Cygnes,* and *Le Pavillon d'Armide.* *Le Spectre de la Rose,* composed to the melting music of Weber's *Invitation à la Valse,* is a fantasy of a girl who falls asleep in her chair after returning from a ball. In her hand she holds a rose which, in her dreams, turns into a spirit that dances with her, kisses her, and departs. *Le Carnaval* brings to life and unites in a slight plot a group of such fabled personages as Pierrot, Harlequin, Columbine, Pantalone and Papillon, animated by Schumann music with Russian orchestration. *Armide* is a figure on a tapestry, who, by magic spell, comes forth in courtly dance with her companion figures and enchants a traveller sleeping in the apartment. *Le Lac des Cygnes* and *Les Sylphides* are practically plotless reveries in the field of pure beauty; of tissue as unsubstantial as the rainbow.

Still a third division is exemplified in *L'Oiseau de Feu* and *Le Dieu Bleu.* As though to test to the utmost the romantic ballet's range of expression, these last deal with occult Eastern religion, calling for a treatment purely mystic.

CHAPTER XIII

A LAYMAN'S ESTIMATE OF CONDITIONS

THAT great dancing is a useful and desirable addition to human happiness needs no argument. Its power to delight the vision and expand the imagination; its value as an example and incentive to an exercise unsurpassed as an ally of health—these and other virtues are obvious. More completely, perhaps, than any of its tributary arts, dancing has the power to impart that indefinable mental well-being that great art aims to give its auditor or spectator. As music is refreshment for one, pictures for another, so the contemplation of dancing is the means of ordering and energising the mind of a third. We of the United States are a beauty-loving people in the main, and almost unanimously attuned to the message of action—so long as we understand its meaning. Once really established among such a people, dancing would take a position of importance second to no other source of national inspiration. In the meantime, there are unorganised cohorts of us to whom good dancing, like good reading, is something of a necessity; and we should like to know what we have a right to expect from the near future.

"The public gets what it wants," is the sophisticated comment almost invariably drawn forth by any discussion along these lines. Which comment exposes its own superficiality; the suggestion of the existence of any one public, in relation to the arts, is absurd.

Patronising dancing there appear, at the very first glance, two publics as widely separated as inhabitants of different planets; each public possessed of appreciations inconceivable to the other, and even contemptible. These are the public that applauds the buxom laziness which substitutes for dancing in the so-called "amusement" known as burlesque, as distinguished from the public that responds to the pure beauty of opera ballet or well-performed ballet pantomime.

Between these two extremes is an intermediate public that is the more or less innocent cause of endless confusion, and whose good nature is an obstacle to the betterment of standards. In the theatre, even when the chaff outweighs the wheat, it applauds everything. The next day Mr. and Mrs. Intermediate Public advise their friends that the production is stupid. Decreasing attendance may warn the manager that something is lacking: but what? As a criticism, absence is not very illuminating. Acts are changed, cablegrams written and lines rewritten, this man discharged, a woman rushed over from Paris. And when all is said and done, the performance perhaps continues to emphasise features that were the cause of bad impressions. For this confusion, the audiences are at least equally to blame with the manager. They owe it to themselves as well as to others to express themselves frankly.

Exactly what grade of dancing this intermediate public really wants is an unsettled question—and one of paramount importance, since it involves a good part of the potential support of good things. Managers infer, each according to his own disposition; and there is rarely material for the formation of inferences in any way exact. For one reason or another, no undertaking serves the purpose of exact experiment; experience does not lead to any unavoidable conclusion. A few wholly good ballet productions have been given in the Untied States during the past few years; they have not been tremendously successful, up to the present, from the point of view of profits. The optimist, however, counts even small profits a success, in the circumstances. Here is an art that employs a language practically unknown to this country; yet it has not failed to impress. But the men who risked the money take another view of it. They consider that they have had a narrow escape from disaster, that the profits are not commensurate with the risks, and that they are well out of a bad affair. Augustin Daly, at the time of his death, was engaged in a course of instructing the public in the appreciation of pantomime, expecting to lose money on it for two or three consecutive years. But the present moment reveals no Augustin Daly among the potential managers of dancing in America. Few are willing to plant seed for a harvest long deferred. And in justice be it added that the equipment and maintenance of *Pygmalion and Galatea* or *L'Enfant Prodigue,* the vehicles of Mr. Daly's missionary efforts in the interests of pantomime, would be a small fraction of the expenses attaching to a first-class production of any of the great mimetic ballets.

The situation is, in all essentials, the same as that through which operatic and orchestral music passed a few years ago. Music lovers put their favoured art on a substantial basis by means of endowments. Any other course in relation to the ballet results in a matter of probabilities and possibilities, but not of certainties. The present interest in dancing, left to itself, may lead to great things. Or it may lead to nothing at all. The renaissance of interest that followed the Kiralfy successes in the sixties and seventies was killed by counterfeits. The same hostile possibilities exist at present.

The above-indicated dependence of the dance on its ability to show immediate profits is only the first of its handicaps. That difficulty would not be light, even though every manager viewed conditions clearly and fairly, as some of them do. Unfortunately, however, there is in the profession a class that has succeeded because of, or in spite of, a belief that good taste does not exist in America. To prove this, they shape every occurrence into an argument. In gathering "names" for the interest of their advertising, they engage a certain number of capable artists. If the productions employing these artists succeed, the cynical manager will construe such success as proof of American worship of reputation, and its power to blind him to a mess of accompanying mediocrity. If, on the contrary, failure attend the enterprise, it proves American inability to appreciate good work. For the success of a really good work of art, these pessimists will find any explanation except that of good work duly appreciated. Skilful publicity, novelty, a public affectation of good taste, the employment of Oriental motifs, any theory, so long as it acknowledges no taste superior to their own. These are the people who, if Madame Pavlowa's present tour, for instance, makes a striking financial success, will inundate the country with pseudo-Russian ballets, perverting everything, unable to see the need of beauty and artistry, bringing all dancing into disrepute.

Let it be clearly understood: these people by no means represent the manager's profession. But they are to an extent in control of the situation, and the person who wants to see dancing is more or less dependent on them as the source of supply. In the absence of any endowed institution, no ballet can be seen except under commercial management—and, as noted, commercial management that cannot or will not knowingly invest in an enterprise that is going to require time to be understood.

The manager desirous of staging a work of genuine choreographic quality finds himself confronted by a discouraging scarcity of even semicompetent material for his ballet—that is, here in America. To bring a *corps de ballet* from Europe, with guarantees covering a minimum number of weeks of work, transportation both ways, and other proper and just requirements, is commercially dangerous. No reasonable blame can be attached to the usual course of engaging such girls as are easily available, fitting steps to their limitations, insisting on the girls and evading the dance, and making much of draperies and coloured lights.

As a direct result of the scarcity of capable ballet people, dance-lovers not infrequently lose the services of a rare artist. No one artist can give a satisfying two-hour public performance of dancing. Saying nothing of variety as a *desideratum* in a programme, the question of physical endurance enters. To rest the *première* between her flights, a *corps de ballet* is indispensable. Without the latter, the former is to be compared to a commander without an army. But the particular case illustrates, where general statement only explains.

On the face of things, Miss Lydia Lopoukowa's determination to take up residence in the United States would seem to mean that American dance-lovers might count on her art as a definite acquisition. After her season with Mordkin, the young woman accepted a position as *première* of a ballet, as good as can be made from native material. A *divertissement* is composed that pleases public and management, and all concerned except the *première* herself. She finds her work circumscribed by the necessity of keeping down to a pitch beyond which the support cannot rise. That the public is pleased is not sufficient; with unrestricted self-expression, and freedom of flight, she could bring that public to a point of enthusiasm. Her art is belittled, and she finds herself in a false position. As soon as contracts permit, she withdraws her energies from the effort to accomplish good in that direction. So, for the lack of a competent ballet, the dance-loving portion of the population is robbed. As to Miss Lopoukowa, she has a taste for and demonstrated ability in the drama. Dancing will give her extraordinary distinction in plays that admit its union with the dramatic action. But under better conditions, her dancing need not have been subordinated to another art.

At this point a question might justly be raised as to whether the interests of the ballet are not being adequately cared for by some of the great opera companies. To such possible question the only answer is negative. Nor are the companies chargeable with any neglect or shortcoming in not giving their ballet departments the relative importance of ballet in European opera organisations. The task of popularising great music alone has been somewhat more than a labour of Hercules. Opera as music now has a supporting patronage; to change the ballet's relative importance would be disturbing, in all probability. Moreover, the Metropolitan (if not the others) has done all that is humanly possible under present conditions, with the principal result of demonstrating that those conditions are to be met by a ballet institution, and nothing less.

At the time of the Metropolitan's organisation, it will be remembered, the world's interest in ballet dancing was at a lower pitch than it ever had been since the dissolution of the Roman Empire; that is, about the middle of the Victorian period. Had the undertaking been no more than that of producing opera in a land already friendly to it, it would have been no more than natural if the Metropolitan directors had accepted the ballet's status as they found it in England. Their task being, however, the production of opera in a country almost hostile to it, a failure to simplify the problem in every possible way would have been bad generalship.

Not finding itself expected to take rank with the ballets of other great opera organisations, the Metropolitan's department of dancing has gone its comfortable gait. It has been under the direction of excellent balletmasters; but they become easy-going, especially after proving to themselves that girls cannot successfully be asked to perform steps for which they lack the foundation of training. To other mollifying influences is added that of a slippery floor in the room dedicated to ballet rehearsal; a room so beautiful and a floor so perfect that to resin it would be a desecration. The dancers, in fear for the intactness of their bones, walk through their numbers as best they can, and ultimately perform them in a manner consistent with rehearsals.

As a step toward relieving the scarcity of ballet people, the Metropolitan founded, about five years ago, a ballet school—an enterprise from which, up to the present, the pupils have rather monopolised the material profits. The arrangement between management and pupil is, in brief, that the pupil shall remain under the school's (free) tuition four years, at the end of which period the Opera has an option on her services for three years, at a salary of twenty dollars a week, a little more or less. If she appears in the *corps de ballet* during her period of study, she is paid proportionately. The school work occupies two hours per day, about nine months of the year. The atmosphere of both school and Opera is wholesome and good; no fault can be found with the arrangement on a basis of fairness; but the number of individuals the school has added to the Opera's ballet is shockingly small. Every *revue,* musical comedy, and other light musical production includes a collection of young women called a ballet; and each year of increased general intelligence in dancing matters adds to the desirability that these ballets should justify the name. The pretty girl, plus coloured lights, drapery, and lively cavorting, no longer constitutes a perfectly secure grip on public approval (except always in burlesque, with which we are not concerned). The result is an insatiable demand for girls who can even half dance. And that demand, in its turn, is a steady drain on the Opera's school. Before she has studied two years, a girl can qualify for a position in an outside concern—a condition of which she never remains in ignorance very long. She thinks it over. Two years more work in the school would insure her a position in the Opera, at weekly pay no greater than the present offer, for a comparatively short season each year. Now, if the Metropolitan ballet had great prestige as a choreographic organisation—a prestige like that of the

Russian ballet, for instance—its more capable members would be sought after as teachers. A connection with it would confer artistic honour and material profit. Unfortunately, such prestige is one of the elements that are lacking. In résumé: continuance with the school insures employment for about half of every year, beginning at a later time, with the chances of advancement almost zero. Whereas, musical comedy and the like offer the probability of employment the year round, minus the time of rehearsing new productions. Present profits are more attractive than the deferred kind; and, a consideration by no means unimportant, a pretty face and a pleasing manner are reasonable grounds on which to hope for a "part." Her contract? The young girl of the present generation has had her own way about everything since the hour of her birth. Experience teaches her that the worst penalty reasonably to be expected is a harmless reproof, soon ended. And her experience is a true guide in this case. As a matter of sentiment, no one likes to oppose the wishes of a girl. As a matter of business, it would be of doubtful advantage for the opera company to take legal steps to enjoin its contract-breaking pupils from appearing in other concerns. Happenings connected with opera and the theatres have a high value in the newspapers; no motive is more popular than that of the persecution of the poor but beautiful girl; the publicity force of the musical comedy employing said girl would busy itself creating for her the rôle of victim. The opera management would find difficulty in securing a true and therefore comparatively uninteresting public statement of its case; indeed, it would be likely to be made to appear, in the eyes of the multitude, as a sort of ogre.

The Metropolitan school furnishes a complete and conclusive test of the possibilities of an opera organisation, as such, in the province of dancing. But even if the Metropolitan ballet were right now at the highest conceivable pitch of perfection, a radical change of policy would be necessary as a preliminary to giving the school its proper power to hold its pupils' allegiance. That is to say, the opportunity to appear in an occasional *divertissement* is not sufficient to hold an ambitious and capable young man or woman through long years of study. In St. Petersburg, the Imperial Opera House dedicates two nights a week to mimetic ballet. The dancers' art on those occasions is subordinate to none. The dance is the thing; and the dancers, according to ability, are given the opportunity to interpret character and motive. In short, they are given the opportunity to express their art as individuals.

Now, one or another of the American opera companies might be willing and able to duplicate the above conditions—conditions without whose aid no ballet reaches a high plane of development. The undertaking, however, would have at least twice the weight of the administration of either ballet or opera alone; it would be accompanied, too, by a risk that the twofold interest would result in confusing or displeasing a portion of the music-lovers who constitute opera's support. The creation, development and maintenance of standards of a great ballet is a combined task and opportunity for dance-lovers themselves, and an end to be reached through the medium of a ballet institution. It may be added that the Russian régime puts music and ballet under the charge of two distinct and separate institutions.

Opera companies whose traditions have been formed during recent years have naturally felt the force of the renaissance of dancing; they have invested their ballets with an importance that would have been considered disproportionate if their formative period had coincided with the mid-Victorian period. The Philadelphia-Chicago company has had a better *corps de ballet* than could logically be expected in view of the limitations of American material; credit is due Sr. Luigi Albertieri, the ballet-master. As *première danseuse* the same company for some years has had Signorina Rosina Galli, a delightful little product of la Scala. In 1913 Sr. Albertieri took the post of ballet-master of the new Century Opera Company, with Miss Albertina Rasch, formerly of the Vienna opera, as *première*. The public's readiness to recognise good work was demonstrated during the Century's first presentation of *The Jewels of the Madonna*. After the act in which the *Tarantella* is danced, the audience demanded that Miss Rasch respond, with the two principal singers, to the curtain-calls.

In Canada, the influence of the times may be noted in the Canadian Royal Opera Company's engagement of Madame Pavlowa and her company to provide the ballet portion of eight performances. Of present interest in the dance throughout North America, there is no manner of doubt. It is perfectly clear that appreciation of choreographic beauty and discernment of skill are rapidly advancing. London has shown its capacity to support four great ballet attractions through the same season, and that a long one; the United States is influenced by England's taste in entertainment. Dancing exhibitions and pageants are now a part of the entertainments of smart society. A masque produced by Mrs. Hawkesworth, in one of the private gardens of Newport, was of a nature to recall the historic festivals of Catherine de Medici. And the nation's taste in entertainment is influenced by smart society. All signs point to a continued and even growing interest in dancing. And it is possible, without other aid or guidance than that interest in dancing in general, that dancing as a great art, an art of deep emotional interpretation, will take its proper place in this land. But, with the multitude of forces of vulgarity, get-rich-quick commercialism, and heedlessness opposed to it, it is doubtful. At the present moment, the high art of dancing is pleasing, and its emotional message partly comprehended. If it were fully comprehended, that art would be an indispensable source of refreshment to the American mind. Consistently repeated for a few years, its idiom would be familiar to a large part of the population. The conditions which this chapter has analysed show, however, that the sufficient and adequate repetition of ballet drama is by no means certain. And this chapter's motive is to emphasise two things: first, if American lovers of dancing wish to insure for themselves the continuous opportunity to see fine representations of that art, they must found a ballet, and an academy upon which it may depend for its artists; second, for such a step no time can be more propitious than the present.

If the vision of an endowed ballet institution in the United States seems lacking on the practical side, it is not amiss to recall a few facts of American history in its relation to music—than whose ambitions of yesterday nothing was thought to be less practical. Thirty years ago the attitude of the United States (particularly the West) toward classical music was less indifferent than scornful. To confess a liking for orchestral or operatic compositions was to brand oneself as queer. Anything connected with music or musicians was deemed a fair mark for newspaper jokers; and they knew their readers. Inevitably, organisations that ventured a tour did so at their financial peril.

Individual singers and performers were protected somewhat by their lesser expenses and their preparedness to render popular ballads; but they too knew well the look of empty benches.

Theodore Thomas pointed out to a group of Chicago people that never, under such conditions, would the adequate performance of great works be other than at rare and uncertain times; that, without fairly frequent hearing of those great works, public taste never would improve. Obviously, the programmes that Mr. Thomas proposed to give, and the manner and frequency with which he proposed to give them, brought up the prophetic vision of considerable money loss; but the funds were subscribed. The result is the Chicago Orchestra: a source of unending happiness to lovers of good music, just pride to the city, and material benefit in no slight degree. Chicago finds itself the place of residence of several thousand music students, and a centre of attraction for many more thousands of occasional pilgrims to the Orchestra's concerts. Lastly, as though to show that idealism is not the idle dissipation that it seems, the Orchestra was reported several years ago to have reached a basis of self-support.

The same history has been virtually duplicated in perhaps a score of cities, needless to enumerate. Even "practical" people admit that most of the orchestras so endowed, though they may have passed through a period of begging people to accept passes to concerts, are now paying their own expenses. The general history of the Metropolitan Opera has already been outlined. Opera in other cities has gone through much the same train of events, slowly changing indifference to interest, and having now arrived at the stage of independence made possible by a demand that grows steadily in volume and intelligence. The number of performances in each city shows a consistent annual growth.

Certainly the taste for dancing of a high class is no less worthy of indulgence and cultivation than the taste for the sister art of music. If music's dependence upon endowment was once more evident than is that of dancing now, then so much less is the difficulty of financing a ballet institution; proportionately less, too, are the hazards and delays to be undergone before the institution arrives at a paying basis.

For the organisation and conduct of such an institution, the Russian ballet and Academy supplies a model that could be followed in most details. American sentiment probably would rebel at so complete a separation of children from parents as the Imperial Academy requires; but a less complete separation would not necessarily be detrimental to results. For actual technical work in dancing, plastic gymnastics, pantomime, music and other courses more than a few hours a day would be beyond the strength of very young pupils, leaving half of each day to attend common school. As the pupil advances, his hours per day in the academy could increase; he could acquire general education after his technical education is accomplished with just as good results as accompany the present reversal of that sequence.

The weak spot that appears in the plan is the possible interference of parents with the school's discipline. The training of a dancer involves hard work and a great deal of it. Although the work be demonstrably beneficial in all ways, the American parents' attitude toward that work and the accompanying discipline would be the question to be settled. Boys, to be sure, are sent sometimes at an early age to military schools, and there brought up under a more or less exact régime. But public sentiment favours the indulgence of the girl in all her wishes. It would be a matter requiring adjustment, and probably susceptible of adjustment. Far greater difficulties have been overcome.

Against the prevailing tendency to abandon the training in order to accept outside engagements, by which the Metropolitan Opera School of Ballet has been too often victimised, the academy could protect itself by requiring each pupil to file a bond as a condition of entrance, the amount to be forfeited if the pupil violates his agreement. Questions of payment, ranking of performers, amount of pensions and the like are details needless to consider in the general plan.

Proper equipment would represent a considerable expenditure: a modern theatre, or the liberal use of one; drill halls, music rooms, gymnasium, baths, etc. As to instructors, the right kind are available. At the outset, ballet-master and most of the dancers would have to be engaged from outside, their number decreasing as the school's products reached the proficiency to take their places. The employment, at the beginning, of finished dancers, would be of advantage in establishing standards for students. Scenery, costumes and orchestra are to be had at the cost of thought and money. Medical and other expenses, taxes, etc., are minor considerations. Now to returns. In considering which, it is understood that such an undertaking may not make expenses at first. But it is not impossible that good management should reduce the losing years to a very small number.

Assuming (say) thirty performances in the home city during the first year: the prestige of that number of performances, kept up to a consistent pitch of excellence, would be nation-wide. As a result of that prestige, a long tour and several short ones would undoubtedly return an excess over salaries and costs. Bear in mind that a commercial undertaking of the sort must figure on recouping a heavy initial expense, and transportation of a company from Europe and return.

Special engagements of artists, in groups or individually, would net the institution a greater or less part of the receipts, according to the terms of individual contracts.

Considering conditions as they are, and looking at the history of music as a fair analogy, it would be safe to assume that local interest in dancing and the mimetic ballet would increase steadily after the institution's first year, increasing income proportionately. On the other side of the account, expenses should begin to decrease after the third year. A wardrobe and a stock of scenery would have been accumulated, their cost reduced to upkeep and occasional additions. More important, pupils by that time would begin to qualify for the ballet, decreasing the pay-roll of European dancers. In eight years, if the institution has been reasonably fortunate, it should have a ballet recruited principally from its own school. These alumni, of whatever grade, it would have at low salaries; salaries at the same time satisfactory to the recipients, whose popularity as private teachers would be about in ratio to the quality of work with which they identified themselves in performances. Stated hours of exemption from duties connected with the ballet and the school would open the way to such extra revenue. The pay of the *première danseuse* of l'Opéra of Paris is small, in relation to the requirements of her position; but teaching and outside performances are said to yield her a comfortable income.

Pension payments would represent a loss more apparent than real, since many pensioners could, with adjustments, serve as teachers and aides in various capacities.

So far as can be learned, the foregoing covers the principal elements of expense and possibilities of revenue. The difficulties would be heavy, but less so than those that have been met and overcome. The ballet institution, achieved, would be a contribution to the fine arts no less glorious than any this country has yet received, an organism whose service to broad æsthetic cultivation has been equalled by few.

On the score of both public education and its correlative, the steady increase of the ballet's earnings, too much emphasis cannot be laid on the advantage the institution would have in its facilities for repeating great works at frequent intervals. We have seen how ground gained by the first Russian season in America was partly lost, through conditions that made it impossible to follow up victories. The choreographic idiom once understood in its fulness, and its public having found itself, the changes of fashion in popular taste would be powerless to affect the dignified status of the art. Under commercial conditions, let the general level of taste sag, or appear to sag, and fine expression is no more. The thousands who have half learned to love the good give it up, and revert to the mediocre; while those who are wholly in sympathy with the good say nothing, stay away from the theatre, and are supposed, by managers, not to exist. Good taste never dies out; it only appears to. The amalgamation of the aristocracy of taste that would be effected by the proposed institution would, in itself, have a tremendous importance. Any basis for computing the potential support for good and honest attractions would be of the utmost advantage to their proprietors. Disclosures of a substantial demand would encourage tours of the best in Europe, while a reliable measure of the limitations of such demand would be no less valuable as a warning against reckless expense. Certainly it is to the interest of the art that good attractions shall be materially profitable.

As to the thought of any tendency of such an institution to take the practice of dancing away from the laity, and confine it to paid exhibitions, the effect would be to the contrary. It would, however, make for a rise of standards. Dancing clubs and pantomime clubs that a little fertilisation would bring to light would find in a quasi-public ballet an inspiration and a guide; and the good to public health and spirits, in the way of such clubs alone, would be pronounced. Also, prevalent impressions concerning the relationship between cleverness, "individuality" and genuine workmanship would be modified, to the betterment of what is known as the American spirit.

CHAPTER XIV

TENDENCIES?

PREVIOUS editions of this book have devoted the space occupied by this chapter to words about an indoor amusement known as ballroom dancing. It was written under coercion, against the wishes of the authors, and never belonged in a book on the dance as an art. That chapter is now melted down into innocuous if not useful type metal. Several pages are thus released for the discussion of a question of live interest to appreciators of the dance: namely, in what conditions is it going to be found in the near future? Any predictions will be furnished by the reader. The causes operating on the art's immediate future are seen in the history of the dance during the past few years. This chapter is concerned with such facts as seem significant, regarded as causes.

In quick review let it be recalled that a dozen years ago this art was newly aroused from a cataleptic state in which it had lain for close to half a century. The awakening was attended by a degree of public interest probably keener than had attached to any artistic movement in history. Civilization had recaptured a half-lost idiom of poetic expression! We seemed upon the threshold of a veritable renaissance of a dormant department of thought. By its own genuineness, the new-discovered beauty created standards and developed critical discernment. The study of the dance attracted young people in thousands. For a period of years the dance was the foremost subject in the interest of the art-loving portion of humanity.

Part of the revived interest was inspired by elaborate and ingenious productions. At least an equal part was due to the amazing dancing of certain individual stars. The productions that bewildered the world ten years ago have lost the attraction of novelty, and they have not been adequately replaced. Most of the stars of a decade ago have retired; the men and women who furnished models of execution and fired public interest. Whence are to come the new stars, the leaders to supply the inspiration indispensable to the art's continuance and development? Soviet Russia? Western Europe? America?

That is what we are about to consider. And the question has an interest even deeper than the artistic: the character of our activities in this real or apparent renaissance is going to furnish an unmistakable measure of certain disputed traits in our national spirit. All arts are an index of the quality of the civilization that produced them; the present furnishes emphatically no exception.

Here was an art transplanted to our soil under peculiarly favorable conditions. Aroused public interest furnished every reasonable promise of support for worthy choreographic undertakings. The new student group was of a high average of intelligence, and quickly showed the desirable qualities of imagination as well as aptitude and persistence. To manifest possibilities was presently added responsibility; responsibility, that is to say, if there is such a thing as responsibility for the care of a beautiful thing. The war came.

The war brought the arts in Europe practically to a halt. War and postwar conditions brought to America not only a wealth of inspiration in the work of dancers; there came also some of the ablest teachers in the world to reinforce the little group already here. European ladies and gentlemen who theretofore had been disposed to deny the existence of American creative ability outside the field of manufacture, at last expressed the conviction that we were about to see the advent of a veritable American School of Art: the dance, as modified by American ideas and shaped by American poetic sense.

It will be seen that most of the art's high practitioners and a large group of its lesser disciples have carried on in a manner consistent with high ideality; that we, the art-loving portion of the public, are the factor of first importance in developments; that various teachers, managers and producers possess both, one, or none of the virtues of honesty and intelligence; these are all formative influences on the dance of the near future. Also we find that an indefinite but unquestionably great part of the art's present hold on public interest is due to one individual.

For the dance means Pavlowa. People say "another Pavlowa" or "a future Pavlowa," when they wish to emphasize their belief in an unknown or future star. The enthusiasm she aroused in 1910 heightens with acquaintance and widens constantly. She has gone into centres of prejudice against the ballet, and in an hour turned hostility into adoration. Her example has affected the character as well as the number of young people in the art. Her ideals are of the highest, and she lives up to them. Her methods of work are an unconscious but effectual crusade against the current mode of slovenly lack of craftsmanship. She is truly the leader of choreographic taste and practise today. Because she is so truly the leader, it will not be amiss to look briefly over her work in range and detail, to the end of ascertaining what are the qualities that leadership requires in addition to the capabilities found in a perfect or even great dancer. Furthermore the time has come when it is possible to establish more definitely than hitherto the place to which Pavlowa is to be assigned in the history of the arts. Her success is not approached in the history of the dance, including as it does both Americas, Europe and the Orient in extent. She is one of the outstanding figures of our time, the holder of an eminence built on her command over beauty and emotion. Yet there is a question whether the very enthusiasm roused by her work has not diverted attention from attributes even greater than the dancing that serves as their outward and visible sign; attributes that can be regarded to better advantage in a quarter-hour of cool retrospection than in the state of inebriate delight with which one sees her performances. For the elements of her art have the perfect union that makes an organism. In appearance it is utterly simple. But simplicity of expression often has been found to retard a just estimate of the thought-content of the work.

The things that Pavlowa does are within every reader's remembrance. The more important matter of how she does them might admit opinion. The authors, therefore, in order to keep this analysis within the bounds of what is universally accepted as to Pavlowa's merits, state of her qualities only such estimates as have been repeatedly recorded by leading critics of London, Paris and New York.

Genius appears, to some extent, to be a matter of natural gifts. Certainly the gods gave Pavlowa everything at their disposal. Intuition, power of intense concentration; alert curiosity, rapid observation, insatiable love of beauty; courage, sympathy and charity. Greatest of all, perhaps, in its contribution to her particular art, is a species of vision into the heart of things; a sensitiveness to what may be called the characteristic state of mind both of animate beings and inanimate things; and receptivity to those impressions which, interpreted into expression, enable Pavlowa to endow flowers and birds and insects with lively and interesting sentiments.

If destiny was concerned in her education, it could not have been more favorable. Pavlowa entered the St. Petersburg academy when it was approaching the peak of its efficiency, and was present through the stimulating period of an artistic upheaval. Better instruction or associations for the training of an artist perhaps never existed.

But of knowledge and skill the gods give none, and teachers only the beginnings. They are bought with the coin of work. At every difficulty aspirations are abandoned; few indeed will toil beyond the attainment of moderate distinction. Pavlowa has endless power to work, endless interest in work. Accepted definitions of finish, or mastery, have meant nothing to her, because to her insatiable interest a step achieved never has meant more nor less than the starting-point of another step.

Take to begin with the technical substructure, the classic ballet: limited as is the number of true "first" men and women, even that little number considerably exceeds the number of those to be deemed complete masters of all departments of the school. Not only is supreme skill required, but skill of as many kinds, almost, as the families of steps. Thus it is seen that perfect turns and *batterie* are rarely accompanied by perfect co-ordination of long movements. Perfect rhythm is unusual. Fine style of one sort or another is a requisite; but of the qualities of majesty, lyrical sweetness, brilliant daintiness, few have more than one. And so nearly impossible is complete command over these many things that it is not demanded. The world justly gives honor to quality, even though limited in range. Yet a review of Pavlowa's repertoire shows her a *prima assoluta* in every department of technique, possessor of styles bewildering in variety. And there, if you please, is one of the keys to this woman's endless power to hold interest: by virtue of command of several distinct fields of attainment, she is a multiple personality. To depth of thought she adds a range that makes her, in effect, several artists, each highly individualized, each superlative of her kind. Her all-round command of technique is only a beginning.

The classic school considers poses with the same care that it gives movement. Pavlowa, always searching added vocabulary, has amplified both its static and dynamic sides, without violence to the fundamentals of either. And she had done a great deal more than that—in the matter of quality of line. What is line? A mark on a surface; the boundary between two areas? Those are designated by the word "line," yes; but owing to poverty of language there is no other word for line that has life: yet as tone differs from noise, or sound, so line may transcend marks. Veronese drew lines that rang, the lines of the Parthenon frieze are a chant of power. Yet, untrammeled as they are by medium, how few painters and sculptors of all time have succeeded in so completely liberating themselves from the limitations of physique as has this woman whose medium is limited to the human body?

To Pavlowa's command of decorative magic of line is at least partly due the "spirituality" so often remarked—especially during recent years. Nor indeed is there any word more appropriate to her ability to deny flesh and blood and weight, her power to put before the eye the living principle of a mood. Perhaps it is this power more than any other that enables her use as subject-matter the most imponderable, impalpable fancies, without ever a suspicion of risk of vagueness; to take the most fragile poetic concept, and say it with unerring clearness.

Poetry is too often considered an art of words. Though wordless, and untranslatable into words, Pavlowa has given the world some exquisite poems. They are addressed, naturally, to the type of imagination which is more approachable through vision than through hearing. To such minds Pavlowa's movement-poems frequently reach a height of eloquence compared with which words seem impotent.

In *Autumn Leaves,* the Chrysanthemum is tossed,

passive, by the heedless *Wind*. Seeing *The Poet,* she adores him as a demi-god, and loves him as a hero; yet timidly. He raises her from the ground; her slow dance is a swooning plea for love. Vaguely puzzled, the unseeing poet leaves her to wither unnoticed. The idea, that of a rudimentary soul pleading for human affection, naturally recalls Fouquet's story, *Undine.* But a comparison between Pavlowa's work and Fouquet's as to beauty reveals the degree to which words are earthbound. Furthermore, to perceptions attuned to the idiom of line and movement, Pavlowa's version appears equally the superior in point of power to stimulate thought.

An older and perhaps better known work is *The Swan.* The arrangement is by Fokine; but Pavlowa's conception and rendering of it, are her own,—as is abundantly demonstrated in the many attempts to imitate it. Through the first movement, the bird floats in gracious enjoyment of the soft-flowing water. Wounded, she reveals none of the horror of physical pain, but is pitiful in her fear at finding herself suddenly helpless; dying, the character of her movement is changed from the short, yet fluid, movement of the second passage into a series of broken gestures that tell something words never have told of resignation to the relinquishment of life. It is poetry released from limitations of words.

In change from such motives are *The Butterfly,* lighter than air, scintillating like a diamond; and the opulent, indolent *California Poppy.* With equal conviction she interprets motives of laughter, of mystery, of exaltation, of tragedy. She is playful, she is majestic. She knows the sentiments of dumb creatures, the states of mind of humanity; and she sings their romance in terms as clear as they are enchanting.

In the manner of representation so far suggested, Pavlowa is seen not as a person, but an instrument of optical music. She has kept distinctly away from realism, which has to do with externals or the surface of nature; and concerned herself with the impalpable, expressing it by means of the combined resources of harmonized movement and decorative design. In keeping with the intent to avoid any approach to imitation of nature, the costumes of these works have been purposely non-committal: variants on the conventional ballet dress, designed to reveal movement, posture and line, but in itself meaningless. The choreography has been purely classic, which is æsthetic and that only. When its detractors call the classic "inhuman" they precisely express its intent. But now, having clarified our remembrance of Pavlowa's use of the classic, we come to a métier of a wholly different sort. The character ballet has the portrayal of humanity as one of its primary purposes. Here is revealed a Pavlowa totally distinct from the person above discussed. A superlatively keen observer of external mannerisms and of human motives, an actress who adds to the devices of her craft the almost occult resources of the dancer. The character ballet choreographically, lies mostly within the field of character dancing. So distinct is the character Pavlowa from the classic Pavlowa, that it is no uncommon thing for spectators unfamiliar with her repertoire to fail to recognize her in successive parts of a performance. Neither uncommon nor strange.

In her character work she rids herself of ballet style to the point of complete change of individuality.

The achievement is the greater in view of a not unusual complication. Though the character ballet is based on character dancing, for the sake of added scope it frequently enriches the leading rôle by free use of classic resources. Dramatic consistency is preserved by making the leading personage a bayadère, for instance; or a country girl inordinately fond of dancing; or a professional dancer. But such increase in scope of the *première's* rôle is usually gained at more or less expense to dramatic consistency. In the complex problem of narration, the expression of mood, and the translation of ballet style into character mannerisms, fidelity to character usually suffers; it becomes evident that the rustic maid is not rustic at all, but an uncompromisingly academic *première danseuse* in peasant costume. And this is not resented, other things being equal, any more than incompleteness in the diverse departments of technique is resented. How can we resent limits of scope? Completeness is too rare to allow us to dwell comfortably on its lack. To be alternately a satisfying dancer and a convincing, illuminating actress is also too rare; a conjunction of the powers of the two is a paradox; impossible. Impossible, but Pavlowa does it. She does it with such perfection of naturalness, such thrilling dramatic effect, that the magnitude of the achievement has hardly been commented on. *Amarilla* is full of instances of her use of this multiple weapon of emotion—this union of histrionic realism with the mood-compelling devices of rhythm and line.

Brought to amuse the guests at a fête, the Gipsy dancer is constrained and timid. Recognizing the *Marquis,* whose betrothal the fête is to celebrate, as a man who has made a conquest of her affections, she wishes to escape. But she is made to perform, and so begins the *adagio.* Mechanically, that number is little more than the familiar set of devices to exploit virtuosity. Pavlowa makes it a condensed romance. Beginning with a slow turn *en attitude,* gripping her brother's tambourine as though to save herself from falling, she raises her face in prayer. Catching sight of the Marquis, she tries to run away. Her brother catches her, gently forces her to continue. Up! With the sweep of a Winged Victory, she strikes the upraised tambourine; abruptly sinking to a kneeling position, she droops like a dead lily. Again up! This time lifted by her brother in a pose of triumph; a tempest of rapid steps, finishing like a jet of flame before the faithless *Marquis,* seeking by the fire of movement to win from him even a glance of the eye. He is indifferent; she, motionless in the *arabesque* that terminated the previous phrase, wilts as though robbed of life.

Opposition of grief and forced gaiety is the motive of the dance. Less than three minutes long, it is the complete revelation of a soul. As Pavlowa performs it, that adagio alone would have brought fame. So would her other *Amarilla* numbers. That bit in which the inert body and arms and the drooping head confess the broken heart, while the trained feet of the dancing girl continue their routine automatically! Technically the steps are of no special consequence;

Pavlowa makes them express the utmost bitterness of dramatic irony.

The *Amarilla* story is admirably suited to ballet construction. It has character interest and dramatic consistency. The Gipsy is doubtless the most famous of Pavlowa's character rôles. But it by no means represents her successful character range. Her Greek is her own evolution; not the unvaried sweetness of the Duncan school, and more piquant than the re-creations of Fokine, and hence sometimes questioned as to its fidelity to "the Greek idea." But regarded in the light of reasonable familiarity with Greek works themselves—not alone the great statues, but hundreds of reliefs, vase decorations and Tanagra figurines—what could be more satisfyingly Hellenic than *Autumn Bacchanale?* or the *Priestess* in *Dionysus?* Passing to the Slavonic still another Pavlowa appears. Her peasant girl in *Russian Dances,* however light in movement, is a peasant in mind and manners; while the steps and their execution reveal not a suspicion of influence outside the Slavonic. Her Mexican dances are said by Mexican connoisseurs to be equally absolute. The list might be considerably increased, if we were to add the fruits of some of her endless experiments, some of which naturally result better than others. Let us then consider only departments in which her absolute mastery is a matter of universal recognition. Leave out, too, schools of character that overlap one another; or merge into one of the above mentioned; and the demi-classic, such as the dancing of the spoiled little girl in *Christmas.* There remain for Pavlowa's repertoire at least three completely dissimilar national families of the dance, beside her limitless command of the classic. The achievement would be incredible if its proof were not easily available by a simple process of mentally reviewing her repertoire.

After all, versatility signifies less than height or depth as the measure of an artist's greatness. It nevertheless is an important part of a star's equipment. Variety, vivid variety, is an essential part of entertainment. Contrast both of matter and of manner. To insure variety (among other things), the great subsidized companies have found it worth while to employ as many as four highly specialized leading women and two leading men. Without variety, it is found (sometimes with pecuniary grief) that appeal is limited to one class of taste, and of interest only a short time. Lack of this necessary condiment has perhaps been as potent as lack of merit in its devastating effect on a number of promising-looking undertakings. If insufficient versatility on the part of leading man and woman is not compensated by the use of specialists, the enterprise fails. Monotony is the capital crime. And the easiest to commit, because an unhappy majority of dancers, though duly impressed with the value of a varied repertoire, fail utterly to note the distinctive mannerisms and states of mind that accompany the several families of national dances. Pavlowa, with her clean distinctions between the schools she represents, has a two-fold advantage. To the entertainment secured by contrasts she adds the sensation of amazement. Amazement at the multiplicity of her abilities. Everybody likes to be amazed. Stars know the importance of it. Pavlowa's arrangements, like Genée's, project a surprise every few seconds: a vivid contrast of long and short, fast and slow, or something equivalent. Genée once said that some such surprise, flashed within the first thirty seconds of a number, was a sure means of getting the attention of any audience. It is of further interest in Pavlowa's work that story—or at least clearly stated motive—is never absent. Her only dances of pure virtuosity occur in ballets, with story interest preceding and following; and even in that protected position, she animates the dance with a wealth of expression.

Every business man knows the value of good will. That advantage Pavlowa has in unlimited measure, and with it an ideal co-operation in all departments. She is square. Square to the point of being quixotic. And she works. She never avails herself of her star's position to avoid the heavy end of the load. To the public she gives generously of her own work always. Her sense of this responsibility was emphasized on an occasion when her *premier* became disabled in mid-performance; she danced the *pas-de-deux* as a solo, and the man's very difficult solo besides. She is modest; her attitude toward her work is essentially that of a student. She is kind. She is carrying a home for Russian refugee orphans, she is equally sympathetic in the little matters of the day's work. She is as courteous to little people as to great people. She has no leading-lady airs. If she has anxieties, she keeps them to herself. If she gets tired, she is never unjust.

Such a person is surrounded by loyalty. Dancers, musicians, stage hands and executive dignitaries delight in doing all that can be done to smooth

Madame Pavlowa's path and help her performances. Such team work money cannot buy.

Nor is her personal side unknown to the world in general, despite the comparative seclusion into which she is placed by her dedication to work. Somehow or other, the fineness of her soul seems to be felt across the footlights. Of even greater importance, from the point of view of the box office if not of sentiment, is the fact that women like her. Without the approval of women, a singer or dancer is destined to a little place. That is a repeatedly demonstrated fact. It would appear, sir, if you think you select the entertainment to which you invite a lady, that you are mistaken. Your chronology is half a century out of the way. Our grandmothers liked Taglioni, and she succeeded; they disliked Ellsler, but she succeeded at least equally, because our grandfathers liked her. Since that time things have changed, have they not?

The whole is equal to the sum of its parts. Many parts of Pavlowa's art elude analysis or description; this sketch is unavoidably inadequate. Nevertheless, if it even partly succeeds, it may freshen our realization, the importance of leadership to the well-being of the art, and our appreciation of the rarity of such a combination of elements as makes leadership possible.

During the years of its existence, the Pavlowa Company has included some notable individuals. Laurent Novikoff, its leading man several years ago and again for the past couple of seasons, is distinguished by virility as a *danseur*, by romance as a mime, and in general by that species of fine thought that achieves interest with simplicity. Of recent years he has reversed an accepted rule of his profession: namely, that after his first few years of work, a *danseur* must lose the brilliance of his small steps—the *batterie*—and prepare a farewell to his lightness. Novikoff has gone right ahead gaining in both. His elevation is easy, grand in style and amazingly strong. His little work has the true crystal sparkle. Since Volinin's retirement, Novikoff and Aveline loom up as the two impressive *danseurs classiques* remaining. But Novikoff, with his authority and his imagination, has a good deal more than the requirements of a *premier danseur,* great as those requirements are.

Volinine, Pavlowa's *premier* for many seasons, is at least temporarily retired. At last reports he was preparing to open a school in Paris. He should achieve brilliant results. The skill that gained him his rank as the most perfect classic dancer of his time was founded on scientific understanding. He was a rare instance of technician by taste and temperament: he laughed with happiness when he met a technical difficulty. But a fine nervous equilibrium that made difficulties easy for him was ultimately broken by anxiety; his parents and brothers were in Russia. At the outbreak of the terror, and during years following, Volinine was unable to get any report of them. It is to be hoped that his retirement is not permanent; in any case there is cause for gratification in that his rare knowledge is not to be lost to the art. He is reported to be preparing to open a school in Paris. His ability to teach, combined with a rare understanding of scientific principles, will be of important service to the art in the years to come.

At the start of the war, Pavlowa and her company

were in Germany, so a number of her Slavonic members were interned. To replace some of the women, she selectd a group of English girls. They were very young; they have grown up in the Pavlowa company, under Madame Pavlowa's personal supervision of their minds, morals and tastes. One of them is Miss Hilda Butsova (name Russianized), who has advanced to leading rôles, and performs them with winning charm. Another, Miss Muriel Stuart, has gained steadily in grace, authority and interest.

Of the men who have made their identities felt, Pianowski always contributes a piquant wit and substantial merit as a dancer. Zalewski is a delightful mime; like Damoslavski, he is a fiery character dancer as well. Another veteran—as years are counted in this too short-lived profession—is Vajinski. Oliveroff—known to his parents and friends as Oliver Grimes—is an American boy who is giving satisfaction in important numbers. Kobeleff has become a teacher, located in New York and highly successful. It is noteworthy, the high average Pavlowa's boys and girls make in constructing sane and successful lives for themselves—whether continuing in her troupe, or in others, or in the retirement of teaching, or in matrimony.

Pavlowa has been fortunate in her musical direction. For nearly fifteen years continuously, this department has had the service of Mr. Theodore Stier. Conducting an orchestra for the accompaniment of dancing, has peculiar and baffling requirements. Mr. Stier's sympathetic skill in it makes him an important contributor to the spirit of performances. Finally and most important of Madame

ADELINE GENEE
From a dry-point by Troy Kinney

Pavlowa's *entourage* is Mr. V. Dandré, her husband. A gentle, cultivated aristocrat of the old régime, he successfully devotes his limitless tact and his varied capabilities to the inconspicuous but infinitely important tasks concerned with the smooth running of a complex mechanism. Yes, he is exactly the husband you would have selected for Madame Pavlowa.

To return to our subject, it will be seen that Pavlowa's art is based on craftsmanship. Which, as an influence, is the most wholesome that could be applied to the arts of today, as tending to counteract that creed which defends sloppy workmanship by the claim of individuality. The value of such individualities as declare themselves expressed in freakish and incompetent workmanship needs no appraiser. One would suppose they would be laughed out of existence. But they are not, and furthermore they are backed by a considerable volume of sanction. As to the dance, whatever may have been Isadora Duncan's original precepts does not matter much. Her ideas are too often used—perhaps distorted—to read in effect as follows: "God has made me in his own image. What is Natural to me is therefore Right. What is difficult for me is False." What could be more attractive? Particularly to the individual of the quack type; of whom droves are found in a profitable entertainment of innocents who think they are learning something in their classes in "nature dancing." Be it emphasized that there are teachers, specialized in the Greek, who have real standards and who really teach. Some of them advise concurrent study in ballet, with good results. But the Greek métier has been peculiarly suited to the soft-spoken incompetent. Success is made easy by the masterfully simple method of encouraging the self-indulgent to quit where difficulty begins. Of this cult the disciples number thousands; and they are a factor to be reckoned with in the dance of tomorrow. Not content with the adulation of parents and friends, they must appear in public. Among the public, they can count on the approval of that ubiquitous element that can recognize an artist by her slim, boyish figure, and devoutly swallows anything bearing the label "Nature." To justify the label it seems necessary only to dispense with shoes and stockings, which *per se* are of no consequence whatever; and with skill and sense, which are essential to anything more edifying than a mere romp. What is the effective difference between meaningless displays of cuticle in recherché halls, and the old-fashioned "girl shows" on Fourteenth Street? An ugly comparison. But the latter is precisely the thing that brought the ballet into disrepute. When they turn their attention away from the flattery of quack teachers and toward facts, a great many young women of today will see that it takes more than bare legs to make a movement poem, and that they have got to have movement poems of intelligible interest if their work is going to get the respect they want it to have.

The true artist's habit of self-criticism often leads him to depreciate his own attainments. Imagination envies technique; and vice versa. In the old St. Petersburg ballet, technique was a common enough possession; and certain of the artists, discovering the virtues of imagination, fell into a way of holding technique as cheap. They had acquired their own skill at such an early age that it ceased to mean anything to them; they proclaimed that imagination was everything. With their right hands these people have sped up the machine, while their left has inadvertently dropped a monkey wrench among the gears. Their virtues and failings are about equally expressed in the famous productions of the Diaghilew troupe: the *Ballet Russe.*

This great organization toured America two eventful seasons, 1915-16 and 1916-17. Notwithstanding previous losses of individual contributors to its sudden fame in Paris in 1909, it was still a magnificent company of dancers. Things began happening at the public dress rehearsal, when it became evident the Mlle. Maclezova, who had been hastily substituted for Mme. Karsavina, was not adequate. Karsavina, it seemed, had suffered a last-minute premonition that if she took ship for America she would be torpedoed. Fortunately Lydia Lopoukowa was in New York. Having adopted America as her home, but finding no satisfactory setting for her work, she had been preparing herself for dramatic work, and indeed seemed to have identified herself with acting. But again fortunately she had—apparently more from habit than purpose—kept up her daily practise at Albertieri's. She was hurriedly called in: had to learn leading rôles with bewildering speed; put up as valiant a fight against fatigue as ever was seen; immediately captured everybody's affections and never fell short of the requirements of a true *première.* She and Bolm were thus the stars. A little later the release of Nijinski from an internment camp in Austria, effected through the efforts of Mr. Penfield, the American ambassador, put his name at the head of the list.

The first season was preceded and accompanied by such a volume of publicity as would have satisfied a political campaign manager. The second had very little; but, so far as New York was concerned, was remarkable for an intermittent stream of letters to the newspapers—letters curiously similar in pattern and even phraseology—protesting the troupe's use of the Metropolitan Opera House, protesting even the use of this and that music for purposes of dance accompaniment. At that time Russia was still an active Ally. It was whispered that the Russian Ballet was in America on a mission of propaganda. And it certainly is true that its art promoted good feeling toward Russia. One may infer nothing or something, as pleases him. The second season's losses (in no way minimized by M. Diaghilew's habitual opulence in every department) ran into the hundreds of thousands. The deficit was paid by Mr. Otto Kahn, as guarantor.

The *corps de ballet* back of the stars and *artistes* was a wonder of versatility, seemingly capable of anything. When its ability was utilized, the results surpassed description. But just as Mikaïl Fokine ultimately became obsessed by emotion and effect to the exclusion of choreographic structure, so M. Diaghilew had discovered the importance of ensemble effect in relation to the ballet. Both gentlemen were right, both were needed, both produced some great expressions. And some of the other kind, too. M. Diaghilew sometimes overlooked the fact that the mission of a dancer is to dance. With the coöperation of Fokine and Nijinski, he invented the Danceless Ballet. We had the spectacle of dancers posturing; sometimes with design and meaning, at best dropping a long step toward the decadence of the dance. In productions not shown in America, Diaghilew also has presented spectacles in which the posturing lacks sometimes design, sometimes meaning, in some cases both. Which, of course, represents the decadence even of the spectacle. But that is out of this discussion. Here we are concerned with the art of the dance.

With reference to choreographic content, the Diaghilew repertoire divides itself roughly into three categories, ranging from pure expositions of dancing, through ballet dramas in which the dance is more or less embellished by narrative and other interests, down to a *genre* in which the dance practically disappears. The first was exemplified in *les Sylphides* and *la Princesse Enchantée*. Both were composed by Fokine, both were masterpieces of pure beauty. Both were classic in structure, consisting of the developments of simple themes through surprising variations into intoxicating climaxes of moving design. Pure dancing for its own sake. Of lesser technicians than Lopoukowa and Nijinski, and the latter's alternates, Idzikovski and Gavriloff, they would have been a depressing exposé of shortcomings. As performed by these admirable artists, *Sylphides* and *la Princesse* and *le Spectre de la Rose*, were sparkling wine of the finest vintage.

Typical of the second class, that of ballet-drama, were *Petrouchka, Schéhérazade, Cléopâtre* and *l'Oiseau de Feu*. These, too, though not of the superlative choreographic interest of *Sylphides* and *Princesse*

Enchantée, were highly satisfying as dance vehicles, and collectively interesting in the range of purposes the dance was made to serve. The pathos of the doll Petrouchka's triviality, yearnings and grief, were carried straight to your heart without stepping outside the terrain of the classic, while dances of character gave the coachmen and nursemaids a flesh-and-blood reality. Of *Schéhérazade* the Oriental premise admitted a suite of arrangements at once exotic and picturesque. Each dance was admirably successful in creating the mood appropriate to the action. In *Cléopâtre* the Queen's revels justified troops of dancing slaves; Egyptians, Jewesses, Greeks; and a dance of love (performed by Bolm and Sokolova) that was a revelation of delicate lyrical fantasy. *L'Oiseau de Feu* was a tale of enchantment, witty and sparkling. The twelve maidens attained exaggerated feminine tenderness in a meltingly fluid Greek number, the motley army of enchanted captives came forth in an amazing riot of character steps, seemingly unrelated yet unified in a definite harmony. In these things Fokine was truly imposing. His power to make movement laugh or cry, plead or threaten, anything he chose, was magic. A poet of motion and a designer of groups.

The above are only instances of the species of genuine ballets, in the true sense of the word, in which the repertoire was rich. To their dressing Bakst and his fellow-painters brought a bewildering opulence of form and color—with opulence married to consistent common sense; everything in conformity with character and locale. That the *décor* was not subordinated to the dancers was resented by individuals to whom the ballet means dancing only. But such protest means rather a declaration of the individual's taste than a criticism of principle. What Diaghilew was after was ensemble, and he got it. A sumptuous picture animated with movement; bewildering with light effects; enchanting with music, which in many cases was composed to suit the story; and—up to this point of the discussion, always making good use of the dance. These wholesome works, underneath all their lavishness and novelty, were a perfectly satisfying realization of rational ideas as to ballet form and structure.

Up to this point it is seen that the dancers did what they and only they can do: they danced. But now we come to a *genre* in which they were asked to compete with Greek ceramic decorations; for that was the self-evident origin of the work of the four nymphs in the much-discussed *Après-Midi d'un Faune*. The comparison was invited and unavoidable, as the nymphs did not dance. They posed, in arbitrary, angular shapes, with profile toward the spectator. But cloth is cloth, and archaic design is a drastic translation of natural forms to severe triangles and rectangles. Such translation was out of reach of soft textures and rounded flesh. That the nymphs' "business" was amusing is not the point. In style, which was the very premise of the undertaking, they fell between stools. They missed the translation of forms to pure ornament, on one side, as far as they had departed from Nature on the other. In trying to make flesh and cloth spell geometry, somebody had stepped into the ancient trap of trying to do with one medium that which another medium would have done better. The stage *décor* consisted of a big set rock and a strikingly handsome back drop; admirably composed, yet sufficiently naturalistic in treatment to create an impression of actuality. The Faun, caught between a Scylla of quasi-archaic nymphs and a Charybdis of an almost naturalistic drop on the other, oscillated in style between the two extremes.

Yet *The Faun* was a success. Debussy's music was ravishing, the lighting a cool suffusion enchantingly harmonious with *décor,* music and idea. Furthermore, police attended the first New York performance. Though nothing occurred to shock even a policeman, either then or later, hope nevertheless sprang eternal that Nijinski, in the title rôle, would do something salacious, as he was rumored to have done in Paris. This last was not the least of the reasons why *The Faun* continued to be talked about, though obviously its many real beauties contributed to its success.

That success marks the advent of a species of representation which with approximate accuracy, may be christened The Danceless Ballet. This monstrosity is by no means always regarded as a butterfly with wings torn off. Pleasing in its color, its possible influence on the art of the dance was not generally considered.

The choreographically decadent tendency was further evidenced the second season in a creation by Nijinski, *Till Eulenspiegel*. Equally sterile as to dancing, *Till* was not even intelligible in its posturing. If its story was comprehensible at all, its comprehension was clearly limited to readers (and possibly writers) of the souvenir program. Certainly, it could make no reasonable claim to be considered drama. If anything, it was spectacle—the word is conveniently elastic. But subtract from *Till* the work of painter, tailor, musician and electrician, and the remainder was zero. Or, to be strictly just, a gaily colored blown egg. But it bore the name of Diaghilew; any question of *Till's* merits, or even the premise on which he stood, could start an argument instantaneously.

The Diaghilew experiments—or novelties, according to your estimate of the man—reach even further radicalism in *Sacre du Printemps* and *Noces*. These works of posture realistically portray—or deride—the uncouthness of primitive man and the peasant. For the grand style of the dancer, they substitute brutish uncouthness; far from picturesque, they are merely ugly. Why produce them? Who knows? Because they are novel? Or because one type of mind believes that a subject which is enshrined in poems or theatres is *ipso facto* to be considered beautiful? And being considered beautiful, is beautiful? on the theory that beauty is subjective, and is a matter of sensation rather than fact. For who is to say what beauty is? Undeveloped taste likes red and orange; people grow to like violet. Who shall say that the entire alphabet of beauty is yet known to humanity? Bernhardt said there is always a graceful way to do even an awkward thing. But who knows but what tomorrow Bernhardt's devices may be deemed quite incompetent? A fidgety world craves an always widening range of dramatic expression, or at least sensation.

Of such casuistry is one side of the argument. It all springs from the same root as the various modern isms in design. The radical is moved by a desperate desire (not always based on incompetence, either) to hack and hammer out a short cut to some new way of conveying emotion, of attaining at the same time a new set of devices for the production of harmony.

However much or little bearing the above has on the aberrations of M. Diaghilew, the rigorous honesty of his great works certainly entitles him to the presumption of sincerity even in his chaotic experiments. Nevertheless, his sincerity does not mitigate the influence his vivid, much-discussed danceless ballets exercise on the dance. To less discerning theatrical managers even the best output of the Ballet Russe has meant nothing more than novelty of subject-matter and gorgeous setting. Whence a flood of polychromatic splurges with dancing that rarely merits the name; and, if these gaudy confections of nudity and noise can successfully claim the high virtue of novelty, they frequently succeed. Pecuniarily, that is. Also dancers, all but the clearest-headed, feel that they almost have the great Diaghilew's blessing on posturing as a substitute for dancing. To make him responsible for all the laziness and obtuseness on the dancing stage would be absurd, of course. But his prestige has been enormous; inevitably the green fruit of his garden has been swallowed with the ripe.

Not much is required to complete the vicious circle. When he starts with the belief that the public wants the lavish and bizarre, the producer requires little dancing, but much nudity. The student of the art is bound to feel misgivings as to the value of continued sacrifices to study. There is easy work and a living for the half-trained. "Will there be an outlet for my best if I perfect myself?" she asks. She can only hope. That a substantial number of ambitious dancers keep right on in the present conditions represents such a fidelity to ideals as deserves a very genuine respect.

Yes, several American girls, and a few boys, have really learned to dance. Their finished work gets them well-paid positions; but positions in which, as a rule, they are at once bidden to forget art and "jazz it up." Does the statement look overdrawn? Preposterous that an employer should not avail himself of his employees' best services! All right. Lydia Kyasht, one of Diaghilew's very brightest stars ten years ago, was brought to Broadway under contract. The pearls of her work were cast in one of those lavish quasi-vaudevilles; nevertheless, the clientage quickly began to show signs of appreciation. In which respect they showed more perception than the management did. Up to the time she had the good fortune to be attacked by typhoid fever (which automatically terminated her contract), the manager was having Kyasht instructed in the turkey trot! His "idea" was that she ultimately should combine it with acrobatic novelties. In tastes and perceptions, this manager is far from unique. Another instance of the same common or simian passion for destruction came under my direct notice in the early adventures of the Cansinos. It is pertinent as a revelation of the criteria by which most—not all, but too many—theatrical managers think about the dance. Mrs. Hawkesworth, who brought them from Madrid, showed them in entertainments of the social leaders, with invariable success. Offered to Tom Shanley, he took them without a second's hesitation; and during their season in his cabaret, they never failed to please. In other words, there was not the shadow of a question of their appeal to that which is called the average taste—which is by no means so depraved as is commonly supposed. It is distinguished from so-called good taste largely by a greater range of assimilation. The Cansinos successfully demonstrated that average taste is perhaps even better pleased with unadulterated wine of Spain than it is with the froth usually thrown before it. But they wanted to get into the theatre; did so, and by a justifiable subterfuge forced their legitimate work onto a management which persisted in grieving, despite the success of the Spanish work. But before getting this contract they "tried out" for managers and managers' "experts" until try-outs became a habit. The verdicts were droll in their uniformity. The formula was as follows:

"Now, you're an artist and I'm an artist, and we can appreciate the fine points of this stuff. But the public! What does the public know about art? Between you and me, not a thing. Not a thing! These kids are dancers; no question about that. Artists. But take a tip from me. If you want to make money on 'em"—(the writer didn't; but what's the use trying to explain such radicalism?)—"if you want to make any money on 'em, you've got to get the clothes off 'em, or else make 'em do something novel—acrobatic, for instance, or both. St. Denis? Clothes off. Genée? Name. Russian Ballet? Name, novelty, *and* clothes off. And that's all there is to it. Now, have these Cansinos get something the public wants, and we can do business. But we're not running an art exhibition; we're here to make money."

The devilish part of it is, these people were speaking in perfect sincerity. They were advising according to their beliefs, the chart by which they travel. They speculate on that which is within the range of their understanding and appreciation, and on that only. And within that scope they must continue to operate if they do not wish to be operated on by court of bankruptcy. A few days after a man begins speculating on things he does not understand, there is just one result, and it is fairly well known.

Moreover, they were half right about the public, regarding matters from the immediate and practical point of view. And that is the point of view from which the matter must be regarded by the man in the theatrical business. Building for the future at present sacrifice is an indulgence; a hazardous undertaking, mercilessly expensive if not successful. If not quickly successful, too. The expenses of a production reach their maximum promptly on opening night, and go right on just the same, attendance or no attendance. Now, one of the peculiarities about the public of cultivated taste is its slowness to assemble—unless as the managers say, a great name can be used as a magnet. There are demonstrably several hundred thousand possessors of good taste in this country; more numerically than there are or ever were in any other country, and probably as great a percentage of the population. Their allegiance to good art is firm once they have given it. But their slowness to take hold is notorious. Justified, of course, by past impositions. But it is not an ethical proposition. The practical aspect of the matter is this: the financially critical period of a production is its first couple of weeks. And that is just the time when, if designed exclusively for cultivated taste, it would lack support, unless it had the attraction of names. Otherwise, hopeless. Without big star names a ballet of angels accompanied by the heavenly choir would be bankrupted by payroll and rent before it could get properly started. Whereas the Jazz Follies stands a good chance of "capacity business" right from the first minute.

It having thus been demonstrated that the ballet's failure of desirable development is due wholly to shortcomings of managers and public, it is now in order to anticlimax the whole argument by the interjection of further complications; which is unfortunate in more ways than one. The way to be interesting, according to the advice of our successful literary friends, is to present one side of the case and one only. No reader can reasonably be asked to keep track of complications. But complication is the very essence of the difficulty in which the dance now stands. If all managers were a cross between a wolf and a turtle, and all dancers combined the proficiency of Genée with the depth of Duse, the situation would be delightfully simple. But neither supposition—even if derived from the foregoing paragraphs—is true. It is therefore suggested to the layman that he skip a few pages, for the two-fold sake of preserving any interest he may have developed in this discussion, at the same time avoiding the indelicacy of which he might accuse himself after having read a few plain remarks directed to the dancers themselves.

Dancers, friends, by and large you are the best people on earth. Certainly no other profession offers greater difficulties than your own, equally certainly there is no profession whose practitioners meet their difficulties more gallantly than you meet and conquer yours. The mastery of the technique of your trade is an achievement before which we others—those of us who know its difficulties—stand in deferential respect. It is a great thing to be able to dance, but it is not enough. It is not enough to earn you a proper living, it is not enough to make you an artist.

For the dance is a *means* of expression, not an expression by itself. Your steps are a vocabulary, your form is a grammar. But do vocabulary and grammar make a poem? Essential, yes; but not the essence. The heart of the poem is the thought, the fancy, the imagining you put into it. Your multiple pirouette finished with a perfectly balanced *attitude* is a singer's vocal exercise perfectly executed. Neither, however perfect, is in itself an expression. Expression in your silent art is in the tone of voice, if you will admit a Hibernianism for the sake of clarity. And there can be no intelligent expression unless there is a thought to be expressed.

When a solo is danced by an artist, a little drama is performed; and the proficient dancer is only one in the cast of characters. That those characters are invisible—all except yourself—takes nothing from their importance; for they are such as Aspiration, Reverie, Ecstasy, Mischief, and Reverence. For these and a legion more invisible spirits you, the dancer, are the medium; but only the medium. It is to fit yourself to serve them as medium that you have toiled these thousand days for perfect beauty of movement. And rejoice that you have toiled. Your colleagues who have neglected technical rigors in the more comfortable companionship of their vanity are deluded. For they are speakers without tongues; though their thoughts be of gold, none will heed their mouthings. Live as they may with the invisible spirits of mood, they will never realize those moods to minds outside their own.

Your art is difficult. All art is difficult. Your difficulties, though great, are not unique. For the art school does not teach art, never did, never will. Because it could not if it tried. When it undertakes more than the technical methods of an art it reproduces a superficial imitation of the master. Can the master tell his thoughts of tomorrow? Can he impart his discipline of thought, or the process by which his mind works? Not at all. If in association with a hundred minds he awakens one of them, at most he has proven that a mind was there. It would have opened itself, as a bud opens into a leaf. The student of painting who has learned how to construct and model a figure is first hurt, then indignant at the world because his academic skill is unnoticed. In the course of time it dawns on him that his draftmanship is as the ability to pen legible letters; if he has vision and feeling, he will then invest his subjects with such qualities of line and form and color as will sing his motive. If he lacks vision and feeling he turns to the freakish, whispers of conspiracies, cries aloud (you've heard the cry!) that the public should be educated up to the artist. Between ourselves, how many artists do you know that are educated up to the public?

Let me introduce at this point a cultivated gentle-

ADOLPH BOLM IN "PRINCE IGOR"
From a dry-point by Troy Kinney

To face page 320

man whose name shall be withheld, though it is by no means unfamiliar. His interest in the dance is sympathetic and discerning. His business is the organization and promotion of theatrical art enterprises. He is, in short, a manager. He is as nice a person as you and I know, and as intelligent; and he is by no means unique among managers, at that. Last summer he earnestly wished to assemble a worthy though small dancing troupe for the present season. Why didn't he? Prepare for a shock: the necessary quality and variety of art could not be got. What he says might equally well have been said by any of several of his colleagues.

"A thing that too many dancers forget is that an art attraction, to stand the slightest chance of success, is under the absolute necessity of having about it something superlatively good. Merely creditable will not do. It ought to have about it something of greatness. Which means, to begin with, a big thought. But big thoughts require a grand execution. Now, in looking around among these scores of hopes, what do I find? Two classes. The first of a few who dance well enough to say something, if they had anything to say; no great fault to be found with their work, but it simply is not interesting. And a second category full of a mess of Nature, Oriental fantasies and Greek legends that they've grabbed in bits from random sources, that means nothing to them, and which they haven't the technique to express even if it did.

"Good academy dancers don't understand why their technical inferiors sometimes get the jobs. It's perfectly simple. A boy or girl that can't dance much sometimes can give a message at least of amiable youth. And that's considerable; anyhow, as compared with an exposé of painstaking work. That's why we buy 'personality.' Who wouldn't rather have both than the one thing alone? But you show me a dancer that has both, and I'll show you a dancer that's getting along very nicely, thanks. Show me one that can dance and has personality and something poetic to say, and I'll show you one that has all the contracts she wants. Or if she hasn't," he added thoughtfully, "one that soon will have."

"All very well," you say. "Supposing all this is true. We admit a lack of those qualities that must be developed largely by professional experience. But in present conditions, how are we to get the experience? The theatre has very few places for anything in the zone between the perfectly meaningless on one side, and perfected art on the other. The immature painter has entrée to exhibitions, where he learns his failings. Where is the immature dancer to get the equivalent?"

It is difficult. That art is hard is repeated so often and so glibly that the words have lost force. But the fact is still there, as emphatically as it was a thousand years ago. And this is inevitable, for a particluar reason: the artist must pay in advance. Except in such conditions as sometimes have been decreed or legislated, the artist pays the world in advance. Because, you see, the coin in which the world pays the artist has a standard value; if the coin is counterfeit or of short weight you can prove it and get quick redress. But the artist cannot agree in advance to deliver work of a specified standard of interest. No field of human effort permits and invites self-deception so plausibly as do the arts; innocently and in good faith artists offer counterfeit and short weight art in exchange for legitimate coin, and fight if the fact is called to their attention. So you must pay in advance. Pay in advance means develop rational interest over and above technique, and demonstrate your command of it. Not to expect interest in that which you will, might or could do.

Proceed as painters do: by group exhibitions. Group, because individual recitals develop smattering knowledge; a half-knowledge of ten things is rubbish; one good thought and the ability to say it with charm is gold. So select your group with an eye on harmonious variety, work out your program on a basis that excuses are of interest to none but their inventors; and when you have something to show, it will be time to think about your theatre.

"But doesn't all this require a great deal more than the qualities of an artist?" you ask. Certainly. Anybody who thinks that the business of being an artist requires only the distinctively art-producing faculties gets his notions from fiction and the stage. Initiative, clear planning and endless determination are unpicturesque, unsung and absolutely essential qualities of the successful artist. So are the ability to do without things, which is possible only if your art is your play as well as your work; and a little cash capital, which sometimes spells independence at a moment when independence is useful. All very prosy; but, despite the implications of mischievous and shallow historians, absolutely essential if you are going to raise your art from the somewhat humiliating posture of a being who "deserves to be supported." Interesting, art is bought and paid for. But in a condition of future and hoped-for interest,—well, what do you think about it, yourself?

But the worst is yet to come. When you arrive at that step of your group organization where it is pertinent to assure yourself that your colleagues have each three good numbers—just three; numbers well composed, with a sentiment read into every phrase, that they have learned to the point that they can render them with easy precision and charm; at that point you are going to be surprised how few are prepared to deliver the best that is in them. And when you learn how many eager individuals haven't even the three acceptable arrangements, with or without the accompaniment of meaning, you are going to have need of patience. You see, a great many of the less fortunate brothers and sisters think they deserve to be engaged on their apparent possibilities. They want to be paid in advance.

For a time you must be two people, the eternal student, and the bread-winner to keep the student alive. It is no easy thing to hold a job kicking the back of your head eight performances a week, and improving your proper art in between times. Call it impossible; this is one of the not uncommon cases in which the impossible has got to be accomplished. When it shall have been accomplished up to the point of producing a genuinely interesting art, accomplished by even a small group that will approximately hang together, you will have the national choreographic situation in your own grip; for there is a big public whose ideals are the same as yours. But it never will preoccupy itself very heartily with

TENDENCIES?

ideals not realized; the task of making them real is yours.

The immediately expedient means of developing the ballet is endowment. But endowment, while capable of speeding up the process of growth and arrival at full bloom, cannot always produce a healthy organism. Diaghilew, subsidized, miraculously produced a century plant in full flower. But, since funds once applied to the arts have been diverted to postwar reliefs, the organization has revealed a surprising lack of power to nourish and water itself. It is as though it had grown over-dependent on the lavishness of production formerly possible. In any event, since the enforced curtailment of physical splendor, the better dancers one by one have dropped away from the Diaghilew troupe. New works, therefore, of necessity if not from choice, have had to be composed in conformity with the limits of mediocre dancers. And a ballet without real dancing needs lavish setting to hold the interest even of novelty seekers. That becomes evident. The vicious circle tightens: reduced total of dancing ability in the troupe, increased need of the freakish as a grab at public interest; increasing freakishness, greater irritation to capable artists, more resignations. The most recently reported defection was of Lopoukowa, who for several years had remained as the last of a once great group.

Pavlowa, on the other hand, is not subsidized and never has been since her début as an independent star. Her tuition and formative experience, of course, were acquired in the old St. Petersburg ballet. But as the head of a private enterprise she has employed brain, of which she has a fine equipment, as a substitute for dollars, of which at first she had comparatively few. She has danced, instead of posturing among novel scenery. She has produced dancing ballets, and consequently built up a ruggedly healthy organization.

For our young dancers one promising field, as fast as they qualify for it, is in "concertizing." This scheme of joint performance with orchestras has not yet been made to show its best possibilities, and has been mussed more or less by soulful incompetents. But the potential attractiveness of the mixed form of entertainment has been demonstrated beyond doubt.

A promising demand for good work is found in the moving picture houses. Not dancing for the films—which up to the present has not amounted to much; but supplementing them as part of the program. Bolm and Fokine and Mme. Sonia Serova have put on some smart arrangements for certain big New York houses. The heaviest handicaps are the weekly change of bill, which cuts very short the time for preparation; and shallow stages, restricting work. Yet the very difficulties have called attention to the importance of the underrated item of arrangement. These little ballets must "get" their spectators quickly. A simple theme must be chosen, so as to be understood; and adhered to, so as to make the rhythm felt. It is no place for self-deception; eccentricity or ugliness under the label of mysticism are not for that kind of a public. What is wanted is narrative; limited to familiar subject-matter, and so much the better; but above all, expressed clearly. The ability to create dance-pantomime stories is rare; and that's the main reason why the art in general is not on a more substantial basis. The composers of movie theatre ballets who do not regard their work merely as a job have in it an extraordinary opportunity. The practise in developing dances consistently with their themes; of creating really interesting stories; of finding their interpretation in broad pantomime and comprehensible symbol—practise in these things is practise in things which accomplished, are of interest to people of all classes and estates. Augment interest with satisfying beauty of execution, and you will have a grand art. And an art which incidentally will create its own supporting public. But the public will not pay much attention to dances that are dances only and without visible significance, unless they are executed with such supreme virtuosity as is seen once in a generation. And even supreme virtuosity generally invests them with motive, if not obvious narrative.

Ruth St. Denis with her professional and matrimonial partner, Ted Shawn, last season made highly successful tours of the United States and England. They secure performers largely from among their own pupils. The St. Denis creed is described in another part of this book. Her work, always widening in range, holds creditably up to her standards. She remains true to the Oriental as a means of expressing the kind of thoughts she likes to think. She has taken a deep interest in teaching, with the result that "Denishawn" is a veritable chain of schools, extending from New York to Los Angeles. Her high faith in the dance, not only as an art, but as a factor in education, are fully shared by Ted Shawn. Both are the essence of sincerity. Their success as dancers and producers is uncompromised by any concessions to shallow taste. The sacrifices Ruth St. Denis made, the obstacles she had to overcome, entitle her to abundant reward; that she is getting it is indeed a cause for satisfaction. Always she has kept good faith with her ideals. Beginning unknown, she introduced her then unknown art to an indifferent world; and the world is the better for it. She never has been too centred on her own interests to be a constant friend of all legitimate branches of the dance.

The Metropolitan and the Chicago Civic Opera Companies are more liberal with the ballet than might justly be asked of organizations dedicated, as they are, primarily to music. Yet by the very importance they give the dance, they invite comparison with the best. Of the Chicago Company it is a little too late and a little too early to write. Adolf Bolm has recently been installed as ballet master. His capabilities qualify him to effect a radical change for the good, if he is given due opportunity. In our older Metropolitan, however, the visible changes during recent years have been few and of minor importance; and in its stationary condition invites examination.

As a preface to discussion of anything pertaining to the Metropolitan Opera, be it said that one feels that expressions of anything but appreciation have some of the indelicacy of looking gift horses in the mouth. It is run at a big annual deficit. In our special field of the dance, it was the Metropolitan Opera that gave America its first vision of the new Russian dancing. Pavlowa and Mordkin were brought to America in 1910, for and by the Metropolitan Opera Company, as an extra attraction;

followed by a similar engagement of Pavlowa and a little company the following season. Those were the very first steps leading to the revival of choreographic interest in this country. Subsequently it has adequately produced *Coq d'Or* and *Petrouchka*.

With its own ballet the opera has been liberal. Whereas it buys singers ready-made, it conducts a ballet school and provides excellent instruction. The present and very capable instructress is Miss Marguerite Curtiss. Her predecessor was Madame Verhoeven, former *première* at the Brussels opera; hers, in turn, Madame Cavallazi, former *première* at La Scala. Nothing lacking in quality of teachers. Of the students who persist the necessary length of time, a due proportion have learned to dance. As they qualify for work on the stage, they are fairly paid; no great bother on that score. In performances the ballet is beautifully costumed, given its due number of minutes of time. When it was found that boys were needed, they were added.

The head of this department is Miss Rosina Galli, famous as one of the most capable dancers in the theatre today. Giuseppe Bonfiglio is thoroughly satisfying as her supporting man and as a *danseur*. Yet as the general result of all this liberality, about the best that its friends can say of the Metropolitan ballet is that it is mildly pleasing. Not great, not a leader. As compared with St. Petersburg or Paris, it has made a very slight impression. In music, the Metropolitan Opera has thrilled the world. Why not also in the dance? Is the dance a less potent art, or of less interest to the public? The answer to such questions is in *Sylphides* and *Amarilla* and a dozen more ballets that concede nothing, either in stimulating power or in vitality, to any music that ever sounded. No, the shortcoming is not in the art, nor in the personnel. When capable dancers fail to interest, the shortcoming is usually in their arrangements.

Arrangement is the most neglected of all the elements of the dance today. Well-considered sequences of movements are exactly as essential to interest, charm, value, or anything else in a dance as are well-considered sequences of tones to the merits of a song. The parallel between the two is exact. The qualities of each has its counterpart in the other. Intrinsically, the two are equally potent as media; both require skill and care for the production of respectable results. Song gives the more to him whose stimuli come best through hearing; but another whose emotions are fed through sight receives more exaltation from the dance. How thoughtfully a worth-while musical composer considers his motive, experiments and eliminates in building up his composition, is familiar knowledge. Singers use infinite care in selecting songs. Yet more often than not you are confronted by a suite of dances scratched together, composed and taught to a *corps de ballet* in a few days, or even hours. The same condition is found in England. Madame Genée emphatically confirms these observations, that better arrangement is the urgent need of the dance today. Few dancers, even, appreciate what arrangement means.

It is not surprising, therefore, to find the importance of movement-composition overlooked by the administration even of a magnificent institution, when that institution exists primarily for the production of music. The Metropolitan ballet has done all that can be expected in the circumstances. If the circumstances were inflexible, they would not be worth mentioning. But they could be changed, so here some of them are.

To the hard and time-consuming work of *première danseuse,* Miss Galli adds the duties of ballet directress. The functions of the latter are to drill the *corps de ballet,* and compose new dances when necessary. A few operas are sung sufficiently often each season to keep their ballet arrangements familiar. Of most of these standbys the choreography, as handed down, consists of dead, symmetrical lines and squares of *coryphées,* plus a meaningless assemblage of academy tricks for the *première;* the logical fruit of the most banal period of dance history.

All right; why not modernize them?

There's the rub. There isn't time. Glance over a month's list of performances, and you wonder how Miss Galli, over and above her daily technical practise, found time to drill her people even in the arrangements established by old tradition. The occasional call for an entirely new group of dances for a new opera brings no relief. Quite the contrary. Such a task should have weeks of undistracted attention. A poem of movement or words or tone may conceivably arrive full-fledged in its author's brain, and yet be found to contain thought. But such inspirations are at best rare. By and large, an interesting work of art has a considered set of ideas, simplified and carefully juxtaposed, and finally wrought into the semblance of spontaneity. It is not the slightest criticism of anybody concerned to observe that the combined tasks of *première danseuse* and ballet directress of an opera company with a huge repertoire leave wholly inadequate time for due study of arrangements. Assistants to drill groups may reduce the pressure somewhat. But they cannot change the fact that the work of a *danseuse* intrudes upon and disturbs a mind that tries to do justice to the exacting work of composition.

A second handicap under which the Metropolitan ballet labors is a steady drain of its better performers. The reason is by no means always money; though opportunities to quintuple one's pay by the simple act of learning a set of tricks of the revue are a test of allegiance. But despite that practically standing inducement, there is a strong preference in favor of the opera and its dignified work. The sore point is the hopelessness of achieving rank in proportion to ability. "Why should I be satisfied with being a *coryphée* as long as I continue to dance?" a girl asks. "I've worked steadily in that ballet for years. I'm one of its best dancers. Yet my position is exactly the same as it was at the start. I'm simply a member of the Metropolitan Opera *corps de ballet*. I get a few dollars more per week than I did five years ago, and in another five years I'll get a little more than I do now. But what good does that do when you feel as though—if you work hard enough and long enough—you'd like to be Somebody?"

You see, between *première* and *coryphée* this ballet offers its young women the hope of just one position. It has one "soloist." Among perhaps two-score competitors for that position if it should become vacant, the individual's chances are an easy problem of arithmetic. To be sure, there is a little self-created distinction between "front-line girls" and "back-line girls." But such make-believe is no adequate encouragement for ambition. These are not disappointed nor broken nor feeble people, nor has-beens. They are the exact reverse: of selected vitality, they have studied with good effect. In terms of work they are paying full price in advance for opportunity and commensurate recognition.

Suggestions that follow are based not on guesswork, but on somewhat intimate acquaintance with the administrative and technical methods of the French National Ballet, in Paris. It has had two and a half centuries of experience. It is the classic model for the great ballet institutions of the world. Its results need no adjectives: here we are concerned with its methods. To begin with, it keeps its people. And that at small expense. Except the stars, the dancers are paid the price of a frugal little living. They are happy in that little living; the difficulty of getting them away from *l'Opera* to other positions is notorious. The administration follows a policy of opportunity commensurate with ability, and a definite designation for each of half a dozen grades of development.

When a girl first sets foot on the classic stage of *l'Opera*, she is an *élève* of the second division. After promotion to the first division she finds ahead of her the ranks of first and second *quadrille*. Next in advancement is a group of a dozen or more *coryphées*. Promotions are based on an annual examination. The *coryphée* advances to the rank of *petit sujet*, the step up from which makes her a *grand sujet*. To that rank there is a pleasant dignity; but it is not a stopping place for ambition. The title of *première danseuse* is at the present moment held by four women. In the Paris ballet the word signifies in effect the ability to adequately dance a leading rôle. Over all is *l'étoile;* the title held these several years by the magnificent Zambeli. Even in this honor *l'Opera* is not parsimonious. For a long period the title was shared by Zambeli and Boni.

The men are similarly graded. There are at present two *premiers danseurs*, Aveline and Ricaux. Following are groups of *messieurs du ballet, coryphés, sujets* and *garçons*.

These little distinctions of rank produce the same lively emulation that exists between class athletic teams in our colleges. They gratify the same craving for recognition of merit that animates athletes in common with admirals, lawyers and civic leaders. The less advanced dancers regard with vast respect their seniors, those entrusted with solos. Respect, but not self-abasement. Ambition and confidence are visible in their enthusiasm. They never tire. Every hour's work is that much progress toward a goal. Their power of sustained attention is amazing, especially in view of their youth. The ages from *élève* to *grand sujet* appear to run from about fifteen to twenty-one. Parenthetically they are not in any shape or manner the overworked and muscle-bound acrobats represented in some of the Degas drawings. On the contrary, they are, though fiercely in earnest, a happy picture of youth and well-being. But what is more to the point, they have no thought of leaving the

Opera. There each has her identity, her respected place, her promise of honors proportionate to abilities.

Perhaps you have been disappointed in the Paris ballet. If so, it is doubtless because you saw it during the summer. The artists relay one another on vacations, and a slump is said to result. Which is unfortunate for the ballet's reputation in this country, since summer is the season of travel. At other times one is impressed that it lives up to its best traditions.

In the Opera the word "tradition," ordinarily so devoid of meaning, assumes vitality and significance. Of its long history nothing is past, because the past is here today, an element in today's work. In the long foyer of statuary, among singers and decorators and composers whose lives are built into the opera, are dancers. Dancers, architects of the dance, who gave the art the form and structure on which it rests today. Their steps and their style are being practised, their identical difficulties will be met at ten tomorrow morning in the ballet room high up in "la Rotonde." By present difficulties we know their thoughts; and conversely it is more easy than otherwise to feel that they know ours; that they are benevolent seniors, yet fellow-workmen; great craftsmen whose precepts as well as standards may be known to him who asks. In the opera's library are preserved their arrangements, their notes, the fruits of their study, along with music, models of scenes and drawings of costumes that embellished their dancing. They are alive; Sallé and Camargo and Noverre and those others who fashioned the dance and conserved its beauty—those practical idealists who held *le Théâtre Nationale de Musique et de la Danse* on its straight course, while other arts of design floundered and governments went to smash. Tremendously alive. Their opinions are as cogent today as though audible. They are active advisors; today's administrators and artists are less their successors than their colleagues. The task of two centuries ago is the task today: to respect the premise on which the art is based; to respect the obligations of the present, and to build for the future.

A big task, but not too big. If its royal founder could look in at the ballet and its methods today, it is difficult to believe that he would be other than pleased with what is being done. He would find in M. Rucher, the *directeur-generale* of the opera, one altogether worthy of his place in the line of executives who have developed the institution. But of all M. Rucher's qualifications, it is doubtful if *le Roi Soleil* would find more pleasure in any than in his intelligent sympathy with the ballet. His friendly interest is a stimulus, naturally and evidently. But greater than that, even, as a means of bringing the dance to full flower, is the adjustment that makes it possible for Léo Staats to do his work. Staats is the ballet-master. His work is arrangement. His wings are not clipped either by lack of material or of time. By grace of complete knowledge of the art and rich resourcefulness in design, and having the Gallic gifts of romance and wit—being a genius, in short—opportunity enables him to make of the ballet all Noverre strove to make it, and a good deal more.

His process of construction resembles the procedure of a capable architect: a series of clearly considered advances from general to particular, each day's work representing a closer approximation toward the desired form. I have had the privilege of watching the development of a couple of Staats' major works, from start to completion. From the point, at least, where the idea begins to assume visible form; the point where, having arrived at a general plan, he begins its visible realization. The latter process, involving a vast amount of testing and comparison of details before Staats is satisfied that he has attained the maximum of interest and beauty, is carried on with the practical aid of a leading dancer; the individual, in fact, by whom the dance is to be performed, who thus learns it while it is being composed. Here is seen one of the advantages in having leading people in excess of the number required by the schedule of performers. It is possible for people concerned in the preparation of new work to be relieved from demands, otherwise excessive, of duties attaching to the concurrent routine. Completion of the solos, *pase-de-deux* and *pas-de-trois* brings the ballet-master to his choral numbers, which are seldom difficult in evolution and are comparatively simple in step. In the not unusual case of their use as introductions for a solo or *pas-de-deux*, the problem is simple. The latter acts as a climax, for which the choral number is preparation; which requires the conformity of both to a common theme. The preparatory, or choral, part is therefore arrived at by simplifying the climax.

Pâdmavâti, an opera-ballet by Albert Roussel, was one of the opera's great and successful undertakings of last season. Each of two solos and a *pas-de-deux* required for its composition about three weeks, five days a week, of sessions varying between one and two hours. A third solo, simpler in motive, developed somewhat more readily. This counts only the time of visible work with the dancers; how much thought outside of that Staats devoted to it all even Maître Staats himself would not know. In striking contrast to the highly charged atmosphere of his sessions with the *corps de ballet,* the periods of creation of the arrangements were cool and deliberate. Days would be spent on a single phrase of steps, no detail of structure, meaning or rendering being too small to consider. For instance, it was suggested that a certain four "pictures"—a sequence which stated the motive of the dance—should be made to conform to a scheme of rectangles and triangles: this would insure easy visibility, and, making the transitions in "dry" movements by contrast, would emphasize fluid character in the steps to follow. After mature discussion from various points of view the idea was found good except in one particular, which was that the proposed dry manner of execution was at variance with the musical directions. M. Roussel, who was present at nearly all these sessions, at this point went to the piano, experimented for a time, and reported that the music might be read so as to conform to the proposed rendering of that portion of the dance.

By such conjunction of alert sensibility and cool science great works are made. Our Metropolitan lacks so little of the ingredients to bring its ballet to an equality with the finest, and is in such an ideal position to carry on and develop the art, that it seems a pity for it to fall short of its opportunity. In concrete terms, it now has in its ballet an investment that pays a moderate return; whereas a small percentage added, wisely applied to that same investment, could be made to multiply the return in terms of prestige, interest, and service to art; to multiply the return many times over.

When this book was written, a study of conditions indicated the desirability of a worthy institution devoted to the ballet primarily if not exclusively. Conditions in relation to such an idea are essentially unchanged; nevertheless, it is not untimely to emphasize the importance of personnel to the value of such undertaking. Since the book's publication, several individuals and groups have successfully solicited money for an institution ostensibly such as the one proposed. These solicitors have ranged in respectability from confidence workers up to sincere well-meaners who have evidently failed to comprehend the necessary quality and magnitude of the plan. Of appeals that have come to the authors none has given any statement as to proposed manner of handling funds; nor as to teaching staff, nor a number of other interesting details. The participation of a man combining the artistic sympathies and financial standing of Mr. Otto Kahn would give the security that would justify contributions. With such security and an adequate subsidy, there need be no uncertainty as to the kind of active heads that such an institution could secure at this time. You could get the best. But there is no visible reason to believe that the idea is worth considering on any basis except the best.

Spain, if it is still to be called the home of the dance, must face the accusation of being an inhospitable home. Public interest has almost abandoned the art, and the acute public criticism that formerly distinguished Spanish audiences from any others in the world has practically disappeared with interest. No instance could more clearly demonstrate the truth that the well-being of an art is primarily in the hands of the public, with the artists little more than instruments of the community's wishes.

Until the recent surrender of his attention to other things, the Spaniard's support of the dance embraced a good deal more than the perfectly finished product. He was a genuine "fan," to the point that promising effort was as interesting to him as promise fulfilled. In one way, even more interesting: on the work and career of an immature artist he could rightly indulge himself in the feeling that he, by his praise and his censure, had been an influence. Though vicariously, he doubtless experienced in full that satisfaction accompanying successes he helped build.

Now, such support for undeveloped and semideveloped artists, coupled with a great volume of intelligent criticism, explains Spain's former ability to develop great artists without aid from institutions or subsidies. It bridged over that period between the acquisition of the academy's precepts, as a starting point, and arrival at the stage of disciplined imagination, authority and nobility of style that spell mastery. During that period, moreover, the artist was employed at the practise of his or her art, and did not fritter away precious years on acrobatic monkey-shines. There was a constant demand for services of every grade from acceptable skill up to supreme genius. Twelve years ago, for instance, every *café cantante* and "*variétés*" offered dancing as the major part of its entertainment; as often as not dances were incorporated in the *Zarzuela*. The entire peninsula was at once a support and a training school for artists of the dance.

But self-modernizing Spain has discovered a violent interest in the rest of the world, and the cinema is at hand to feed it. News films or anything else that will give a glimpse of the houses and faces and clothes used by other people are in strong demand. It is part of the wave of discontent. Spaniards are asking what is the matter with Spain, what is the rest of the world like. The easy acceptance of the new government is only one of many symptoms of the national state of mind. But that is neither here nor there. So far as the dance is concerned, celluloid comes cheaper and at present is found more interesting.

On top of this comes the dance of the ball-room. If there were two separate and distinct words to distinguish ball-room amusement from the choregraphic art, it might emphasize the fact that the two are as unrelated as pinochle and polo. But the needed words do not exist, so it can only be said that in Spain ball-room dancing is pushing out dancing. There again Spanish conditions have been peculiar. Of the old typically Spanish dances, few permitted a man to touch a woman's hand; only one permitted the man's arm around the woman's waist. And as that one—*la Malagueña y el Torero*—was hardly within the limits of amateur skill, it didn't affect popular customs. But now, just as the old Iberian self-sufficiency breaks down, comes this mode from Paris, sanctioning the familiar embrace. For the proprietor of the *café cantante* what could be simpler? A group of gaudily costumed females flounder through a few

Spanish numbers on the platform. Quality would be wasted, because nobody pays any attention—until they come down to one-step and *paso-doble* among the tables, with whomever wants them as partners. The direct effect on standards is obvious. One of the indirect effects is the practical exclusion of boys from the art. Another is the destruction of opportunity for ambitious girls. They can no longer earn while they learn. To arrive at professional maturity, they must acquire the necessary professional experience at their own expense; occasional fiestas and benefits furnish no livelihood. Reduced to this precarious means of development, genuine ambition has become, for the time at least, a pretty nearly extinct virtue. The academies are attended, to be sure; but very few students are interested in foundation. As Maestro Jose Otero put it: "Formerly people wanted to learn to dance. Now they want to learn dances."

Let it not be understood that the Spanish dance is dead. Pastora Imperio, reviving the old fandango, is truly great. She is copied to the extent that her adoption of the train skirt of the Gipsy has completely extinguished that garishly adorned bell-shaped affair of a dozen years ago. Argentina is popular and has lost nothing of the pleasing quality she has shown in this country. Carmen Salom, Laura Santelmo and Isabela Ruiz are of recent arrival in public favor; clever, appreciative of the dignity pertinent to their school, endowed with fire yet to reach its height. Doubtless there are still others worth attention. But in the main the art is pitifully bastardized by violence and speed; or haphazard admixture of the *flamenco* with the classic; or other frantic artifices to hold diminishing public attention. Tortola Valencia, successful as an artist of interpretation, is self-avowedly not a Spanish dancer in the orthodox sense. Argentinita, whose *garrotin* was—but what's the use? Like most of the other great figures, Argentinita has retired.

Yet, however depressing today's conditions affecting the Spanish dance as a grand art, it is far from dead as a popular art. Maestro Otero took us to a *fiesta de la cruz de Mayo* in Sevilla. It was a night gathering in a patio shared by a cluster of apartment houses; a neighborhood religious observance, with a great illuminated cross as its symbol. A golden voice sang religious songs—*Saetas* among them, that heartbreaking half-Arab melody with its wailing chant of the crucifixion. Yet religious feeling, intense as it was, intermittently gave way to a tempest of gaiety, and *Sevillanas* and *Soleares* and even *Tangos* were danced with a whole heart. Otero had not intended to dance; protested that he was too old; but when Señoritas fall on their knees and importune,—*vaya!* what is a man to do? It was all exceedingly pleasing. And it showed that the roots of the dance are still alive in Spanish soil.

For these people were poor. And the poor are they who have evolved and preserved popular arts. In a land lacking organizations to keep the poor amused, the poor—if they are good for anything—employ considerable cerebral activity in amusing themselves; even to the point of creating national arts. The poor community's active participation in the dance means very genuine choreographic vitality. Whereas the dilettante's activities more often mean a momentary fashion. Spain has her share of young ladies who perform three dances indifferently, and Maestro Otero writes that he has as pupils the children of one of the royal cousins; which may be significant, or may mean nothing but a caprice. The well-to-do amateur is not dependent on his art for entertainment, nor committed to it for a livelihood; it never means as much to him as he thinks it does.

Heretofore the honor of being the home of the dance has been claimed by London; and, in the light of Spain's present lack of becoming affection for the art, might seem to merit the title by default. But the new number of *The Dancing Times* arriving at the moment of writing contains an expression of hope that London *again* may become the home of the dance. If not yet the home, it certainly is the hotel; a hotel with almshouse attached. For London, along with joy in the good, has shown astonishing tolerance of the bad and indifferent. It competes with Paris as the favorite resting-place of expatriated Eastern Europeans. And in the process of reaching a comprehension of that fact, the American in London discovers a profound moral. Never, never, never let it be said again, or even hinted, that bluff is peculiarly an American attribute. Our softly lighted and harmoniously tinted concert halls are subject to invasions of soul and bluff unaccompanied by any trace of artistic sense or skill. That's true. But here's the difference: in America these Parnassian maids cut very little figure. Whereas in London, all that seems necessary is to claim ex-membership in the imperial ballet and be consistently incoherent. The latter is accepted for mysticism. No, not quite accepted, either; the action is negative. London audiences seem to combine with good taste, a species of distrust of their own perspicacity, and a predisposition to believe the artist is sincere; as though saying: "We don't understand it, of course; but possibly there is something in it. The only way to find out is to become so accustomed to it that one's perceptions can get past its surprising first impressions. And if the chap has something to say, as he seems to think he has, he certainly is entitled to attention." America's attitude is less amiable, sometimes doubtless unjust; but in the prevailing lack of artistic omniscience, probably more wholesome as an influence. Confronted by meritricious mysticism, America bluntly says: "It looks like nonsense to me." That collection of futuristic posturists called The Swedish Ballet seems to be able to play London weeks at a stretch. Its American tour finished about the time it started. On the face of it, one might say that America would, by its demand for intelligibility, deprive itself of the delicate and the subtle. Yet Pavlowa and Ruth St. Denis use motives as tenuous as air, and nowhere are they better supported or—seemingly—understood, than here in America. Londoners seem prepared, in order to get a new set of thoughts, to spring into the air after them, abandoning both foot-holds and hand-holds. We, in effect, refuse to take our feet off the solid ground of artistic rationality. A new art that invites our company must proceed into the unknown from the known by sure steps, never abandoning a good grip on the known. If new arts of any value can be developed by any other than this step-by-step process—which is at least debatable—their development will take place in London or Paris. Meantime both are passive victims of absurd counterfeits. Paris perhaps does not encourage the noisy witlessness that envelops New York. But, a martyr to her own reputation for discernment, she fears to call nonsense nonsense, lest future historians find evidence that she was aesthetically fallible today.

This book has been criticised as stressing the importance of the classic ballet to the point of representing that the ballet is the only genuine school of the dance. Such was not the intention. Other schools have solidity of form, an adequate vocabulary of expression, and a rich content of thought. If none of them achieve the magic of lightness, some of them lend themselves to the monumental. If some of them lack the brilliant, they have a compensating interest of the sinuous. There is something important in all schools worthy of cultivation. But the subject of souls and counterfeits brings up one most emphatic reason for the ballet's supreme importance: it is the only school that has definite standards of execution. Its movements and positions are precise. It has methods of exact training. Its requirements cover most nearly the whole scope of dancing; it is recognized as an invaluable aid to mastery of almost every occidental school. It has standards. Of other schools, execution admits debate. The ballet reveals mastery or exposes incompetence. For many reasons, therefore, it is the school best capable of protecting the art, as a whole, from slumping down to tedious mediocrity in the hands of conscious and unconscious impostors. The mortal Marsyas challenged Apollo to a competition in playing the lyre. After exposing the man's presumption, the god killed and skinned him, and hung his skin on the limb of a tree. Today the descendants of Marsyas would possess themselves wholly of the theatre of the dance. The dance needs an Apollo; the classic ballet, more nearly than any other, has proven its competence to act as Apollo's apostle.

London, as though in compensation for charity to the bad, gets also the best and an abundance of it. Sheshinskaia, *étoile*, and Legat, ballet-master of the old St. Petersburg organization; Karsavina, and various lesser but worth-while artists, unknown to America, are familiar to Britons. Artists are loaned by the Paris ballet for special occasions. At all times London gives the lover of dancing a far richer variety than is to be had here. Nor is there any lack of teachers, beginning with Cecchetti, the dean of the classic. His half-century of professional experience, beginning as a *danseur* at Milan; followed by many years as finishing teacher at St. Petersburg; and lastly a series of years as ballet-master intermittently for Pavlowa and Diaghilew—this long stretch of work has brought the years of the maestro to well over seventy and tired him not in the least. He demonstrates the most difficult steps with ease and style; a livelier mind does not exist; for excellence he has an unlimited reservoir of enthusiasm, and the sting of a wasp for shams. The schools of Novikoff, Kyasht and Karsavina also are famous.

More notable as a sign of lasting vitality, however, is an undertaking of certain leading English dancers and teachers themselves, acting concertedly under the name of The Operatic Association. Although of recent origin, it is already visibly influential in the general betterment of choreographic standards. Its origin is due to Mme. Genée; who is English in sympathies, through long residence in London; and also by marriage to a particularly delightful British gentleman. In retirement from the stage she found a certain amount of unaccustomed leisure. Having seen a good deal of difficulty undergone by ballet directors and young British dancers because of a lack of uniformity in nomenclature and execution of steps, which of course traced directly back to teachers, Mme. Genée offered the British teachers a gratuitous course of instruction aimed at the establishment of proper standardization. Mr. Philip J. S. Richardson instantly saw the importance of the idea as related to the hoped-for British ballet, and published it in his magazine, *The Dancing Times*. The teachers recognized the value of Mme. Genée's offer, and needed no urging. As the potential usefulness of a permanent organization became apparent, Mme. Genée and Mr. Richardson have continued to stand by with encouragement and counsel. It is only natural, as is reported, Mme. Genée's instruction has effected not only the proposed standardization, but a nation-wide improvement in quality of work. To the end of proving to Anglo-Saxon self-depreciation that there is an Anglo-Saxon imagination, the association has given a number of successful performances. Tangible results of the combined activities are presented in the form of a set of reports from managers of London theatres, showing a conspicuous twelve months' increase in the number of dancers employed. Nothing is said as to quality of work demanded and permitted;

quantity is encouraging, at least. But the great benefit this association and its members are receiving never will be adequately reported, because it cannot be measured. In coming under the leadership of Mme. Genée, the British dancers are benefiting not only by her superlative knowledge, not only by her rare power to reduce technical magic to scientific explanation; whether consciously or not, they hardly can help absorbing some of that high ideality for the art, and serene faith in its value to the world, that enter into Mme. Genée's greatness as an artist. In proportion as they have added to themselves these qualities it will be found that they have added strength to themselves individually, and to the cause for which they are working.

Of the stars that brightened the world ten years ago, most have been accounted for in preceding paragraphs. Mordkin (by last reports) is in Petrograd, dancing in the national ballet at the modest remuneration of a pood of flour—or its equivalent—per performance. Rumor also had it that a couple of unsuccessful attempts to leave Russia brought him a warning that a third attempt would be punished by death. About Nijinski the one evident fact is that he has been out of the theatre for several years, during which reports and denials of his death have been frequent. The most nearly credible information is to the effect that he spent some years in a sanitarium in Switzerland, broken down mentally; and that he recently has been brought to Paris in a condition to warrant hope of his recovery. Isadora Duncan's comings and goings, and her periodical denunciations of American taste, are familiar enough without repetition. Loïe Fuller's fire dances, all her well-remembered devices of light and silk, are kept alive by her pupils. The old tricks, and some new ones. A recent exhibition in Paris achieved striking effects in a shadow dance. Shadows of varying size were cast on a plain back drop by means of causing dancers to pass through the spreading ray of a powerful lamp, which was placed on the floor just behind the proscenium arch. According to the dancer's distance from the lamp, shadows varied from life (appproximately) to gigantic, and accomplished most amusing effects of impossible jumps, impossibly fast retreat into the distance, and vice versa. It is understood that the Fuller school uses the dance as a part, and only a part, of a general education. So it is with extra enjoyment that one sees in these girls in possession not only of piquant vivacity, but of good style. Their vocabulary is limited; but what they do they do nicely.

New York for several years has been the home of Fokine and Fokina. As dancers, their interest is essentially historical. An intermittent series of recitals by whose means they introduced themselves to America hardly augmented their reputation, their merit in character numbers having been cancelled by the appearance of being out of practise in the classic. M. Fokine is a powerful believer in "personality"; a commodity which, however desirable as an adjunct to the classic, and however serviceable in character work, fails as a substitute for classic form. A second activity of M. Fokine is teaching, in which he has built up a prosperous business. But his chief interest, of course, is as a composer. And that interest exists chiefly as an instance of the power of the vicious circle hereinbefore mentioned. The author of *Schéhérazade, Thamar, Petrouchka, le Spectre de la Rose* and a half-score more masterpieces did his great work while he was with Diaghilew. Since his residence here he had done big, glittering, turbulent things; and some mildly pleasing things; and some mildly borous things. But of ballets or arrangements fit to mention in the same year with the works that made his fame, not one. Of all the depressing circumstances into which the dance has fallen, this of the miring of Fokine's genius is one of the most discouraging. Whose fault is it? Partly his own, perhaps. Partly his employers' if you regard them as stewards of the art—which they almost perfectly frankly are not. But the real fault, companions in love of the dance, is yours and mine. We number well up in the hundreds of thousands; but of all the groups united by a common taste, we are quite the most invertebrate. We do not say what we want, we do not refuse what we do not want. Because it is set before us, we eat the gaudily-embellished pudding of chaff, and get indigestion. But in another week we come back for more, humbly thanking God if the mixture contains a little wheat and is fairly free from evil odors.

Bolm had a fine idea in his *Ballet Intime*. As the name implies, this was a compact organization equipped to give a program essentially of solos and small group numbers. The company included Roshanara, fascinating in the India dances in which she is an absolute artist. Ratan Devi, the musician, accompanied her with Indian instruments and songs; and also added very acceptable musical numbers to the program. Another member of the company was Michio Itow, whose *Fox Dance* and other numbers showed the very height of Japanese cleverness. Rita Zalmani, remembered as one of Pavlowa's artists, was the *première classique*. With her Bolm did one of the old *Dance of Death* ballets, and as solos used a number of bits from his famous character rolls. The class of entertainment offered by this brilliant group will be correctly imagined.

On all accounts, the *Ballet Intime* merited a long and successful career. And it might have had it, except for a sneeze. Its history began in New York in August, for such undertakings, the least propitious month in the calendar. The choice of that time was prompted by a promise of certain social leaders to guarantee a season at Newport, or some such place; so a couple of weeks in New York, even at an immediate loss, were deemed advisable as a preliminary. But it happened that a society personage sneezed. Bolm, on 'phoning to make final arrangements, was told to wait; an epidemic was about to break out. Hysteria, of course, neither more nor less. But there was nothing imaginary about the effect on the *Ballet Intime*. Waiting was above all the thing the artists could not afford. For most of them it was necessary to get engagements without delay.

Roshanara is perhaps unique among dancers of Occidental blood in the respect that she learned her India dances in India, from Hindu teachers. Which gives her work a special interest, apart from its intrinsic merits, in relation to a current superstition. Through repeated assertion it has come to be pas-

From an etching by Troy Kinney

ROSHANARA
In her *Nautch*, accompanied by Ratan Devi

To face page 352

sively agreed that the West will not accept Hindu dances in their natural state; that we can enjoy them only in the denatured condition of translations, adaptations, or what not. Interesting if true. But several of Roshanara's numbers were Indian classics, danced by her exactly as danced by Hindus for Hindus; her accompaniment was sometimes an Occidental orchestration of Indian melodies, but more often exactly as sung and played in India, even to the use of Indian instruments. These numbers took one irresistibly to another world. But it was not a world in which we required a guide, nor in which we felt in the least alien. Type of movement and of line were, of course, completely exotic; but their beauty was none the less evident, none the less compelling. The story, where any was used, had the condensed interest usual in old folk tales. The *Nautch* (perhaps her richest number in point of narrative content) was light in motive, sparkling with drolleries that delighted the audiences unanimously. And all this was expressed in a vocabulary of pantomime which, though new, was sufficiently close to nature to make its comprehension immediate and easy. In short, that *Nautch* might well be regarded as an ideal of structure for narrative dances in general; at least as regards clearness.

But in method the Hindu has a peculiar advantage. It is possible for her to make a clean demarcation between her dance proper and her pantomime. Pantomime passages alternate with dance, the latter appearing as a refrain between the narrative stanzas. The Hindu's advantage is that she can give herself over to pantomime—arms, head, and body—without loss of rhythm; because, by small or even imperceptible movements of the feet, she can jingle the bells that adorn her ankles. Thus when *Rhada the Celestial Milkmaid* milks the goat, or stops her journey to listen to the flute of *Krishna*, the pulse of her dance never loses its beat.

Roshanara danced with Pavlowa a season in Great Britain. She played two successful seasons of vaudeville in this country, leaving that field largely on account of managers' insistence on meddling with her work. She has "concertized" intermittently and successfully. But during the few past years her activity has been curtailed by persistent bad health. Nevertheless she has spread her knowledge to numerous pupils, and put a lot of good incisive thought into productions that she has directed. At present she is shaping material for a work on the grammar of movement; which, with her clear thought and broad knowledge, should be an important contribution to the literature of the dance.

So Hindu dancing is added to the list of branches in which competent instruction can now be had in America. For opportunity to study, our young people have little to ask, so far as New York at least is concerned. Good teachers are reported to have been found in all parts of the country. But New York alone contains variety and quality of dance instruction that makes it one of the world's most desirable centres for the study of the art. Albertieri; Vestoff and Kobeleff, formerly of Pavlowa's company; and Tarasoff, once of the Diaghilew troupe, are doing good work in the classic. To the grace commonly imparted to students of the Greek métier Mme. Sonia Serova adds truth of movement and a pleasing element of brilliancy. To pupils who lack aptitude in the last quality she recommends a period of training in ballet technique. Mme. Aurora Arriaza, native of Sevilla and one-time pupil of Otero, teaches the dances of Spain. Denishawn, with its all-round training, already has been mentioned. Of Slavonic character dances the teachers are legion. Of instruction in dances indeed New York is peculiarly a forcing-bed during the summer. Chalif, inexhaustibly clever in the composition of effective, easy, story-telling arrangements, was the first to attract out-of-town teachers in droves to summer courses. With quick drill in a new set of arrangements he provides music and choreographic directions complete, and sends them back as missionaries of the art. The demand for this type of knowledge has spread till it includes most of the leading studios in New York.

But it is not the intention to turn this chapter into a list of honest and able teachers. It is sufficient to say that it will not be for lack of quality or quantity of instruction if the dance in America goes back to mediocrity in the next few years. Whether it will or not is a question of interest to such people as are better for an occasional hour of contemplation of the poetry of motion. It is a question of even greater interest as an expression of the somewhat distracted spirit of these present times. That a vast number of us consider the dance worth while is demonstrated by the amount of money we spend on teaching it in public schools. It has become a familiar feature in women's colleges and girls' schools, and is the subject of tremendously popular summer courses in at least two of the great universities. There need be no debate about the existence of a great interest, on the part of both students and of a very considerable public.

In the face of such interest, including as it does a really extraordinary degree of critical judgment, that which is now happening and failing to happen is at least paradoxical. We, who patronize the best of music, fiction and painting, have practically surrendered control of this other art, the dance, to a group of line-of-at-least-resistance self-seekers, whose average artistic non-intelligence is notorious and self-evident. Pearls to which we fell heir we entrusted to jackdaws, and complacently accept gaudy trinkets in exchange. Constructive people, as we like with more or less truth to call ourselves, we annually spend a huge sum in the instruction of our youth, engage their interest and virtually commit them to a profession, then by our apathy force them to live by a travesty of the profession for which they studied to fit themselves. Wanting the best, in these ten years we have produced from among ourselves a mass of the merely acceptable. In all other matters alert and eager to co-operate with the man or woman who seems capable of creation, we passively encourage conditions that limit the developing dancers to the condition of "promising." Our great universities are presumably dedicated to the conservation of high standards of excellence: insofar as they have concerned themselves with the dance they have thus far failed to rise above a miserable mediocrity.

An art is an index, a very sensitive index, of the civilization in which it is practised. A formidable quantity has been written about the American spirit. The condition of the dance in this country ten years from now will be more illuminating than any ton of literature on the subject of present-day American mentality.

Except as Pavlowa has had them in her company, the Russian stars have manifested neither inclination nor ability to re-assemble themselves for purposes of worthy ballet production. The plant has gone to seed; it is evident that the old organism will not take root. It is easy to say "let it die; when we want a new bouquet we can buy a new one at the florist's." The possible error is, whether there will be any florist a few years from now. *L'Opéra*, up to the present impossible to get people away. Russia, by all reports, is non-productive of new talent. Milan, comatose. London, at best doubtful. Stockholm—did you see the Swedish Ballet? When Pavlowa retires, the leadership necessary to a continuance even of struggle for the preservation of this art must come—if it comes at all—from one of three sources: the as yet unforeseeable (which after all is the deciding factor in most things); or the dancers; or ourselves, the art-loving portion of the public.

To expect the dancers to dominate such bewildering conditions is unreasonable in view of a certain indispensable adjunct of their profession; namely, youth. Even if they have the talent for organization, before they have time to develop it we retire them from the theatre. Among the arts the dance is unique in the respect that the world demands of its practitioners that they be young in years while experienced in artistry. Yet that is not saying that these American dancers may not develop the organizing and administrative abilities to show their best capabilities in a worthy manner. For these are no ordinary young people. Like all professions, they have among their number the lazy, the stupid, the affected, the petty shrewd; none of whom affect things much. But the good element possesses that combination of sincerity and determination and intelligent idealism that has a way of accomplishing results. Can they overcome the handicaps of their own inexperience in affairs of organization? Can they add its burden to the requirements of adequate study? Will they be wise in their selection of advisers and allies? The answers to these questions perhaps contain the future history of the art.

If we, the public, are to assume the guidance in the matter, we have two methods open to us. The first, more natural and more surely effectual is to tell the theatrical business, in words and the more eloquent language of money, what we want and what we do not want. This method is open to the objection that up to the present, at least, it is beyond our inclinations, or perhaps capabilities. The second way is that heretofore discussed: the national ballet institution. Such an organization, to be effectual promptly, or to be an influence more permanent than one person's life, must be a big undertaking. With a big subsidy it could secure the best of instruction, the best of composers, and an adequate plant for training and performances. Governed disinterestedly and with insight and firmness, it would be a constructive institution Governed otherwise it would become the prey of petty job-seekers, a hollow shell of art and a detriment. It is an undertaking for big people to handle in a big way. On a lesser scale it would fall so far behind the accepted and therefore essential standards of our public and quasi-public art institutions that it would be only another handicap to the progress of the dance.

The foregoing is a fairly complete sketch of the history of the dance from 1914 to 1924. Whether the authors are correct in their inferences as to tendencies and in their selections as to significance, they do not know. If they knew, this chapter would finish with a prophecy. As the matter stands, A can guess as well as B whether the amazing phenomenon we have seen is the beginning of an artistic renaissance, or on the other hand a mere volcanic eruption destined to subside to nothing. All we really know is this: that we of today have seen a pillar of fire such as perhaps never before has arisen from the arts of mankind; that we have seen beauty in such profusion and of such poignancy as has been given to few generations of dwellers on the face of this earth.

BIBLIOGRAPHY

LA DANSE GRECQUE ANTIQUE: *Maurice Emmanuel.*—Traces the origin of a number of steps to ancient Greece, by analysis of poses of dancing, figures on ceramics, etc. Good explanation of ballet steps. (French.)

A GRAMMAR OF THE ART OF DANCING: *Friedrich Albert Zorn.*—Explains a system of choreographic writing by means of symbols to indicate positions and movements. By means (partly) of symbols explains ballet steps, also several ballroom dances. Exact and complete. (Written in German; translated into English and other languages.)

L'ACADEMIE IMPERIALE DE MUSIQUE: *Castil-Blaze.*—"Histoire litteraire, musicale, choréographique, pittoresque, morale, critique, facétieuse, politique et galante de ce théâtre." (From 1645 to 1855.) Contains much history and anecdote of Roman Empire and Middle Ages, with descriptions of mediæval ambulatory ballets, etc. (French.)

LES PENSÉES: *J.-J. Rousseau.*—Defends the dance against attacks of English. Rare; frequently missing from (supposedly) complete editions of the author. (French.)

MEMOIRS ET JOURNAUX: *Pierre de l'Estoile.*—A collection of anecdotes of the court of Henry III. A mine of information and gossip in relation to masques, etc., in the period described. (French.)

DES BALLETS ANCIENS ET MODERNES, SELON LES RÉGLES DU THÉÂTRE: *Claude François Ménestrier.* 1682.—Author was a Jesuit priest. Book includes extensive list of ballets produced in France up to year of its publication.

ORCHESOGRAPHIE: *Thoinet-Arbeau* (anagram of *Jean Tabourot*). 1589.—Author was Canon of Langres and Maître de Chapelle of Henry III. The first book devoted to the dance. Comments on all aspects of dancing in France of his time. (French)

THE CODE OF TERPSICHORE.—LE CODE COMPLET DE LA DANSE.—TRAITÉ HISTORIQUE THÉORIQUE ET PRATIQUE DE L'ART DE LA DANSE, DE LA PANTOMIME, DES BALLETS: *Carlo Blasis.*—Of the three books named, the first is in English; its material is more or less repeated in the other two, which are in French. A standard for the use of ballet-masters especially. Authoritative on matters pertaining to ballet technique, questionable on character dances, wholly untrustworthy on Spanish.

LETTRES SUR LA DANSE ET LES BALLETS: *M. Noverre,* ballet-master of the Duke of Würtemburg, l'Opéra of Paris, and other operas. 1760.—Classic. Author was the prophet of and leader to the modern ballet. A broad and comprehensive work on art, as well as authoritative on stage direction, ballet technique, and history. (French.)

DE LA SALTATION THÉÂTRALE: *M. de l'Aulnaye.* 1790.— Dancing and pantomime in antiquity. Contains a catalogue (thought by some authorities to be complete) of dances of ancient Greece. (French.)

DANCING AND DANCERS OF TODAY: *Caroline and Charles Caffin.* 1912.—Special attention to biographies of contemporary dancers. (English.)

LETTRES À SOPHIE SUR LA DANSE: *A. Baron.* 1825.—History, folk-dances and balls of Middle Ages. A chapter is devoted to dancing of Hebrews. (French.)

LA DICTIONNAIRE DE LA DANSE: *G. Desrat.*—Recent. Extremely useful. In dictionary form presents wide range of information.

A HISTORY OF DANCING: *G. Vuillier.* 1898.—Translated from original French into English and Italian. Read-

BIBLIOGRAPHY 363

able history of the art from antiquity to latter 19th century; many descriptions of early ballets and masques are quoted from Ménestrier, De l'Estoile and others.

MODERN DANCING AND DANCERS: *J. E. Crawford Flitch.* 1912.—History of ballet in England, biographical-analytical sketches of individuals of latter 19th century, details of Russian ballet in London. Delightfully written. (English.)

TRATADO DE BAILES: Jose Otero, famous master in Seville. 1912.—Expression of the spirit of Spanish dancing. Much amusing reminiscence. (Spanish.)

DICTIONNAIRE DE DANSE: *Charles Compan.* 1802.—Detailed instructions in social dances of the period. (French.)

THE ART OF TERPSICHORE: *Luigi Albertieri.* 1923.—"An Elementary, Theoretical, Physical and Practical Treatise of Dancing." A text on ballet technique; sound, scientific and thorough. Indispensable to teachers, useful to students.

THE MASTER OF THE RUSSIAN BALLET: (*The Memoirs of Cav. Enrico Cecchetti*) *Olga Racster.* With an introduction by Anna Pavlowa. 1923. An entertaining biography covering over a half-century of professional life of the dean of the art. Picturesque sketches of dancer's hardships and successes. Sidelights on early career of most of present Russian stars, with whom Cecchetti has been associated as teacher and ballet-master.

NOTE.—The above-named works are not arranged in order either of chronology or importance.

INDEX

ADAGIO, 95.
Albert, dancer, 109.
Albertieri, Luigi, ballet-master; definition *balloné*, 74; Century Opera Company, 279; teacher, 307, 354. See *bibliography*.
Alegrias, Spanish dance, 134.
Alexander VI. See *Pope*.
Allard, Mlle., dancer, 107.
Allemande, the, court dance, 52.
Almées, the, tribe of dancers, 210.
Amarilla, ballet-drama, 296, 297, 298.
Anacreon, 8.
Anderson, John Murray, dancer; old court dances, 52.
Animals, danced representations of, 19.
Anisfeldt, Boris, designer stage decorations, 264.
Anne of Austria, 49.
Antoinette, Marie, 53.
Arabesque (posture), 78.
Arabs, dancing of, 196 *et seq.*
Arbeau, Thoinet (anagram of Jehan Tabourot), Canon of Langres, choreographic historian. Ridicules opposition to dancing, 31. Hints on deportment, 55. See *Church*.
Argentina, dancer, 342.
Ariosto, *Suppositi*, performance in Vatican, 44.
Aristides, 8.
Aristodemus, dancer as ambassador, 8.
Ark of Covenant. See *David*.
Arms, positions of, ballet, 67. See *Flamenco, Arabs*.
Arrangement. See *Composition*.
Arriaza, Aurora, teacher, 355.
Artificiality, charge of against ballet, 62, 63.
Assemblé (step), 69.
Attitude, 84.
Aveline, *premier danseur*, l'Opéra, Paris, 303, 334.
Awakening of the Soul, dance, Egyptian, 210, 211.

BACCHU-BER, Savoyard observance, 186.
Bacon, Francis, composer of masques, 48.
Bakst, Léon; designer stage decorations, costumes, choreographer. Compared to Noverre, 105. Part in Romantic movement, 248. Relation to Diaghilew productions, 310.
Ballet Academy, French National. Founded, 49; Influence, 100. See *Opéra, le*.
Ballet Academy, Metropolitan Opera. See *Metropolitan Opera*.
Ballet Academy, Russian Imperial. See *Russian*.
Ballet, Classic, its artistic function, 60, 61; 89-91, 96. See *Expression*. Conserver of standards, 346, 347. See *Pavlowa et seq*.
Ballet dancers, effects of scarcity in America, 273-277.
Ballet (le) Comique de la Reine, 46.
Ballet Russe. See *Diaghilew, Russian Ballet*.
Ballet Theater, American, outline for conduct of, 282-287.
Ballet technique, ballet steps, 65-97.
Ballet, Russian. See *Russian Ballet*.
Balloné, 60, 73.
Baltarazini. See *Beaujoyeulx*.
Bathyllus, 25 *et seq.*
Battement, 71, 72.
Beaujoyeulx, ballet-master, 45.
Belgium, dances of, 182 *et seq*.
Bible, The; references to dancing, 5.
Black Crook, The, 231 *et seq.*
Blasis, Carlo, ballet-master, writer on dancing, 110.
Bolero, the, Spanish dance, 146, 148.
Bolm, Adolf, dancer, 248; *premier danseur* Diaghilew troupe, 307, 310. Choreographer, 326. Ballet Intime, 351, 352.
Bonfanti, Marie, dancer, teacher, 232.
Bonfiglio, Giuseppe, *premier danseur*

365

INDEX

Metropolitan Opera, 329.
Boucher, designed stage decorations, 104.
Bourrée, la, French dance, 52, 54, 183.
Branle, family of dances; *B. du Haut Barrois, B. des Lavandières, B. des Ermites, B. des* Flambeaux, 55.
Brisé (step), 73.
Brunelleschi, stage decorations, 44.
Bulerias, Spanish dance, 134.
Burlesque, 229.

CABRIOLE, 72.
Cachucha, the, Spanish dance, 111, 140.
Camargo, dancer, 50 *et seq.* Place in art, 59 *et seq.* Influence on costume, 100. Quality of work, 107. Continuing influence, 335.
Canadian Royal Opera Company, ballet, 279.
Can-Can, The, dance of Montmartre, 229.
Cansino, Antonio, teacher, 124.
Cansino, Eduardo, dancer, observer
Cansino, Elisa, dancer, 135. of work of Gipsies, 126, 134.
Carmencita, dancer, 139. Influence in America, 239.
Carnaval, le, ballet drama, 268.
Caryatis, dance. Sacred to Diana, 13.
Castanets, Spanish use of, 131, 147, 148, 151, 152.
Caucasus, The, dancing in, 217.
Cavallazi, Malvina, preface.
Cecca, stage decorations, 44.
Cecchetti, Enrico, ballet-master, teacher, 74, 89, 347. See *bibliography.*
Cerezo, teacher, 146.
Cerito, Fanny, dancer, 118.
Chaconne, the, court dance, 52, 55.
Chalif, Louis, teacher, 355.
Changement (step), 69.
Chaplin, Nellie, reviver of old English dances, teacher, 173.
Characteristic dancing, contribution to ballet, 53. See *Pavlowa,* 296 *et seq.*
Charles I, King of England, 48.
Chassé, 68.
China, dancing in, 224.
Chirinski-Chichmatoff, Princess, dancer; defines characteristic dancing, 193. Russian Court Dance, 195.

Dancing in the Caucasus, 217.
Church, the Christian, St. Basil attributes dancing to angels, Emperor Julian reproved by St. Gregory, 30. Canon of Langres ridicules opposition to dancing, 31. Mozarabic mass, St. Isidore, 32. Abuses complained of, 33. Anecdote of the *Fandango,* 141. Lerida Cathedral, Seville Cathedral, 142. Scotland, 167.
Church, the Christian, relation to dancing. See *Pope.*
Cicero, 27.
Ciociara, the, Italian dance, 162.
Clayton, Bessie, dancer, 93.
Cléopâtre, ballet drama, 266; relative value, 309.
Cobblers' Dance, the, Swedish, 182.
Cobra Dance (India), 220.
Coles, Miss Cowper, reviver of old English dances, teacher, 173.
Collins, Lottie, dancer, 230.
Columbina, 157.
Composition (choreographic), general principles, 89, 90, 91. Noverre's influences, 105. Arabic, 196 *et seq.,* 204. Fokine (hypothetical example), 264. Analogy to wordpoems, 294, 295; to sculpture, 299. Ballet structures compared, 309-313. Content of imagination, 319. Possibilities, 326. Neglected, 330, 331. In le ballet de l'Opéra, 336-338. See *Fokine.* See *Expression.*
Contredanse, type of dance, 184.
Coopers, Munich's dance of, 186.
Cordax, Ancient Greek dance, 20.
Corybantes, taught mankind, to dance, 7.
Coppini, Ettore, dancer, ballet-master, 233.
Cossack Dance, the, Russian, 190.
Cou-de-pied, sur le. See *Pirouette.*
Counter-time, Spanish use of, 126, 130.
Country dance. See *Contredanse.*
Coupé, 68.
Courante, the, court dance, 52, 56.
Court Dances, seventeenth century, 52 *et seq.*
Crawford, Margaret, 53, 169.
Cybele. See *Corybantes.*
Czardas, the, Hungarian dance, 190, 192.

INDEX

DALDANS, the, Swedish dance, 182.
Dancing Times, the (publication), 344, 348.
Danse caracteristique, la. See *characteristic dancing*.
Dauberval, dancer, 108.
da Vinci, Leonardo, stage decorations, 44.
David, danced before Ark of Covenant, 5.
de Botta, Bergonzio, ballet masque, 37 *et seq.*
Debussy, musical composer, 312.
Decoration, analogy to dance, p. 2 of preface, 96, 97, 98. Arabic, 196 *et seq.* Egyptian, 209, 212. See *Composition; Bakst.*
del Sarto, Andrea, stage decorations, 44.
de Medici, Catherine. Place in history of ballet, 44; organizer of, performer in, grand ballet, 46.
de Medici, Lorenzo, 45.
de Staël, Madame, appreciation of *Tarantella*, 160.
de Valois, Marguerite, 54.
Dervishes (Whirling), 90, 216. See *Religions, non-Christian.*
Developpé, 84.
Diaghilew, Sergius, manager, 251, 252. American tours, influence, 307-314. Consequences of modernistic experiments, 325.
Dieu (le) Bleu, ballet drama, 268.
Dionysia, dances, sacred to Bacchus, 13.
Duncan, Isadora, dancer. Source of inspiration, 11. Her artistic beliefs, 241 *et seq.;* early career, 243 *et seq.;* influence on ballet, 246; application of her precepts, 305. See *Russian Ballet, Expression.*

ÉCHAPPÉ, 70.
Eggs, Dance of (India), 220.
Egypt, Ancient, dancing in, 4.
Egypt, latter-day, dancing in, 209 *et seq.*
Elevation, defined, 75.
Elizabeth, Queen of England, 48.
Ellsler, Fanny, dancer, 110 *et seq.* In America, 116. Episode leading to retirement, 117. Influence, 228. See *Taglioni.*
Emmeleia, group of ancient Greek dances, 11.
Enchainement, defined, its function in composition, 61.

Endymatia, group of ancient Greek dances, 11, 12.
Entrechat, step, used by Camargo, 60. Execution, 72, 73. Relation to ballet costume, 100. Question of origin, 146.
Ethologues, school of pantomimists, 16.
Expression, abstract, 60, 61. In ballet composition, 89, 90, 91. Noverre's ideals, 105. Spanish Gipsy, 124 *et seq.* Sevillanas, 138, 139. St. Denis, 221. Duncan, 243-246. Bakst, 248, 249. Russian recreation of best Greek dramatic form, 251, 319, 320. See *Pavlowa*, 290-302; and *Staats.* See *Decoration, Composition.*
Extravaganza, 229.

FANDANGO, the, Spanish dance, 141, 142, 154, 342. See *Imperio.*
Fantaisie, Fantasia (Arab), 207.
Farandole, the, French dance, 183.
Farruca, the, Spanish dance, 127 *et seq.*
Fatma, dancer, 199.
Faune, l'Après-Midi d'un, spectacle, 311, 312.
Feet, positions of. Ballet, 66.
Feis, Irish festival, 177-179.
Feu, la Danse de. See *Fuller.*
Fight with Shadow. Ancient Greek dance, 19.
Flamenco, type of Spanish dance, 124 *et seq.*
Fling, see *Highland Fling.*
Flour Dance, The (Arab), 205.
Fokine, Mikail, choreographer, teacher, dancer, ballet-master, 246. Heads Romantic movement, 247. Hypothetical instance of composition, 264. Composer The Swan, 295; mixed influence, 308, 309, 310. Minor compositions, 326. In America, 350, 351.
Folk-dancing, influences upon it. Place in dancing, etc., 164 *et seq.* See *Characteristic Dancing.*
Forlana, the, Italian dance, 156 *et seq.*
Fouetté, 75, 76.
France, folk-dances of, 183 *et seq.*
Fuller, Loïe, dancer, 235 *et seq.;* teacher, 350.

INDEX

GADITANAE. See *Spanish dancing*.
Gaelic League, the, attitude toward dancing, 178.
Gaillarde, the, court dance, 43, 52, 55.
Galeazzo, Duke of Milan. See *de Botta.*
Galli, Rosina, dancer, 279; *première danseuse* Metropolitan Opera, 329, 331.
Gardel, Maximilian, dancer. Rebelled against mask, 102. Example of effect of French Revolution, 108.
Garrotin, the, Spanish dance, 127, 134.
Gautier, Theophile, appreciation of Ellsler, 110.
Gavotte, the, court dance, 52, 53.
Gavriloff, dancer, 309.
Geisha, 225.
Geltzer, Katarina, dancer, 254.
Genée, Adeline, instance of virtuosity, 84. Influence, 239. Value of surprise, 301. See *Operatic Association.*
Genée, Adeline, re-creations of art of historic dancers, 59.
Germany, dancing in, 184.
Gigue, the, Italian dance, 43, 162. See *Jig.*
Ginsberg, Baron, 252.
Gipsy, Spanish, type of dancing, 124. Pantomime, 125, 126. Relation to Spanish dancing, 128 *et seq.*
Gitanita, La, dancer, 94 *et seq.*
Glazounow, musical composer, 248.
Glissade, Glissé, 68.
Gluck, musical composer, 105.
Grahn, Lucille, dancer, 118.
Greece, ancient, dancing in, 6 *et seq.* Present day, 189, 190.
Greeting, Dance of (Arab), 202.
Grisi, Carlotta, dancer, 118.
Guimard, Madeleine, dancer, 107.
Guerrero, Rosario, dancer, 139. Influence, 239.
Gustavus III, King of Sweden, influence on dancing, 181.
Gymnopædia, group of ancient Greek dances, 11, 12.

HAMADSHA, Mohammedan observance, 208 *et seq.* See *Religions.*
Handkercheif Dance, The (Arab), 205.
Harlequin, 157.

Hazélius, Dr., 180.
Hebrews, dancing of, 5, 45.
Henry IV, King of France, 48.
Henry VIII, King of England, 48.
Herodias, daughter of, 5.
Highland Fling, the, Scotch dance, 167 *et seq.*
Hill, Thomas, dancer, 175 *et seq.*
Hippoclides, 20.
Historians, their neglect of dancing, 9 *et seq.*
Holland, dances of, 182 *et seq.*
Horace, 27.
Hormos, dance of ancient Greece, 7.
Hornpipe, the, Irish dance, 174 *et seq.*
Hornpipe, the *Sailor's,* characteristic dance, 171.
Hula-Hula, The, Hawaiian dance, 223.
Hungary. See *Slavonic dances.*
Hyporchema, group of ancient Greek dances, 11.

IAMBIC, dance, sacred to Mars, 13.
Idzikovski, Stanislaus, dancer, 309.
Imperio, Pastora, dancer, 342.
India, dancing in, 218 *et seq.* See *Roshanara.* See *St. Denis.*
Inns of Court, produced masque, 48.
Ireland, dances of, 174 *et seq.*
Israel, children of. See *Moses.*
Italian characteristic dances, details of costume, 159.
Itow, Michio, Japanese dancer, 352.

JALEO, informal accompaniment. Spanish dancing, 126.
Japan, dancing in, 225 *et seq.*
Jarrett and Palmer, producers, 231.
Javillier, dancer, 108.
Jeremiah, Book of, 5.
Jeté, 70, 71. *Jeté tour, j. en tournant,* 71.
Jig, the Irish dance, 174 *et seq.*
John the Baptist. See *Herodias, daughter of.*
Jones, Inigo, stage decoration, 48.
Jonson, Ben, composer of masques, 48.
Jota aragonesa la, Spanish dance, 124, 150-152.
Jota valenciana, la, Spanish dance, 153.
Judges, Book of, 5.
Julian, Emperor. See *Church.*
Jump, effect of length analysed, 86, 87.

INDEX

KADRILJS, the, Swedish dance, 181.
Kahn, Otto. Guarantor Diaghilew tour, 308. See 339.
Karsavina, Thamara, dancer, 248; teacher, 347.
Kiralfy brothers, dancers, producers, 232 et seq.
Kobeleff, Constantin, dancer, teacher, 304, 354.
Kolia, ancient Greek dance, 19.
Kolo, the, Servian dance, 189.
Kyasht, Lydia, dancer, facing p. 247. On Broadway, 315; teacher, 347.

LA GAI, Louise, dancer, definition *balloné,* 74; in Italian dances, 157 et seq.
Lac (le) des Cygnes, ballet, 268.
Lany, dancer, 108.
Le Brun, Father Pierre. See *Church.*
Leo X. See *Pope.*
Lezginkà, dance of the Caucasus, 217.
Lind, Jenny, singer, 118.
London, public criticism in, 344, 345.
Long, Patrick J., dancer, 176.
Lopoukowa, Lydia, dancer. Basis of academic training, 89. Slavonic dances, 191. Part in Romantic movement, 248. Metropolitan Opera, 254. Describes curriculum Imperial Academy, 261 et seq.; affected by American conditions, 273, 274. Première *danseuse* Diaghilew troupe, 307.
Lou Gué, 37.
Louis XIII, performer in ballets, 48.
Louis XIV. See *Ballet Academy, French National.*
Ludiones, 25.
Lycurgus, regulations and recommendations concerning dancing, 7, 8.

MACCABEES, 5.
Malagueña (la) y el Torero, Spanish dance, 143, 144; castanets in *la Jota,* 147.
Malagueñas las, Spanish dance, 144.
Managers, influence on dancing: Chicago World's Fair, 237; Jarrett and Palmer, *The Black Crook,* etc., 232 et seq.; imitators, 233. Sergius Diaghilew, 251, 252. Public's share in blame for American conditions, 270. Exceptional undesirables, 272. Commercial exigencies, 273.

Managers (theatrical) relation to the dance, 314-318, 321, 322.
Manchegas, Spanish dance, 144.
Mandelkern, Joseph, manager, 248.
Marianas, Spanish dance, 134.
Mary, Queen of Scotland, 169.
Mascagni, Theodore, dancer, 156.
Mask. Origin, 18 (inference of Mme. L. Nelidow), 249. Persistence, 101, 102.
Masque, early steps and elaboration, 36 et seq.
Mâtelot, the, Dutch dance, 182.
Mazurka, the, Russian dance, 190, 192.
Memphitic, group of ancient Greek dances, 15.
Ménestrier, Father, choreographic historian, 29.
Metropolitan Opera Company. Russian ballet, 254. Relation to music and dancing, 255, 274-279, 328-333, 338.
Military training, dance in, 14, 15.
Minuet, the, 52. M. *du Dauphin,* M. *de la Reine,* M. *d'Exaudet,* M. *de la Cour,* 57.
Mirror, figure of Minuet, 57. See *Bavarian.*
Mohammed. See *Religions, non-Christian.*
Monteverde, musical composer, 39.
Moor. See *Spanish dancing,* also *Oriental dancing.*
Morality of dancing. See *Church: Religions, non-Christian; Sex; Tango.*
Mordkin, Mikail, dancer. Part in Romantic movement, 248. Metropolitan Opera, 254. In Soviet Russia, 349.
Moresca, the, 43.
Moritas, las, Spanish dance, 134.
Morra, la. See *Tarantella.*
Morris Dances, 172.
Moses; bids children of Israel dance, 5.
Mourning, choreographic expression of, Greeks (ancient), 13. Spanish Gipsies, 126. Arabs, 207.
Moving pictures, relation to the dance, 326; in Spain, 341.
Mozarabe. See *Church.*
Mozart, musical composer, collaborated with Noverre, 106.
Municipal ballets, 6, 8.
Music, analogy to. See *Expression.*

INDEX

NAGEL, Fred, dancer, 188.
Nagel, Mrs. Fred, dancer, 188.
Napoleon (Emperor), ballet in Egypt, 109.
Naturalism, consideration of. See *Ballet, Classic.*
Nautch, 221, 353.
Nemours, Duke of, *Ballet of Gouty,* 49.
Nicomedes, mother a dancer, 8.
Nijinski, Waslaw, dancer, 247, 248. Star of Diaghilew troupe, 307. Influence, 309. In *l'Après Midi d'un Faune,* 309. Retirement, 349.
Noblet, dancer, 109.
Noverre, M., ballet-master. Reforms in French ballet, 103. Collaboration with Gluck, 105. Ballet compositions, 106. Continuing influence, 335.
Novikoff, Laurent, dancer, mime, 302, 306; teacher, 347.

OBERTASS, the, Polish dance, 192.
Oiseau (le) de Feu, ballet drama, 268; relative value, 309.
Opera, ballet's place in, 118, 119. See *Metropolitan Opera.*
Opéra (le) French National, organization of ballet, 333-336.
Operatic Association, the (London), 347-349.
Oriental dancing: distinguished from Occidental, 213-215. See *Roshanara.* See *St. Denis, Composition.*
Otero, dancer, 139, 239.
Otero, Jose, teacher, writer on Spanish dancing, 124, 342, 344. See *bibliography.*

PANADEROS, *los,* Spanish dance, 149.
Pantalone, Doctor, 157.
Pantomime, distinguished from abstract expression, 62 *et seq.* Noverre, 107. Spanish Gipsy, 125. Arabic, 200 *et seq.* Greek, 249, 250. Rome, 250. Augustin Daly's interest in, 271. See *Expression.*
Paris, criticism in, 346.
Pas de Basque (step), 74, 75.
Pas de Bourrée (step), 74.
Pas de Chat, 85.
Pas de Chevala, 85.
Passecaille, the, court dance, 52.
Passepied, the, court dance, 52.
Pavane, the, court dance, 43, 56.
Pavillon (le) d'Armide, 268.

Pavlowa, Anna, dancer; academic discipline, 89. Instance of virtuosity, 92. Part in Romantic movement, 248. Metropolitan, Opera, 254. Canadian Royal Opera Company, 279. Analytical sketch of her art, 290-302. Not subsidized, 325.
Perchtentanz of Salzburg, 184, 185, 186.
Petrouchka, ballet, 309.
Philip of Macedon, wife a dancer, 8.
Piqué tour, 89.
Pirouette, 76-81, 83.
Pirouette, defined, 76, 79. *Fouetté p.,* 76, 77; variations, 78. *P. sur le Cou-de-pied,* 79, 80; *P. composées,* 81.
Pito, finger-snapping, accompaniment Spanish dancing, 131.
Plato, his valuation of dancing, 4, 7.
Plié, 75, 76.
Pointe, sur la: in ancient Greece, 88; erroneous ideas concerning, 93; instances of, barefoot, 93, 94.
Poland. See *Slavonic dances.*
Polka, the, 181.
Pope Alexander VI, 45.
Pope Eugenius IV, 31.
Pope Leo X, 45.
Pope Sixtus IV, 45.
Pope Zacharias, 32.
Prevost, Françoise, dancer, 49.
Prince Igor, ballet drama, 266.
Princesse Enchantée, la, ballet, 309.
Public (American) in relation to dancing, 229, 232, 233, 269 *et seq.*
Pylades, 25 *et seq.*
Pyrrhic, group of ancient Greek dances, 15.

QUADRILLE, see *Contredanse.*

RAPHAEL, stage decorations, 44.
Rasch, Albertina, dancer, 279.
Reel of Tulloch, the, Scotch dance, 170.
Reel, the, Irish dance, 174 *et seq.*
Reel, the, Scotch dance, 170.
Relevé, 69, 70.
Religions, non-Christian, Greek, 6 *et seq.*
Religions, non-Christian, relation to dancing. Egyptian, 4. Greek, 4, 11 *et seq.* Roman, 24, 25. Mohammedan, 196 *et seq.* Dervishes, 216. Hamadsha, 208 *et seq.* India, 224.

INDEX

René, King of Provence, 36.
Renversé, its æsthetic significance, 61.
Revolution, French, effect on dancing, 108.
Riario, Cardinal, composed ballet, 45.
Richelieu, Cardinal, composer ballet, 49.
Rimski-Korsakow, musical composer, 248.
Rincce Fadha, the, early Irish dance, 177.
Roger (Sir) de Coverley, the, English dance, 177.
Romantic Revolution, the Russian. See *Russian Ballet.*
Rome, dance in, 22 *et seq.*
Romeo, Angelo, dancer, 80.
Rond de Jambe, 81.
Rose and the Dagger, The, pantomime, 139.
Roshanara, dancer, teacher, 351-353.
Russia, characteristic dances. See *Slavonic dances.*
Russia, Court Dance of, 195.
Russian Ballet, for comparison. See *Ballet, Classic.*
Russian Ballet. One field of its new material, 58. Artistic sanity, 99. Isadora Duncan influence, 241-247. Re-creates best of Greek drama, 251. Plays in Paris, 252. Metropolitan Opera, 254. Misrepresentative appearances, 255. Relation to Imperial Academy, 257 *et seq.* Compared with Classic, 263. Scope, 266-268. See *Ballet, Classic.*
Russian (Imperial) Ballet Academy: favored ward of government, 245; conditions of entrance, 257, 258; disposal of pupils, 258, 259; curriculum, 259-261; care of pupils, 262; synopsis of history, 262, 263. Influence of Romanticism, 263-266.

SAILOR'S *Hornpipe.* See *Hornpipe.*
St. Basil, dance in his *Epistle to St. Gregory,* 30. See *Church.*
St. Carlo Borroméo, canonisation of, 35 *et seq.*
St. Denis, Ruth, dancer. Influence, 199. *Cobra dance,* 220. Her contribution to art, 221, 222, 223. Teacher, 327, 355.
St. Isidore, choreographic composer. See *Church.*
Salic priests, 24.

Sallé, de, Marie, dancer, 49, 335.
Sallust, observations, 27.
Saltarello, the, Italian dance, 43, 163.
Samuel, Book of, 5.
Saraband, the, court dance, 52, 54.
Saracco-Brignole, Elise, dancer, teacher, 156.
Saracco, George, dancer, balletmaster, 233.
Saturnalia, dances of ancient Rome, 25.
Serpentine. See *Fuller.*
Scandinavian, dances of, 180 *et seq.*
Schéhérazade, ballet drama: Volinine in, 86; in character, 268; relative value, 309.
Schuhplatteltanz of Bavaria, 187 *et seq.*
Scotch Reel, the. See *Reel.*
Seguidillas, type of Spanish dance, 136, 141, 144.
Seises of Seville. See *Church.*
Serova, Sonia, choreographer, 326; teacher, 354.
Sevillanas, las, Spanish dance, 136-140 incl. Instance of a competition, 94.
Seville Cathedral. See *Church.*
Sex, dance in relation to, 8, 24. Ellsler and Camargo contrasted, 110, 111, 115. Spanish Classic and Flamenco contrasted, 128. Chicago World's Fair, 199, 238. Arabian *Handkerchief Dance,* 205. One manager's belief, 239.
Shawn, Ted, dancer, teacher, 327, 355.
Shean Treuse, the, Scotch dance, 171.
Shiloh, daughters of. See *Judges.*
Siciliana, the, Italian dance, 43, 163.
Sikinnis. Ancient Greek dance, 20.
Simplicity, Greek and Roman compared, 22 *et seq.*
Sixtus IV, see *Pope.*
Skansen, the, 180.
Skralât, the, Swedish dance, 181.
Slavonic dances, 190 *et seq.*
Socrates, 8.
Soleares, las, Spanish dance, 152.
Sophocles, 8.
Spanish dancing costume, details of, 135, 142, 143, 149, 153.
Spanish dancing, its place in history: Carthaginian province, Roman entertainment, 121; Moorish influence, 122; Century of Gold, 122. Decline, 339-343.
Spear, ancient Greek dance of, 19.

INDEX

Spectre (le) de la Rose, ballet drama, 268.
Spilled Meal, dance of, 19.
Staats, Léo, dancer, ballet-master l'Opéra, choreographer, 80. Instance of methods, 336, 337.
Steps, classes of, definition of, 67, 68.
Stoige, Otto. See *Pirouette*.
Strathspey, the Scotch dance, 171.
Style, ballet, some elements of, 91, 92, 93, 96, 97. Russian and Classic compared, 263-266.
Sur la pointe, les pointes, position, æsthetic significance, 61. In ancient Greece, 88.
Sweden, dances of, 180 et seq.
Sword Dance (Scotch), the, 167.
Sword Dance (Turkish), 216.
Sylphide, la, ballet, 116.
Sylphides, les, ballet, 268, 309.
Szolo, the, Hungarian dance, 193.

TABOUROT, Jehan. See *Arbeau*.
Taglioni, Marie, dancer, contributor to ballet steps, 58, 112. Reference by Thackeray, 110. Individuality, 111. Rivalry with Ellsler, 114 et seq. Performance for Queen Victoria, 118. Influence, 228.
Tango, the, Spanish dance, 127 et seq.
Tarantella, the, Italian dance, 158.
Tarasoff, Ivan, teacher, 354.
Tcherepnin, musical composer, 248.
Temps, definition, 67.
Tencita, dancer, 154.
Till Eulenspiegel, spectacle, 312.
Time markers, 17. See *Castanets*.
Toe-dancing. See *pointe, sur*.
Tordion, the, court dance, 52, 54.

Toreo Español, Spanish dance, 155.
Tour. See *Pirouette*.
Tourists, dancing for. Tangier, etc., 205. Egypt, 210.
Treaty, Anglo-French concerning dancers' contracts, 109.
Tulloch. See *Reel*.
Turkey, dancing in, 216.

VAFVA *Vadna*, the, Swedish dance, 181.
Vestoff, teacher, 354.
Vestris, Auguste, dancer, 102.
Vestris, Gaëtan, dancer, teacher, 102.
Victoria (Queen) influence on dancing, 118.
Vingakersdans, the, Swedish dance, 182.
Virginia Reel, the, American dance, 177.
Vito, el, Spanish dance, 155.
Volinine, Alexander; instance of virtuosity, 86; academic basis, 89; part in Romantic movement, 248. Metropolitan Opera, 254. Retirement, 303.
Volte, the, court dance, 52.

Waltz, the. Probable origin, 75. Universality, 183. The Rheinlander Waltz, 188.
White Fawn, The, ballet spectacle, 233.
World's Fair, Chicago, 238.

ZAMBELLI, Carlotta, dancer, 78; danseuse etoile l'Opéra, Paris, 334.
Zarabanda, the, old Spanish dance, 122. See *Saraband*.
Zourna, dancer, 199 et seq.

THE END